WOMEN AND FAMILY IN CONTEMPORARY JAPAN

Japanese women have often been singled out for their strong commitment to the role of housewife and mother. But today they are postponing marriage and bearing fewer children, and Japan has become one of the least fertile and fastest aging countries in the world. Why have so many Japanese women opted out of family life? To answer this question, the author draws on in-depth interviews and extensive survey data to examine Japanese mothers' perspectives and experiences of marriage, parenting, and family life. Her goal is to understand how, as introspective, self-aware individuals, these women interpret and respond to the barriers and opportunities afforded within the structural and ideological contexts of contemporary Japan. The findings suggest a need for changes in the structure of both the workplace and the education system to provide women with the opportunity to find a fulfilling balance between work and family life.

Susan D. Holloway obtained a Ph.D. in developmental psychology and early childhood education from Stanford University in 1983. She has been conducting research on Japan since 1980 and was the recipient of a Fulbright Award in 1994 to study and write about family and schooling in Japan. She is the author of *Through My Own Eyes: Single Mothers and the Cultures of Poverty* (with Bruce Fuller) and *Contested Childhood: Diversity and Change in Japanese Preschools*. In addition, she has authored more than fifty articles and book chapters on family and schooling in cultural contexts. Holloway has taught at the University of Maryland, College Park; Harvard University; and the University of California, Berkeley, where she has been a faculty member in the Graduate School of Education since 1996.

Women and Family in Contemporary Japan

SUSAN D. HOLLOWAY

University of California, Berkeley

CAMBRIDGE
UNIVERSITY PRESS

CAMBRIDGE UNIVERSITY PRESS
Cambridge, New York, Melbourne, Madrid, Cape Town, Singapore,
São Paulo, Delhi, Dubai, Tokyo

Cambridge University Press
32 Avenue of the Americas, New York, NY 10013-2473, USA

www.cambridge.org
Information on this title: www.cambridge.org/9780521180375

First published 2010

Printed in the United States of America

A catalog record for this publication is available from the British Library.

Library of Congress Cataloging in Publication data
Holloway, Susan D.
Women and family in contemporary Japan / Susan D. Holloway.
p.   cm.
Includes bibliographical references and index.
ISBN 978-0-521-19227-9 (hardback)
1. Women – Japan.   2. Family – Japan.   I. Title.
HQ1762.H643   2010
306.850973–dc22   2010001369

ISBN 978-0-521-19227-9 Hardback
ISBN 978-0-521-18037-5 Paperback

Contents

Preface

In 1990, in an article in the *Annual Review of Anthropology* entitled "Women's Voices: Their Critique of the Anthropology of Japan" Mariko Tamanoi argued forcefully that the perspectives of Japanese women have received shockingly little attention in the academic literature:

Before women's perspectives can be integrated successfully into the study of Japanese culture and history, we must listen to what women have to say about their own experiences, emotions, and thoughts. Their voices, not yet sufficiently explored, may lead to different views of Japanese culture and history. Thus, to focus on women is not to ghettoize them but to include their subjective experience in the study of Japan. It means seeing Japanese culture and history from the vantage points of women, who in recounting their experiences and emotions must talk about the lives of their male partners and/or competitors as well. (p. 18)

Tamanoi's call for closer study of Japanese women's perspectives is still relevant today. Although a growing number of anthropologists, political scientists, and sociologists have focused on recent changes in the Japanese family, relatively few have focused directly on the voices of contemporary Japanese mothers. As a psychologist, I wanted to focus on women's perceptions of what the role of mother entails and how they evaluate themselves in that role. In light of the initial evidence that many Japanese mothers perceived themselves as inadequate, I also hoped to uncover what types of experiences bolstered (or diminished) their sense of confidence – referred to by psychologists as self-efficacy – in pursuing this role. And I was determined to see how these self-perceptions set the stage for their actions as parents.

These insights into women's perceptions, experiences, and emotions lie at the heart of this book, but they cannot be properly understood without a detailed consideration of the social institutions that have created some types of opportunity and denied others. In contemporary Japan, the educational system and the workplace are the two institutional contexts whose policies and practices most directly affect women's lives. In this book, I attend to the tension between these structural forces and women's individual thoughts, feelings, and perceptions of agency. I also focus on the immediate social context of the family and examine the support that family members provide (or fail to provide) to young mothers. I have been particularly interested in exploring women's perceptions of their husbands, examining the ways that husbands promote mothers' sense of parenting competence as well as the ways that they contribute to its erosion.

Psychologists often ignore the historical dimension of social phenomena in Japan; to address that gap I have directed significant attention to governmental family policies that have shaped women's lives over the past 125 years. At the turn of the twentieth century, officials in the newly reconstituted Japanese government sought ways to bind the citizens together and build their allegiance to a central state. Recognizing that women had a powerful role to play in this nation-building exercise, these officials discarded traditional Confucian perceptions of women and crafted an image of them as capable citizens and mothers. Though it sounds repressive and confining to contemporary ears, women's new identity as *ryōsai kenbo* – good wife and wise mother – signaled an expansion of women's opportunities. The notion of good wife encompassed both contributing to the family and state through productive labor and engagement with civic institutions and fulfilling duties in the home. And the concept of wise mother implied that women could actually be wise!

Over time, the notion of what it means to be a good wife and wise mother has continued to evolve, and it is still debated in contemporary Japan. I hope to capture these changing and contested images in this book. At the heart of the book is a longitudinal research project that I initiated in 2000. A key aspect of the work is a series of four interviews conducted over a three-year period with each of 16 mothers living in the Osaka area. Additionally, we conducted three surveys with a larger group of 116 mothers in Osaka and Sapporo. All of the major findings that emerged from analysis of the interviews were also supported by results from the surveys.

Overview of the Book

The book is divided into four parts. Part I, Chapters 1 and 2, introduces the theoretical frame of the research and provides an overview of the research site and participants. In Part II, I explore mothers' perceptions about themselves and their family members. Chapter 3 begins with an historical overview of societal expectations for Japanese mothers from the mid-1800s to the present time. This analysis forms the backdrop for understanding our participants' views about the nature of mothering. In Chapter 4, I explore several crucial cultural models pertaining to the common practice of *hansei*, or self-reflection, and use them to help understand these women's tendency to reflect carefully on their parenting behavior and to judge themselves harshly for failing to live up to their own standards.

In Part III of the book, I explore the conditions that give rise to women's role definition and evaluation of themselves as parents. Chapter 5 takes a close look at the women's early family experiences, particularly focusing on the ways that their own parents had nurtured – or curtailed – their early dreams about the future. I also examine how these early family dynamics continue to be echoed in their current interactions with their own children. Chapter 6 begins with an overview of the institution of marriage in modern Japan. I then take a close look at what these women expect from their husbands and examine how well their husbands live up to these expectations.

Part IV of the book provides insight into these women's actual behavior, beginning in Chapter 7 with the issue of child rearing and discipline. I illustrate the high standards that mothers set for their own parenting but show that they often do not have a strong network of supportive relations to help them accomplish these goals. In Chapter 8, I focus on the ways that mothers support their children's schooling, both at home and at school. A central theme of this chapter is how the parents' own educational experiences affected their confidence in their ability to provide support for their children's academic achievement. I also show how the demands of the school system shape women's beliefs about their role in supporting their children's achievement. In Chapter 9 I examine the circumstances and motivating factors behind the women's varied trajectories through the world of work. Many of the women began early adulthood with well-formulated aspirations regarding employment but were unable to combine full-time work with parenting. Chapter 10 sums up the major findings of the book and discusses their implications for family policies and practices in Japan. I conclude with an examination of the theoretical implications of this work for the study of parenting, social institutions, and individual agency in Japan.

Author's Background and Acknowledgments

I have been conducting research in Japan since the mid-1980s, when I was a graduate student involved in a cross-national project examining parenting practices in Japan and the United States. Subsequent to receiving a doctorate in developmental psychology and early education, I continued to study the role of Japanese parents in preparing children for school. Like many other Western observers, I was intrigued by Japan's postwar economic success and interested in understanding Japanese society's commitment to education. At the time, I was more wrapped up in documenting the instrumental value of Japanese mothers' efforts than in discovering how they themselves constructed and understood their role.

My interest in the personal experiences and perspectives of Japanese mothers began in the 1990s, when I conducted a project on Japanese preschools. In contrast to the positive image of Japanese women that was permeating Western academic literature at the time, the preschool directors that I interviewed frequently characterized mothers as sybaritic tennis players or sake-sloshing shoppers. I sometimes had to suppress feelings of annoyance at these criticisms, but I didn't pay that much attention to them. Then one day, a small event made me think more carefully about the discourses surrounding what it means to be a good parent. I was on my way to an interview at a preschool, accompanied by my research associate, a Japanese woman in her mid-fifties. We had arrived a bit early and stopped in a coffee shop near the school to kill time. Noticing many female customers, my associate casually mentioned that it still surprised her to see housewives hanging around in public during the middle of the day. Unlike the preschool directors, she did not express criticism of women for spending time on leisure activities; still, the fact that they were doing so was noteworthy to her. It made me realize that it wasn't just a few grouchy men who were attending so carefully to mothers' everyday activities. I became increasingly curious about what it would be like to be a mother in a society in which having a mid-morning cup of coffee with a friend made you conspicuous.

Because of my own experience in wrestling with the best way to balance work and family commitments, I tried to be as conscious as possible of the position from which I conducted my research. I was highly aware of the fact that some scholars "seem to have begun their work with a certain indignation towards the supposed submissiveness of Japanese women to patriarchal authority," as Tamanoi put it (1990, p. 19). How ironic it would have been, if I were to join the noisy chorus of those who criticize Japanese women, albeit from a feminist rather than traditionalist perspective. I tried not to judge these women in terms of my personal and political beliefs, but rather attempted to immerse myself in the task of understanding their own perspectives.

Of course, the fact that I am not Japanese is also a significant factor that shaped not only how I viewed the participants but also how they viewed the project. One strategy for offsetting the limitations of my outsider status has been to work as closely as possible with Japanese colleagues. As the current research was just getting under way, two talented doctoral students joined the project: Sawako Suzuki, now an assistant professor at Saint Mary's College of California, and Yoko Yamamoto, currently a postdoctoral researcher at Brown University. Both women were involved in every step of the study and were crucial to its success. They participated in the initial phase of recruiting our sample, were involved in developing all the surveys and interview protocols, conducted many of the interviews, and participated in all phases of data analysis and write-up. I count myself as extremely fortunate to have had the opportunity to work with these two talented women.

A number of other undergraduate and graduate students at the University of California, Berkeley, contributed to the project as well. Kazuko Behrens, now a faculty member at Texas Tech University, was deeply involved in early pilot work. She was also instrumental in developing the ideas for the first survey, recruiting the Sapporo sample, and conducting the first round of interviews in Sapporo. I received valuable assistance from a variety of UC Berkeley students, including Melike Acar, Soung Bae, Jamie Chen, Sari Leivant Sanghvi, Jessica Mindnich, Kyoko Onoda, Jessica Taisey Petrie, and Lynna Tsou, all of whom participated in the coding and analysis of the data. Stephanie Lo and Sira Park provided competent and valued assistance with library research and proofread the manuscript. I also benefited from discussion of an early draft of the book with students in my research group at UC Berkeley: Melike Acar, Shana Cohen, Irenka Domínguez-Pareto, Olivia Flint, Manuela Groth, Laura Lara, Ayumi Nagase, David Neufeld, Sira Park, Patti Solomon-Rice, Tanya Soohoo, and Lisa Wadors Verne. I am very thankful to Yoko Yamamoto and Bruce Fuller, who also read and commented extensively on the full manuscript. Sarah Serafim provided much-appreciated assistance with the job of copyediting. I thank Simina Calin and Jeanie Lee at Cambridge University Press for shepherding the manuscript through the publication process.

I am appreciative of a small grant from the Spencer Foundation, which enabled me to begin the project in 2000. Over the subsequent years, Sawako Suzuki and Yoko Yamamoto received additional funding from UC Berkeley to support their work on the project. This project has been largely a labor of love, and it would not have been possible without the willingness of many people to become involved on a volunteer basis, which advanced the work on all fronts.

I deeply appreciate the help of several preschool directors in Sapporo and Osaka prefecture in recruiting women for the study. I do not name them or their schools in order to preserve the anonymity of the women in the sample. For similar reasons of confidentiality I cannot thank the study participants by name, but I wish nevertheless to extend my heartfelt appreciation to them for participating in this project. I am particularly grateful to the 16 women who invited us to their homes and shared their thoughts and feelings with Sawako, Yoko, and me.

A host of other friends and colleagues have contributed to this work in important ways, both direct and indirect. I owe much to Keiko Kashiwagi, who is a pioneer in the study of Japanese women. I have learned a lot from her research and also from her personal example about what it takes to succeed professionally as a woman in Japan. Professor Kashiwagi, Hiroshi Azuma, and the late Robert Hess were my earliest mentors in this field, and I am truly thankful for all of their wisdom and guidance.

Throughout the last 15 years, I have received good counsel and valuable insights about social conditions in Japan from Noboru Takahashi at Osaka Kyoiku Daigaku. Long discussions during hikes on Mount Tamalpais with Marty Blum, Miriam Kuppermann, and Laura Myers have helped me deal with the problems and opportunities afforded by this project and just about everything else of importance in my life.

During the period in which this project was conducted, my children, Caitlin and Dylan, have grown up and they are now pursuing their own professional and academic dreams. I thank them for their lifelong tolerance of my Japan addiction. Bruce Fuller has listened with apparent interest to every idea I've ever had about Japanese women and has contributed significantly to the interpretations and analysis presented in this book. His steadfast partnership in our family life has enabled me to experience fulfillment in my professional career as well as joy in being a wife and mother.

PART I

"Good Wives, Wise Mothers": Parenting and Family Life in Cultural Context

During the last half of the twentieth century, Western scholars and media experts often singled out Japanese women for their strong commitment to the roles of housewife and mother. Seemingly untouched by the gender revolution occurring around the globe, Japanese women tended to marry young, then drop out of the labor market and devote themselves to raising children and caring for their hardworking husbands. But events in contemporary Japan suggest that this exceptional pattern no longer holds true. Many Japanese women are postponing marriage and bearing fewer children – or avoiding these activities altogether.

In 1947, the average Japanese woman could be counted on to have 4.5 children in her lifetime. Just over 60 years later, the number has dropped to 1.3 (National Institute of Population and Social Security Research, 2003). In a few short decades, Japan has become one of the least fertile and fastest aging countries in the world. The country's population, now 127 million people, is projected to drop to 90 million by 2055. By that time, one in four Japanese citizens will be 75 years or older, according to projections by the Japan Center for Economic Research (JCER) (2007; see also Kaneko et al., 2008a).

This drop will undoubtedly have far-reaching effects on the economy of Japan, currently the second largest in the world. The shrinking workforce is one of the government's biggest concerns in light of estimates that the working-age population will drop to 44.5 million people by 2050, less than 70 percent of the 2005 level (Japan Center for Economic Research, 2007). While forecasts by the JCER suggest that initial declines in the labor force will be offset in the next decade by rising participation of women in the labor force, the longer-term picture is not encouraging. Indeed, the JCER predicts that the growth rate of Japan's economy will fall to zero in the 2040s.

Why are so many Japanese women opting out of the business of being "good wives and wise mothers," the role they have been encouraged to take ever since the birth of the modern Japanese state? Analysts from a variety of disciplines have weighed in with possible answers to this question. From demographers we learn that Japanese women are waiting longer to get married, thereby shortening the number of years they are fertile and married, two preconditions to bearing children in a country where only 2 percent of children are born out of wedlock (National Institute of Population and Social Security Research, 2003). From economists, we learn that Japanese worry about the cost of having children (Kaneko et al., 2008b; Ogawa, Retherford, & Matsukura, 2009).[1] And from public policy experts, we learn that Japan ranks 22nd out of 29 Organization for Economic Co-operation and Development (OECD) countries in its ratio of total social expenditures to GDP (OECD, 2003). One result of this fiscal stringency is that child care is in short supply and of uneven quality (Holloway, 2000).

Japanese politicians have pronounced on the birth rate issue as well. Conservatives have criticized women who opt for a career instead of homemaking, calling them selfish and unpatriotic. For example, in 2003, former prime minister Yoshiro Mori, a member of a government commission charged with finding solutions to the population crisis, publicly attributed Japan's falling birth rate to the fact that Japanese women were too highly educated (French, 2003). He also expressed his opinion that the government should not provide a retirement pension to women who had dodged their civic duty to have children (Frederick, 2003). Perceiving Western influences as a root cause of Japanese women's "abandonment" of family life, conservative politicians have even pushed to revoke Article 24 of the Japanese constitution, which gives women such things as the right to own property and obtain a divorce. Indeed, a recent government report asserted that the equal rights clause has promoted "egoism in postwar Japan, leading to the collapse of family and community" (Beech, 2005).

For their part, moderates have tried to steer the debate in a different direction. Most official government rhetoric has acknowledged fertility decisions

---

[1] In fact, at slightly over 13 million yen (roughly $113,000 at the 2005 exchange rate), this cost is not particularly high relative to many Western countries. For example, the U.S. Department of Agriculture (2005) estimated the cost for a middle-income family at $250,000 in the United States, and a comparable estimate of raising a child in Melbourne, Australia, is just over $211,000 (U.S. dollars) (Henman, 2006). Although the higher cost of rearing a child is somewhat offset by the relatively higher personal income in the United States (where the personal average disposable income in 2007 was 19,776 international dollars compared to 12,076 in Japan) there is relatively little difference between the personal average in Japan and that of Australia (13,296 international dollars) (World Salaries Group, 2007).

to be a matter of individual choice, and politicians have passed measures providing parents with funds to offset the costs of child rearing. For instance, a law effective in 2005 provided qualified parents of children younger than age 7 with an allowance of approximately $50 a month for the first and second children and $100 a month for every child thereafter. This allowance was doubled for the first and second children in 2007 (Ministry of Health, Labor and Welfare Website, 2008). The government has had less success, however, in compelling employers to eliminate sexist employment practices that prevent women from staying in the labor force after having a child; nor has there been much progress in creating a culture of work that doesn't preclude the worker's active participation in family life (Miller, 2003; National Institute of Population and Social Security Research, 2003; Schoppa, 2006). So far, neither the harsh rhetoric of the conservatives nor the enticements offered by the moderates has succeeded in reversing the birth rate's downward trend.

[margin handwritten note: trying to motivate parents/women to have more children (§§§ incentives)]

What Is the Subjective Experience of Japanese Mothers?

In spite of Japanese officials' deep concern about the declining birth rate, they have paid surprisingly little attention to the viewpoint of the women who are to make these important decisions. Nor, until relatively recently, have many scholars attempted to understand women's perspectives either. Over the last several decades, psychologists in Japan and Western countries have focused on mothers' role in supporting children's development more than on understanding mothers' own experiences. As Keiko Kashiwagi (1998) notes, most academics have viewed Japanese women as an "environment" for producing children rather than as individuals whose own beliefs and feelings should be considered apart from their skill in producing high-achieving children. It would be ironic indeed if scholarly attention were again turned to Japanese women only because they are – literally – the "environment" for producing children in a country concerned about the declining birth rate.

[margin handwritten note: not JUST baby-makers]

In fact, my interest lies less in the declining birth rate per se than in what it reveals about the condition of women in Japan. I suspect that most women in Japan as elsewhere would like to become mothers if societal conditions permitted them to have children and to live a full, satisfying life. The declining birth rate is thus an indicator that women's status is problematic (see also Rosenbluth, 2007). What is going on in Japan that makes many women feel uncertain about becoming wives and mothers? What *is* it like to be a mother in contemporary Japan?

[bottom handwritten note: women may want to have children, but status + other factors discourage them?]

Data from opinion polls and surveys suggest that Japanese women's perceptions of the role of wife are ambivalent at best (Ohinata, 2001). Schoppa (2006, pp. 75–76) cites a comparative survey conducted in the late 1990s by the Ministry of Education finding that only 46 percent of Japanese women were satisfied with their family life, compared to 67 percent in the United States, 72 percent in Britain, and 53 percent in Korea. Findings from Japan and the United States collected in the mid-1990s suggest that Japanese women view marriage significantly less favorably than American women do. For example, only 51 percent of unmarried Japanese women indicated that they expected to be happier married than unmarried, compared to 69 percent of American women (Tsuya, Mason, & Bumpass, 2004).

Compared to their counterparts in the West and in other Asian countries, more Japanese women with children view child rearing as a complex job with few emotional rewards. A recent survey reported by Hirao (2007a, p. 70) found that only 47 percent of Japanese parents thought it was "always enjoyable to raise children," whereas 64 percent of parents in South Korea and 67 percent of parents in the United States responded positively to this question. When asked whether they thought raising children was fun, only 46 percent of Japanese parents agreed, compared to 67 percent of American parents (National Women's Education Center, Japan, 2005). Yet another recent survey comparing child-rearing attitudes in five Asian nations indicated that mothers in Tokyo felt more frustrated about child rearing than mothers in Seoul, Beijing, Shanghai, and Taipei (Benesse Educational Research Institute, 2006a).

Furthermore, despite the many accolades that they receive from observers in foreign countries, most Japanese women think they are doing a lousy job at parenting and are plagued by anxiety and self-doubt. For example, nearly half of mothers in one survey described themselves as "not very confident" or "not confident" about child rearing (Shwalb, Kawai, Shoji, & Tsunetsugu, 1995). Comparative studies find that Japanese mothers are less confident about child rearing than are mothers in seven other industrialized countries (Bornstein et al., 1998).

What's the problem with lacking self-confidence as a parent? According to psychologist Albert Bandura, individuals who evaluate themselves as unable to take a particular action – who lack what he calls self-efficacy – tend to become so overwhelmed by negative thoughts and feelings that they are less willing to exert effort when faced with difficult situations, and are likely to give up rather than respond with resilience (1982; 1997). Research findings bear out Bandura's theoretical assertions. People who feel efficacious in rearing their children are indeed better able to cope with challenging situations than those who lack confidence in their parenting skills (Ardelt & Eccles, 2001; Bandura, Barbaranelli, Caprara, & Pastorelli, 1996; Coleman & Karraker, 1997; Oettingen, 1995; Olioff & Aboud, 1991; Silver, Bauman, & Ireys, 1995; Teti & Gelfand, 1991; Williams et al., 1987).[2]

Indeed, some observers view mothers' lack of parenting confidence – a condition the Japanese media call "child-rearing neurosis" (*ikuji fuan*) – as one of the most serious problems facing families in contemporary Japan (Kazui, 1997; Shwalb, Kawai, Shoji, & Tsunetsugu, 1997). In one study focusing on Japanese mothers of toddlers and preschoolers, researchers found that mothers' lack of confidence in their child-rearing practices made them "unable to cope decisively and firmly with their children's opposition and assertion" (Ujie, 1997, p. 482). Kashiwagi (1998) argues that the anxiety and frustration experienced by many Japanese mothers can result in a feeling of detachment from their children. Her studies show that the more women engage in full-time child rearing (thereby fulfilling the "traditional" role), the *less* likely they are to experience a feeling of "oneness" with their children, often purported in Japan to be a "natural" expression of the maternal instinct.

[handwritten margin note: lack of confidence doesn't allow them to be firm w/ child]

So, given the importance of feeling successful at accomplishing valued tasks, what is it like for a Japanese woman to go through her daily life perceiving that she is failing at the role that many in her society deem to be of utmost importance for women? This is a question that captivated me when I began the research for this book. I was also curious to learn how, if women are indeed lacking in parenting self-efficacy, they have managed to be such good parents. After all, outside observers often look at the high achievement and positive social development of most Japanese children and conclude that their parents must be doing *something* right.

My exploration of these questions draws upon an ecocultural approach to parenting.[3] Within this perspective, parents in a society are thought to develop goals and care strategies (i.e., cultural models) that maximize the likelihood of their children's physical survival and the attainment of

---

[2]   Self-efficacy is one of several similar psychological constructs that pertain to the individual's perception of agency or control (e.g., locus of control, personal control, mastery, etc.). I use the construct of self-efficacy because it has a well-developed theoretical frame as well as a substantial body of related empirical work. It has made some inroads in the sociological literature as well (Hitlin & Long, 2009), where it is seen as a useful tool for analyzing the possibilities of individual action within a context of institutional power.

[3]   This approach was pioneered by anthropologists Beatrice Whiting and John Whiting, along with their colleagues and former students including Sarah Harkness, Robert LeVine, Sarah LeVine, Charles Super, and Thomas Weisner (e.g., Harkness & Super, 1992, 2002; LeVine et al., 1994; Weisner, 2002; Whiting & Edwards, 1988; Whiting & Whiting, 1975).

culturally valued skills and characteristics. The adoption of an ecocultural approach to parenting thus rests upon three analytic levels: individual, cultural, and institutional. With respect to the first level, that of the individual, I am particularly interested in perceptions of agency or self-efficacy as a variable that differs across individual parents. I seek to understand how women conceptualize the role of mother, what criteria they use for self-evaluation, and whether their self-evaluation is stable over time. I am also curious about the factors that contribute to women's perception of themselves as effective or ineffective parents. I look extensively at how their self-perceptions are shaped by their own experiences as children, in the context of their marriages, and by their involvement in the world of work. Additionally, I acknowledge unique personal attributes that shape their response to these experiences – for example, a certain sense of humor might help one woman shrug off criticism from her husband, while another would feel deeply wounded by similar comments. And finally, I am concerned with the ways in which women's self-efficacy is linked to their interactions with their children and support for their achievement in school.

The second level that forms the conceptual foundation of this book is that of *culture*, particularly the collective representations – or cultural models – of family life that are available to Japanese women as they negotiate the demands of daily life. The notion of a cultural model refers to a collectively constructed belief about how things are or how they should be.[4] For example, in the realm of parenting, some Japanese people may believe that children should be indulged up until the age of three years, after which they should be treated more strictly. In addition to beliefs and values, cultural models also include behavior sequences used to deal with routine situations.

Although cultural models of child rearing are collectively constructed, this does not mean that they necessarily emerge at the level of a national group (or an ethnic group); nor do all members of a group necessarily agree with the dominant cultural models (Gjerde, 2004). Even in Japan, a relatively homogeneous country, there are of course many disagreements about how children should be raised and educated (Holloway, 2000). Anthropologists often describe cultural models as being "tacit" or "taken for granted," but the ones that I will be describing are more likely to be a target of conscious reflection. In other work, I have referred to these as "declared" models because they are consciously evaluated and declared as the beliefs held by

---

[4] Some writers prefer the terms "cultural concerns" or "discourses" because these terms are associated with a notion of fluidity or "an instability that allows different interest groups to suit their own interest and promote their own representation" (Gjerde, 2004, p. 146).

a certain individual (Holloway, Fuller, Rambaud, & Eggers-Piérola, 1997). Parents may sometimes approach child rearing on the basis of tacit assumptions and models, but most parents in modern communities are exposed to other models by observing other parents, talking with their children's teachers, and accessing various forms of media. This is the space in which individual agency comes into play as parents evaluate various approaches and appropriate those they find of value into their own parenting repertoire. To understand why a parent acts the way she does, it is essential to identify the models that are available to members of a certain community but also to acknowledge "individuals' self-consciousness, individuality, and ability to transcend their own culture" (Gjerde, 2004, p. 140).

The third analytic level pertains to the ways in which *public policies and institutions* help to define the role of wife and mother and shape the opportunities available to Japanese women. Certainly, the rapid changes that have occurred in Japan during the past century have resulted in new institutional forces that press parents to prepare their children for life in a complex, largely urban society. Institutional interests are capable of using cultural models strategically. For example, the Japanese government has worked actively at various points to re-invigorate certain "traditional" values that it deemed crucial to the continued economic success of the country, including thrift, hard work, and docility. When Japanese business leaders, politicians, and bureaucrats encounter opposition on some issue, they frequently accuse the dissenters of being poisoned by "Western individualism" or castigate them for being "un-Japanese" (Mouer & Sugimoto, 1986). This technique has been an effective way for these institutional actors to suppress women's attempts to break out of constraints on their activities as mothers and employees, as we will see later in the book.

In recent years, Gjerde (2004) and others have urged cultural psychologists to identify those in a society who possess the "hegemonic voice" – that is, those who have the power to shape and promote certain cultural models and to suppress others. Writing about Japan, psychologists sometimes assume that Japanese people are homogeneous with respect to cultural values, and that they arrived at this state of homogeneity through processes such as "symbiosis" which are power neutral. In contrast, other scholars have focused on the way that authority is wielded in the family, school, community, and workplace (Holloway, 2000; Sugimoto, 2003), and argue that while it may come in a guise that is ostensibly benign or indirect, Japanese "friendly authoritarianism" can nevertheless be highly effective and demands careful consideration.

What Is a Good Wife and Wise Mother?

The phrase "good wife, wise mother" (*ryōsai kenbo*) was coined by Masanao Nakamura in the 1870s. It reflects the realization by Japanese government officials in charge of facilitating Japan's swift transition to modernity that women could contribute to the new nation by taking a more active role in child rearing, as well as by engaging in patriotic activities and by contributing to the family's income (Patessio, 2006; Sievers, 1981). Within a few short decades, however, the meaning of the phrase shifted as government officials pushed women out of the public realm, took away the few legal rights they had previously held, and identified child rearing rather than productive labor as their primary role. In the years subsequent to the Second World War, women's rights were instated in the new constitution, but the image of good wife and wise mother retained a conservative flavor. In the postwar years, government prioritization of the maternal role was further underscored by new policies making it difficult for women with children to participate in the labor force. For the men in the "iron triangle" of business, bureaucracy, and politics, the ideal workforce was composed of hard-working men supported at home by "professional housewives." The phrase "good wives, wise mothers" is still heard today, but its meaning has taken on a negative connotation to women who perceive it as emblematic of the ways in which government and business interests have limited women's opportunities to work outside the home.

Indeed, in the twenty-first century, the limits of the government's attempts to promote the more conservative aspects of the good wife, wise mother image have become increasingly apparent. If Japanese citizens were faithfully absorbing the cultural models being promoted by their government, Japanese homes would still be bursting with children, but they are not. This is where our inquiry begins – to examine how, as introspective, self-aware, and creative individuals, Japanese women themselves think about their obligations as mothers, wives, and human beings.

2

Locating the Research in Space and Time

Listening to Women's Voices

Throughout this book, I will focus on the stories of four women – Junko, Chihiro, Asako, and Miyuki. Their narratives illustrate the themes that figure prominently in the accounts of the larger group of participants – their parenting goals and self-evaluation, their struggles to create a life that somehow reflects their childhood dreams and aspirations, their experiences as wives, and their participation in the contexts of school and work. Becoming familiar with the "whole story" of at least a few individuals makes it easier to see how their lifetimes of experiences and relationships are interrelated and also to gain a deeper sense of how the institutional features of work and schooling set the stage for their parenting efforts. In this chapter, I introduce the four women. I then describe the communities in which they were living and characterize the societal and political conditions affecting their lives during the data collection period.

I supplement the narratives of these four focal mothers with material from 12 other mothers in our interview study. These 16 women were in turn selected from a larger sample of 116 women to whom we had already administered a parenting survey. In selecting 16 women for a series of in-depth interviews, the research team's goal was to include some women who were confident in their parenting and others who were less confident. As noted in Chapter 1, my interest in the notion of self-efficacy was sparked by research indicating that Japanese mothers were convinced that they were not good parents, in spite of much evidence to the contrary. Our reading of the literature on self-reflection and self-evaluation in Japan led us to suspect that additional work was needed to tease apart the elements of this important construct in order to understand how it functions in Japan. In order to ensure variability among the 16 women with respect to parenting self-efficacy, we examined the scores from a parenting self-efficacy scale included in the first survey of 116 women, and selected eight individuals who were above the average in terms of self-efficacy and eight who were below the average (the scale items can be viewed in Appendix A).

Additionally, we selected women of varying socioeconomic status, as most previous scholarship on Japanese families has focused on the middle class. Accordingly, we made sure that eight of the 16 were high school graduates and eight had graduated with either two- or four-year college degrees. The women were interviewed four times, twice when their child was in preschool, once in first grade, and once in second grade. Basic demographic characteristics for this group can be found in Table 2.1. In this book, the interview data from these 16 women are supplemented by findings from our surveys conducted with 116 mothers when their children were in preschool, first grade, and second grade. Demographic data for the 116 mothers and details concerning our research methods can be found in Appendix B.

In selecting the four focal women for this book, I chose two who expressed considerable self-doubt about their parenting abilities (Junko and Chihiro) and two who felt much more efficacious as mothers (Asako and Miyuki). Two of the focal mothers were high school graduates (Junko and Asako), one was a graduate of a two-year college (Miyuki), and one held a degree from a four-year university (Chihiro).

Junko. Frank and funny, Junko /joon-koh/ lived up to the reputation of Osaka residents as comedians and storytellers. When I met her for our interview, I remember thinking that she looked more like a college student than a 30-year-old mother of two, with her hair dyed brown and cut in a fashionable style and eyes ringed with dark eyeliner and a heavy application of mascara. Listening to her husky laugh, it was easy for me to imagine her as a mischievous young girl, challenging her parents and teachers with her rebellious behavior but charming them at the same time.

In spite of her spunky personality, Junko's parenting self-efficacy was not high. In the first interview, she described how difficult it was for her to find the right way to discipline her children:

I've never really been confident about child rearing. Like, how I scold, for example. I'm not very good at getting my child to understand what I'm trying to say. I've never been articulate enough. I always say unnecessary things and I can't seem to get my child to understand his actions. So I can't seem to do anything except raise my voice and slap his butt. Yeah, I guess I don't really have much

TABLE 2.1. *Characteristics of participants*

Name	Mother's education	Mother's employment[a]	Children	Husband's education	Family income[b]
Asako	High school	Not employed	2 sons	High school	Medium/high
Beni	2-year college	Not employed	2 sons, 1 daughter	Vocational school	Low/medium
Chihiro	4-year college	Part-time	1 son, 1 daughter	4-year college	Low/medium
Hiromi	High school	Full-time	1 son, 1 daughter	High school	Low/medium
Junko	High school	Part-time	1 son, 1 daughter	4-year college	Low
Kayoko	Junior high	Not employed	2 daughters	High school	Low
Mari	2-year college	Not employed	1 son, 1 daughter	4-year college	High
Masayo	4-year college	Full-time	2 sons	4-year college	Medium/high
Miho	High school	Not employed	2 daughters	High school	Medium/high
Miyuki	2-year college	Part-time	2 daughters, 1 son	Vocational school	Low
Naoko	4-year college	Part-time	2 sons	4-year college	Medium/high
Reiko	2-year college	Part-time	1 son, 1 daughter	4-year college	Medium/high
Risa	High school	Part-time	2 daughters, 1 son	High school	Low
Sakura	High school	Part-time	2 sons, 1 daughter	High school	Low/medium
Yasuko	High school	Part-time	2 daughters, 1 son	High school	Low/medium
Yuri	College	Part-time	1 daughter	4-year college	Low/medium

Note: The names of the four focal mothers (Asako, Chihiro, Junko, Miyuki) are indicated by italics. Shaded cells indicate mothers with relatively high parenting self-efficacy on first survey. Two mothers (Sakura and Masayo) dropped out of the study after the second interview.

[a] Employment status at time of final interview.

[b] Income categories reported at first contact with families: Low = 3,000,000–5,000,000 yen (approximately $28,302 to $47,170 U.S. at 2000 exchange rate of 106 yen per dollar); Low/Medium = 5,000,000–7,000,000 yen ($47,170 to $66,038); Medium/high = 7,000,000–10,000,000 yen ($66,038 to $94,340); High = more than 10,000,000 yen ($94,340).

confidence when it comes to getting my child to understand. It's because I can't explain things as gently as the preschool teachers do.[1]

Junko believed that parents should be strict and "tell them [their children] that wrong is wrong." But she regretted that she did not know how to mix strictness with affection, remarking "I am not really nice or kind to my children." She also worried about her ability to support her children's academic development. She herself had barely made it through high school, and she was convinced that she lacked the necessary intelligence to support her children's achievement in school.

Junko had few people to turn to for support and advice about rearing children. She had been married for just under ten years when we first met her, and she and her husband were not on good terms. Although his position in a family-owned business afforded flexibility and ample free time, he was not involved in child rearing and performed few household activities. Junko did not respect her husband's values or ideas about child rearing and never asked him for help or support when she was worried or had a problem. She described herself as unable to connect with her children's teachers, nor did she rely on the mothers of her children's classmates for information or advice. Instead, she relieved her feelings of stress by taking walks with a friend, doing piecework at home (assembling circuit boards), and listening to CDs of her favorite pop singers.

Chihiro. Sturdily built and bursting with energy, Chihiro /chee-hee-roh/ is nevertheless one of the less efficacious mothers in our sample. Chihiro applied herself conscientiously to the role of mother, but, despite her efforts, she did not feel that she was doing a good job of being a parent: "Sometimes I wonder if I am qualified to be a parent, because from a child's perspective I'm not that great." Not only did she have difficulty understanding the thoughts and feelings of her children, but she also felt a sense of detachment – even hostility – toward her daughter in particular.

In spite of her grave self-doubts about her parenting skill, she was a continual presence at her children's schools, observing and monitoring classroom activities, organizing events for the PTA, or engaging in routine office work to help out the staff administrators. I have an enduring mental image of her navigating her minivan through the narrow streets of Osaka, ferrying

[1] To preserve the anonymity of the women and their families I have used pseudonyms for them and altered certain details that would permit identification. All quotations are taken nearly verbatim (leaving out disfluencies for the sake of readability) from English translations of interview transcripts. To reduce the length of the quotations, I have occasionally left out repetitive or digressive elements; I indicate such omissions with ellipses.

her children from one lesson to the next. She preferred these activities to shopping or meeting friends for lunch – activities that consumed the lives of many women in her well-off community. To earn extra money and to fill her free time, she had also taken an entry-level position at a copy shop, a position well below the status and pay level of the work she had performed prior to marrying and having children.

Even as an adolescent Chihiro knew that she wanted to participate actively in civic life. She eagerly took on leadership positions at her high school and earned excellent grades. She dreamed of becoming an architect but was forced to give up this dream when she learned that no college within commuting distance of her parents' home offered a major in architecture. Her father would not allow her to live away from home, so she shifted her sights to the study of industrial design and gained admission to a well-regarded local university. She graduated with honors in four years and eventually took a job with a prominent design firm. Chihiro loved the challenge of designing new products and enjoyed interacting with her colleagues and clients. She even liked commuting with the (mostly male) salaried workers, getting to know the "regulars" and joking with them on the long train ride to work.

As much as she enjoyed working, Chihiro's professional life lasted only a few years. When she married, her parents expressed doubt that she had the physical stamina to work and raise a family. She decided it was best to quit her job, but later came to regret that she had not found a way to continue working while her children were young. Throughout our interviews, she spoke of her frustration with life as a housewife and mother, and her longing to return to school or to go back to the working world.

Like Junko, Chihiro seemed to lack a sense of support from those around her. She reported having a somewhat distant relationship with her husband, whose work required him to leave the house well before dawn every day. She was more likely to get help and advice about child rearing from her mother and father, but they tended more to criticize and give advice than to listen to her private feelings. And her sense of privacy prohibited her from confiding in other women; she preferred to keep her friendships light and to avoid serious topics. Chihiro dreamed of a different life, although she was not sure what exactly she was looking for:

Well, I think that I'm longing for a stimulation that I'm not getting from life now. I want to see the outside world. I feel that there are so many things I can learn like going to school, studying, getting a job. It's like starting anew, although I don't know what I'll become, or when I'll change. But to do those things, I need my own time. That is, not as a mother, nor as a housewife, but my own personal time. I just want that little bit of personal time.

Asako. Asako (/ah-sah-koh/) arrived at the first interview in a formal suit, with carefully applied makeup. I came to appreciate the significance of this effort to dress up when we learned that she was a serious athlete and generally preferred wearing a comfortable tracksuit to anything formal or traditionally feminine. Asako's gesture of respect toward us was characteristic of her approach to life, which focused on maintaining harmonious and respectful relationships with others. Her lifelong involvement in athletics had required that she fight traditional expectations about females, but it also helped her develop a set of moral guidelines that brought joy and meaning to her life. Gentle, calm, and serious, she appeared to move through life with a sense of purpose and enjoyment.

Asako was one of the most confident mothers in our sample. She was highly self-reflective but had found a way to avoid obsessive rumination about her parenting practices. As she remarked in our first interview, "If you think really hard about [parenting], and keep thinking and thinking about it, maybe you might think it's a very difficult thing, but as long as you hold onto your beliefs and stick to them, as long as you think like that, I think it's OK."

Asako's aspirations for her son were consistent with her personal philosophy of life; she hoped that, above all, he would develop a sense of empathy and consideration for others. She helped him cultivate these sensitivities by watching over him as he learned from interacting with other children and from experiences he had in nature. While Asako herself had been an indifferent student and was glad to take a job after graduating from high school, she wanted her son to experience academic success. She was able to use his enthusiasm for trains as a basis for learning activities and she felt comfortable interacting with his teachers.

Asako appeared to derive this sense of parenting self-efficacy partly from the supportive actions of her husband. He had a steady job with a company that required no overtime and was only a short distance from their home. He spent his free time with his family rather than at a bar or *pachinko* (Japanese pinball) parlor, and he had formed a very close relationship with their son. Unlike some fathers, whose interaction with their children was limited to bathing together and watching television, Asako's husband took their son on errands, played sports with him, and took him on train rides just for the fun of it. Asako frequently consulted with her husband on child-rearing matters, and the two of them worked together to encourage their son's interests.

Asako told us that they approached discipline as a team: "My husband and I decided not to get mad at the same time. We've been talking about it since he was little. So when his father is scolding him I don't say anything. And when I am scolding him my husband doesn't say anything and watches us from the side." Asako's husband shared her love of soccer and respected her skill as an athlete, another factor that contributed to the strength of their partnership.

Asako was not employed, nor did she express a desire to move back into the workplace. She had quit her job with little regret when she got married. Shortly before our final interview, she gave birth to a second son. Her plans for the future focused on providing a home for her husband and children, and continuing to participate in soccer at a serious but non-professional level.

Miyuki. When I entered Miyuki's /mee-yoo-kee/ small kitchen for our interview, the first thing I noticed were platters heaped with food, including home-made *takoyaki* (fried octopus). With a wide smile, Miyuki motioned my colleague Sawako and me to the table. In spite of all the effort involved, she had decided to make homemade *takoyaki* after learning in a previous conversation with Sawako that it was one of her favorite dishes. This thoughtfulness and concern for the welfare of others were characteristic of Miyuki, the consummate Japanese homemaker. Another of Miyuki's characteristics was a knack for finding a constructive lesson in almost every experience, no matter how challenging. She viewed virtually everything that happened as an opportunity for learning and rarely complained about anything.

When I think of Miyuki, I picture her in the pink apron decorated with cartoon animals that she was wearing the day of our *takoyaki* lunch. But her outwardly sweet, feminine appearance was somewhat deceiving. For one thing, in spite of her girlish manner, Miyuki expressed a strong sense of parenting self-efficacy. She seemed to reflect carefully on her performance in the role of wife and mother of three children, but did not succumb to negative self-evaluation and considered her own needs and preferences in addition to those of her family members. She evaluated herself as a mother according to the amount of effort she expended, not according to the actual results in terms of her children's behavior, and she did not hold herself to any type of universal standard:

I think there are many kinds of mothers. I think it's pointless to say that this kind of mother is good or that kind is good. I think that I am myself and I've never thought about imitating other mothers … As a mother, I don't think there is a "perfect mother." I think that it's good enough to be my kind of mother. For example, I'm not good at sewing, but I can at least sew wiping cloths (*zōkin*). I can at least sew a tiny bag. Even if it's not well done, at least I can do it.

Miyuki's confidence as a parent stemmed partly from her experience (previous to marriage) as a preschool teacher. She felt that the training she received in the course of obtaining her associate's degree in early childhood education, along with her classroom experiences, contributed to her sense that each child is unique and that the job of the parent or teacher is to learn how best to support that individual child. Perhaps not surprisingly, given her own background, Miyuki was strongly oriented toward fostering her children's academic achievement. All three children were enrolled in a variety of after-school programs, and Miyuki was well informed about what each child was learning there as well as in their regular school. She kept in close touch with their teachers and worked with them to help her children address any areas of weak performance. In spite of her focus on supporting her children's achievement, she nevertheless seemed to approach her life with a sense of enjoyment and frequently remarked that it was fun to be a mother.

Miyuki's husband worked long hours to maintain a middle-class lifestyle for his family. When he was home, in spite of his exhaustion he willingly interacted with the children. Miyuki mentioned on several occasions that she felt comfortable discussing her worries and problems with her husband, even though he frequently did not appear to be listening carefully. His advice, although sometimes harshly critical of her, helped her come to a satisfactory resolution of most issues. Miyuki's essentially sweet and accommodating nature again showed itself to be tempered with a strong sense of purpose. She knew how to get what she needed from her husband and did not hesitate to take the steps to make it happen.

In spite of her love of teaching, Miyuki had made the hard decision to quit her job when she got married. By the time she was ready to re-enter the job market – when her third child entered elementary school – she was told by the municipal authorities in charge of hiring teachers that she was too old to return to her former position. After months of looking for work, she took a part-time job as a clerk at a convenience store. In spite of the mundane nature of the position, she appreciated the opportunity to get out of house and to gain some new skills. Always optimistic, she believed that her work experience was helping her become a better mother by exposing her to a variety of people, teaching her new skills, and giving her a sense of accomplishment as a person. When we last spoke with her, she indicated her belief that it would be unwise to take on a more serious or time-consuming job because she anticipated caring for her husband's parents when they became elderly or ill.

Community Context of the Research

The 16 women who participated in our interviews were all from Osaka prefecture. At the core of the prefecture is Osaka City, a "mega city" with a population of over 2.5 million people situated on 222 densely populated square kilometers. Osaka's history dates back to the seventh century, when it served as the port of arrival for envoys from China and Korea. Its seaside location and proximity to several large rivers made it a natural choice for the development of maritime transportation, and it developed as a center of international trade as well as the central dispersal point for shipping goods throughout Japan. Starting in the late 1500s, it served as Japan's political capital as well, but this status was lost when the capital was moved to Tokyo (then called Edo) in the seventeenth century. However, commerce and popular culture flourished in the subsequent 200 years, and the citizens of Osaka developed a reputation within Japan as open minded, outgoing, and entrepreneurial. Subsequent to the Meiji Restoration in the late nineteenth century, the area experienced a period of economic stagnation. As the region's economic base shifted from trade and finance to industry, it became the site of many factories, which have contributed to serious environmental degradation that continues to the present day.

The variability in family socioeconomic status (SES) is wider in Osaka prefecture than in most other parts of Japan, with the areas to the north having a far greater proportion of college educated families than those in the south (Mizuuchi, Kato, & Oshiro, 2008). Some of the more affluent mothers in our study lived in Takatsuki City, situated at the northern edge of the prefecture. With a population of over 354,000 people, Takatsuki City is a relatively new community whose residents generally own or rent units in medium-rise apartment buildings. In the commercial area surrounding the train station, boutiques selling trendy clothes are interspersed with stores catering to the more sober tastes of the older generation. Women can be seen meeting for lunch in spacious restaurants serving gourmet dishes with a European flair. Florists, bakeries, and other stores offering a wide variety of consumer goods signal the relatively affluent nature of this community.

Most of the working-class mothers in our sample lived in the Nishiyodogawa ward of Osaka City. Unlike Takatsuki City, which is primarily residential, Nishiyodogawa features a mixture of housing, light industry, and retail establishments. Over 95,000 citizens live in an area of just 14.23 square kilometers, which is over three times the density of New York City. Much of the area is home to small apartment buildings, convenience stores, and modest retail establishments, together with coffee shops and family-owned restaurants often with just two or three tables and a lunch counter. The narrow streets are crowded with pedestrians, cyclists, and cars. In some parts of the neighborhood, older buildings have been recently torn down and replaced with office buildings, warehouses, and larger stores, and the once-narrow streets widened to permit two lanes of traffic.

The Nishiyodogawa area is infamous for its problems with pollution. In the early part of the twentieth century, rapid industrialization triggered pollution and environmental degradation in Osaka. Citizen protests in the 1930s led to the enactment of Japan's first statutory controls on particulates by Osaka Prefecture, but Japan's military buildup later in the decade triggered further construction of heavy and chemical industry factories. Osaka was bombed heavily during the Second World War, and it is estimated that a quarter of the city was damaged or destroyed. Osaka's industrial sector suffered a huge blow, but the government moved quickly to develop it anew. To achieve this rapid growth, it again sacrificed the environment. As a result, the combination of industrial and automobile emissions has contributed to widespread asthma, chronic bronchitis, and emphysema in Osaka. The Nishiyodogawa area has been particularly hard-hit, both due to its proximity to several major highways, including the Hanshin Expressway, and because it is an industrial zone. In 1995, a lawsuit brought by pollution victims in the Nishiyodogawa area was decided in their favor. However, despite the ongoing efforts of government, citizens, and businesses to improve the environment, the government's goal of a community so free of pollution that the scent of the official ward flower – the *Camellia sasanqua* – can be detected in the air has yet to be achieved.

In general, I noticed subtle social class differences in the housing options and furnishings in the homes we visited. Most of the less educated women lived in apartments in large, multi-story buildings that were three or four decades old, although one lived in an older single family home. The apartments typically consisted of two or three small bedrooms, a bathroom, and a combination living and dining room adjoining a kitchen area. In most units, the living room was light and airy due to the presence of a large sliding glass door along one wall; however, a few apartments located in older buildings lacked a source of natural light in the main living rooms. In the homes of the high school graduates, the décor often included posters of cartoon characters from Disney or Sanrio (e.g., Hello Kitty). One mother had even upholstered her sofa with fabric embossed with the familiar Kitty, using a similar fabric in contrasting colors for curtains. The apartments tended not to have a lot of furniture, but a lack of storage space sometimes contributed to a cluttered feeling.

Most of the more educated mothers also lived in apartments, although two among the 16 we interviewed (Chihiro and Miyuki) lived in detached homes. The furnishings in Takatsuki homes were more expensive than those in the homes of the less educated women, and they were more likely to include Western elements such as glass cases for displaying knickknacks, including family photos and souvenirs from trips to Hawaii or other foreign countries.

Contemporary Conditions for Families in Osaka

During the 1980s, Japan became an economic superpower, inspiring pride at home and envy abroad. However, 1989 marked the peak of the "bubble economy," and the following year stock prices began to fall precipitously. Many citizens attained a middle-class lifestyle during the 1980s, with money to travel abroad and purchase luxury goods, but the gap between the rich and the poor also widened during that time. During the 1990s, the closing or downsizing of firms and factories hit less affluent citizens particularly hard. Eager to save money on part-time labor, companies continued to offer women low wages for temporary work with no benefits, and the wage gap between men and women widened (Tipton, 2008). Corporations also attempted to become more efficient by discontinuing the usual Japanese practice of inevitable promotion and "lifetime employment," creating a sense of anxiety among many Japanese workers about their financial future. The participants in our study questioned the value of higher education, with some believing that an entrepreneurial spirit would prove more valuable to their own children's economic future than a diploma from a prestigious university.

The economic and political problems of the 1990s were accompanied by several other troubling events that gave many Japanese a feeling that their country was headed in the wrong direction. In January of 1995, the year that many of the children in this study were born, the city of Kobe experienced the devastating Hanshin Earthquake, which took 6,434 lives. Living approximately 50 kilometers from the quake's epicenter, close enough to feel the tremors, the people of Osaka were deeply affected by this tragic loss. Many believed that the government had failed in its fundamental duty to protect its citizens, both before and after the earthquake, and some were also dismayed by the initial inability of the community itself to organize and care for the victims. Several mothers in our study mentioned lessons about civic responsibility that they had learned from undergoing that traumatic experience. The nation was further traumatized in March of that year, when members of a terrorist group released sarin gas in the Tokyo subway system, killing twelve people and creating massive panic among many thousands. The fact that many of the terrorists were students or recent graduates of prestigious universities caused many to question whether Japan's preoccupation with academic credentials had occurred at the expense of basic human values.

Around the same time, there were several sensational crimes in the Kansai area involving children, including the gruesome murder of two children in 1997 by a 14-year-old Kobe boy (Smith & Sueda, 2008) and the stabbing death in 2001 of eight elementary school children ("Stabbing suspect aimed to harass relatives," 2001). These crimes strongly affected the women in our study, and they reported taking increased precautions to monitor their children's whereabouts. The fact that the crimes were committed by individuals who had grown up in seemingly normal, middle-class families made some mothers in our study nervous about their own children's mental health.

In addition to these extreme incidents, there were other troubling trends among the nation's youth. Although Japanese students continued to perform well on international tests, many Japanese observers believed that the school system was in crisis (Tsuneyoshi, 2004). Newspapers frequently reported on the phenomenon of the "collapsed classroom" (*gakkyū hōkai*), in which rebellious students openly challenged their teachers and refused to pay attention or do any work (French, 2002; Otake, 2002; see also Yoder, 2004). An increasing number of students were reported to have developed "school phobia" and refused to go to school at all (Yoneyama, 2000). Bullying became a serious concern of many Japanese educators (Ando, Asakura, & Simons-Morton, 2005). And finally, a growing number of adolescents declared their intention to forgo professional goals and became so-called "freeters," individuals who float freely from one low-paying job to the next rather than settling down (Kosugi, 2006). For the most part, these problems continue to be of significant concern today.

Politicians and the public at large have offered many explanations for these problems in the schools. Conservatives have tended to blame parents for spoiling their children, and worry openly about the corruption of Japan by the Western values of individualism and materialism. They have criticized the schools for allowing too many women to become teachers, and have called for a reinstatement of the traditional curriculum – including "moral education" – and corporal punishment. Liberals locate the problem in the rigid and unimaginative curriculum found in the schools, and also cite the pressures created by the high school and college examination system.

By the end of the 1990s, the Ministry of Education had implemented reforms more in line with the liberal analysis. The goal of the new policies – which were dubbed "relaxed" (*yūtori*) education – was nurturing students to become curious, active problem solvers rather than mere compliant consumers of factual material. They sought to reduce the demands on students and increase the amount of time they had available for social interaction, sports, and hobbies. The school week was reduced from five and a half days to five days by eliminating classes on Saturdays. In order to accommodate the reduced number of classroom hours, they effected a 30 percent reduction in the curriculum (Tsuneyoshi, 2004). They continued the focus on discovery learning, and also introduced a period for integrated study (*sōgōteki gakushū no jikan*).

These reforms were quite controversial. Some vocal "back to basics" critics decried the negative effects of diluting the curriculum; others expressed concern that elite families would now be more likely to send their children to special cram schools or to private schools, where the number of hours had not been reduced, thus widening the achievement gap between the haves and have-nots. The families in our study were directly affected by the "relaxed education" reforms, because their children began the first grade in April of 2001. As we will see in Chapter 8, some mothers were happy about the changes and expressed satisfaction with the schools, whereas others were less optimistic. Those who worried about declining standards attempted to offset any gaps in the curriculum by arranging for after-school supplementary classes and keeping a close eye on their children's progress.

In fact, in the years subsequent to these reforms, the achievement of Japanese students on international examinations has dropped precipitously. One international assessment (Program for International Student Assessment) ranked Japanese students at the very top in math in 2000, but they dropped to sixth in 2003 and tenth in 2006. In reading, they dropped from eighth in 2000 to fourteenth in 2003 and fifteenth in 2006 (Organisation for Economic Co-operation and Development Website, 2008). Following this sharp decline, the Ministry of Education announced plans to conduct a thorough national achievement examination in elementary and junior high school, to be followed by a reformulation of educational guidelines in January of 2008. The new guidelines mandated an increase in the number of lesson-hours, an increase in the extent of subject matter, the addition of English language activities in elementary school, and increased instruction in "moral values" (Benesse Educational Research Institute, 2008a; Manzo,

2008). An influential government advisory group called for a return to Saturday classes, but so far this measure has not been adopted ("Education rebuilding council submits second report," 2007).

Historically, residents of Osaka have a reputation for being somewhat less education-oriented than their counterparts in Tokyo. In its official education policy, Osaka City focuses on human rights rather than academic achievement and emphasizes the importance of producing well-rounded students who are thoughtful, considerate, and healthy in body and mind (Official Website of Osaka City, 2008). Students from Osaka City, which includes the working-class area where the less educated mothers in our sample lived, performed below students from the wealthier Takatsuki City, whose performance was close to the the national average ("Osaka prefecture results on national achievement test," 2008). A survey administered along with the national achievement test found that, compared to the national average, students in Osaka reported somewhat more relaxed daily habits, less study time, less homework, and less enrollment in supplementary schooling. Teachers in Osaka were also more critical of their students' motivation to learn, ability to attend to their lessons, and general manners. In light of Osaka's distinctive characteristics, it is important to exercise caution in generalizing the results of our study to other regions in Japan. Whenever possible, we supplement the results of our study by describing comparable research conducted in other geographical areas.

PART II

3

What Is a Wise Mother?

[Good mothers] are dynamic and busy but they are also kind. They don't express their kindness openly but they have an internal kindness, the real kind inside. (Chihiro, college educated, low self-efficacy mother of two)

I don't know. Maybe [a good mother is] a person who can say, "It's right" when it is right and the person who doesn't do anything wrong, or who doesn't bother other people especially in a public place, so a person who can scold their children. (Junko, high school educated, low self-efficacy mother of two)

Well, when the child has problems or has hit the wall, if I could be a source of security just by being next to him. It's not like I can say something or do something for him, but if I could provide a sense of security or be near him and if that could help him overcome the issue on his own. (Asako, high school educated, high self-efficacy mother of two)

These comments by three of the focal mothers in our study introduce some of the key elements of being a "wise mother" that have characterized Japanese child rearing in the past as well as the present. In these excerpts, Chihiro, the frustrated industrial design engineer, ponders the affective side of parenting. Asako, the serene and confident athlete, focuses more on socialization, expressing her view that a mother should be a watchful presence but let children learn through experiencing the natural consequences of their actions rather than by being explicitly taught how to behave. And Junko, the spunky working-class lover of pop music, describes her as a teacher who should instruct her child about proper behavior.

We focus in this chapter on understanding the varied representations that Japanese women have constructed about the role of mother. I am particularly interested in how individuals develop characterizations of motherhood as they draw upon and interpret the representations that are available as part of their sociohistorical legacy. To unpack this idea, let's begin with a definition of terms. In the past, many social scientists – particularly in sociology – have used the term "role" to refer to a mother's understanding of the range of activities that she believes to be important, necessary, and permissible for her to take on behalf of the child. Traditionally, social scientists have seen a mother's role definition as reflecting the expectations held by those around her, including family members, the media, and school personnel. More recently, scholars have moved away from the position that role-related understandings are simply transmitted from society to the individual, and have embraced the idea that individuals construct role understandings based on representations of, for example, motherhood available in a given community. Thus, according to this perspective, each woman perceives the expectations of others, and constructs a role by integrating these selective perceptions with her own personal experiences and values. As Everingham (1994) has argued, "mothering involves more than the instrumental act of meeting the child's needs. It also involves more than the imposition of normatively held beliefs and values. The uncovering of the interpretive action of the mother exposes the mother as a critical agent, reflecting upon and responding to the agency of her child in a particular sociocultural setting, and in the process, actively constructing cultural meanings and forms of subjectivity within that milieu" (p. 8). As notions of interpretation and agency have become more prominent in theoretical formulations, so too has the view that perceptions of what it means to be a mother may be fragmentary, shifting, and situational. The term "role" – with its connotations of stability and integration – no longer seems apt, and has been increasingly replaced by such terms as "discourses," "cultural concerns," "subjectivities," and "representations" (Gjerde, 2004).

In order to describe the representations of motherhood available and used in contemporary times, I first look at how notions about motherhood have changed during the modern period. I begin by exploring the ways in which government officials, reformers, and business leaders have defined and shaped motherhood since the Meiji Restoration in 1868, when Japan emerged from 250 years as an isolated feudal state and began its transition to modern democracy. The historical perspective illuminates how and why representations of motherhood have changed in response to the perceived requirements of the modern nation-state. I then turn to the women that we interviewed, and describe their own perceptions of what it means to be a good mother, focusing particularly on the differences – as well as the similarities – in ideas about good parenting between the early modern and contemporary eras. I focus on the ways that our participants have integrated older cultural models about what it means to be a good mother with the normative expectations of their own family members, friends, and acquaintances, as well as of their children's teachers and other professionals.

Families and Child Rearing in Nineteenth-Century Japan

During the latter part of the nineteenth century and early part of the twentieth, the very notion of family was quite different from what it is today. Prior to the Meiji Restoration in 1868, family life among the wealthier classes was organized around the extended household (*ie*), an assortment of individuals that typically included the head of the family, his wife and children, his parents, and assorted unmarried relatives, as well as servants, lodgers, apprentices, and sometimes even concubines and their children (Lebra, 1984). Household activities were organized around ensuring economic productivity and maintaining household continuity by honoring ancestors and producing descendants (Hendry, 1981). Husbands and wives were not viewed as being romantic partners, nor was marriage intended chiefly to provide emotional fulfillment to the couple (Inoue & Ehara, 1999). Rather, marriages were arranged by senior members of the *ie* in order to advance its economic position and social status.

In contrast with their central position in contemporary families, young mothers had very little social status within the extended household. Social power in the *ie* was determined by generational status as well as by gender. Consistent with Confucian philosophy, elders were held in high respect, and men had significantly more status than women. Only those women who married the head of a household had a chance of someday becoming powerful when their mothers-in-law were no longer managing the daily operation of the *ie*.[1] Younger married women were among the lowest level members of the household by virtue of age, gender, and outsider status. They were expected to adapt to the norms of their husband's household and to contribute their labor to the family enterprise. If a wife did not produce a male heir or successfully conform to household practices, she could be sent back to her natal family.

Consistent with their marginal status in the *ie*, young mothers were not entrusted with the exclusive care of their children. Children were considered to belong to the household, not to their biological parents, and responsibility for child rearing was distributed across all adult members of the household

---

[1] The harsh treatment meted out by formidable mothers-in-law has been a frequent theme of historical and fictional narratives (e.g., Mishima, 1941).

(Yamamura, 1986). Mothers were expected to carry out the physically demanding aspects of housework, while the relatively easy job of providing child care for infants fell to the mother-in-law and other relatives. In wealthier families, wet nurses, apprentices, and nannies also assisted with child care. In any case, rearing young children was viewed as a fairly simple matter of ensuring the child's physical well-being rather than requiring careful cultivation of his or her psychological or intellectual development (Uno, 1999, p. 24).

[handwritten margin note: more important for child to be healthy than emotionally]

The amount and quality of attention that each child received from family members was also determined by his or her position in the social structure. Within the *ie* system, the eldest son was usually named as the successor and sole heir to the household property. Therefore, this child was seen as very valuable to the household and was given more affection and attention, as well as better food and warmer clothing, than the girls and later-born boys (Uno, 1999). In her memoir, Mishima (1941) describes the custom of giving warm rice to the head of the household and his heir, while everyone else – women and girls, younger brothers, and servants – ate old rice every day: "The delicious warm rice and the stale, crumbling old rice marked the principal order of our family life" (p. 45).

[handwritten margin note: social status even between children]

In elite families, first-born boys were taught occupational skills as well as customs related to the veneration of ancestors and perpetuation of the household's status. These teaching responsibilities were considered too important to delegate to women, whom Japanese Confucian thinkers viewed as morally inferior to men. As Uno (1999) writes, "Especially in the literate classes, old ideas tended to undermine mothers' relationships with their children, because early modern advice tracts held that women's many faults impeded their ability properly to socialize children. Children would become better adults if reared by more virtuous males" (p. 37).

During the nineteenth century, as government officials struggled to unify the country in the wake of its new status as a nation and member of the international community, they seized upon the idea of using the family as a core metaphor for a new "family state" (Morioka, 1986). Following a long internal debate, the *ie* structure rather than the individual was designated as the key unit in civil law. The Meiji Civil Code, enacted in 1898, granted the head of the *ie* "wide-ranging power over subordinate members of the family, including the right to approve marriages or adoptions, the authority to determine where family members lived, and the capacity to control family property" (Ito, 2008, p. 28).

Concomitant with this "re-invention" of the *ie* as the official family unit, the notion was also extended and used as a metaphor for the state: "The family ruled by its patriarch operated on the same principles as the nation ruled by the emperor; the observance of hierarchy and the enactment of proper roles, based upon position and gender, were paramount in each. An often-stated component of the master analogy was the idea that the relationship of subject to emperor mirrored the relationship of son to father" (Ito, 2008, p. 26). White (2002) points out that while the values of the *ie* were "rational, bureaucratic, and therefore 'modern,'" they were also "clothed in the vague assumptions of an eternal and unique Japanese heritage and experience and were therefore unassailably 'traditional'" (p. 47).

Even as the *ie* system was formally instantiated as a way of preserving patriarchal relations and organizing allegiance to the nation-state, members of the new national government were beginning to redefine family relations in ways that were consistent with the thinking of educators and social reformers bent on rejecting "feudal" norms. These reformers drew on Western ideas, adapted them to Japanese cultural values, and promulgated them in girls' high school classrooms and in women's magazines (Sand, 2003). One prominent reformer was Yoshiharu Iwamoto, principal of the Meiji School for Women, editor of Japan's first major women's magazine, *Jogaku Zasshi*, and founder of a publishing company specializing in books about women (Brownstein, 1980; Patessio, 2006). Writing primarily during the 1890s, Iwamoto sought to free Japanese citizens from what he characterized as an outmoded feudal system of family relations. To achieve this goal, Iwamoto favored reducing family membership to the core elements of husband, wife, and children, and urged the exclusion of adopted children, concubines, extended family members, lodgers, and servants from the household. Iwamoto initially promoted conjugal love as the core of the new family, but eventually realized that this Western idea would not be readily accepted in Japan. He also came to see that it would not be easy to eliminate the presence of the grandparent generation in the household.

[margin note:] hard to get rid of "tradition"

Reformers such as Iwamoto were convinced that it was essential for Japanese women to occupy a more central role in the care and education of their children than they had in the feudal era. These influential writers insisted that the home should be seen as an educational environment for children and promoted the image of the modern housewife as a "domestic manager and moral instructor" (Sand, 2003, p. 24). In high school classrooms and women's magazines, educators and reformers provided concrete, detailed instructions about family life: "Since the moral discourse of domesticity was alien, others were not content to leave the form the family gathering should take to chance. To make its moral value self-evident, champions of the *katei* [home] gave the family circle a ceremonial character,

[margin note:] mothers can teach their kids too

providing specific protocols for its enactment and investing it with symbolic significance" (Sand, 2003, p. 29). Whereas men in the feudal era tended to spend their free time engaged in activities with other men, modern reformers sought to integrate them into the family unit. Advocates of the switch from *ie* to *katei* characterized meal times as an opportunity for conversation between parents and children, and encouraged family members to spend their leisure time engaged in wholesome activities like poetry declamation and singing.

These reforms intersected with changes occurring in several government agencies subsequent to the Meiji Restoration in 1868. As noted earlier, members of the newly formed Home Ministry began to re-evaluate women's capabilities in the hope that they could be relied upon to take a more active role in civic life, including working outside the home, managing the household in a frugal manner, and volunteering during times of war or national emergencies. Nolte and Hastings (1991) argue that these bureaucrats envisioned "an ideal woman who … would be modest, courageous, frugal, literate, hardworking, and productive" (p. 172). In contrast to the Western "cult of domesticity," this "constellation of virtues was so appropriate for economic growth that we might term it a 'cult of productivity'" (p. 172). Meanwhile, officials at the Ministry of Education were developing a somewhat different view of the role that women could play in the new nation-state. While they also believed that women could be encouraged to play a productive role in modern society, they did not think that civic participation should be emphasized. Rather, they believed that women's engagement in the home was of more value to the nation (Nolte & Hastings, 1991).

By 1899, both images of women's role – domesticity and productivity – were surfacing in government documents. The phrase "good wife, wise mother" (*ryōsai kenbo*) began to appear in the curriculum of elite girls' schools, and by 1911 had found its way into the ethics textbooks of all elementary schools (Uno, 1999). This phrase combined the Ministry of Education's focus on motherhood with the notion of a "good wife" who was a frugal household manager and possibly even a wage earner. Thus, "a new ensemble of family norms" had taken shape in Japan (Sand, 2003, p. 54).

Ideas from the West about the role of the mother continued to be influential into the 1920s, particularly in the writing of child-care and education experts. The new emphasis on mothers' domestic responsibilities notwithstanding, the reality was that most women were required to focus on the productive aspects of their role, because their labor in the fields and shops was essential to the family's economic security. Working-class mothers still relied on grandparents, babysitters, and older siblings to care for their children. The national government was willing to provide substantial financial support to child-care centers, acknowledging as late as the 1930s that they were essential to "increasing the labor efficiency and improving the household" (cited by Uno, 1999, p. 136).

This tension in government rhetoric between the idea of the "good wife," with its connotation of household productivity, and that of the "wise mother," with its focus on child rearing, did not dissipate until after the Second World War. The government formally discontinued the *ie* household structure, and government publications increasingly emphasized the importance of mothers serving as the child's exclusive caregiver. No doubt this intensification of the discourse of domesticity was prompted by economic factors. The emerging postwar economy demanded a reliable workforce of full-time employees who could be counted on to devote considerable time and energy to their jobs. By defining women as "professional housewives," business and government officials hoped to ensure that men would not be distracted by household responsibilities, expecting women to form a pool of part-time workers who could be hired and laid off as business conditions demanded. And as schooling became the major sorting mechanism to supply workers for the burgeoning industrial infrastructure, women were expected to work in tandem with the education system to provide a stable, supportive environment conducive to children's academic progress (Allison, 1996). The demanding role of adjunct educator was seen as incompatible with full-time participation in the workforce or civic society.

The early reformers' insistence on leaving behind feudal ideas continued to manifest itself in the full-scale adoption of a "modern" scientific approach to homemaking. Throughout the early and mid-twentieth century, Japanese women increasingly looked to classes, books, and magazines for advice from experts on how to maintain a household and rear their children. At the same time, the power and influence of the older generation waned considerably. Ronald Dore, whose fieldwork in Tokyo during the early 1950s captured this dramatic time of transition, provided this description of how mothers increasingly drew upon modern ideas to buttress their status within the family:

The young bride in the traditionally-oriented society of a hundred, or even fifty, years ago, accepted her mother-in-law's advice concerning the care and weaning of her children as the accumulated wisdom of the centuries, observed the superstitions she was taught and was generally prepared to grant that the mother-in-law always knew best. But in modern Japan new authorities have arisen to challenge tradition. The school and the woman's magazine teach new methods of hygiene, a new "nutritional" way of looking at food, new theories about the appropriate time and ways of weaning children, new ideas about the arrangement of kitchens. These all have the backing of the authority of science, and in the acceptance of that authority is implied the assumption that the newer a theory is the more likely it is to be right, in contrast to the old view that tradition alone is an adequate guarantee of truth. (1958, p. 129)

During the heyday of the "professional housewife" (*sengyō shufu*) – the 1970s – women expressed a "strong investment and satisfaction in the selves they had developed as mothers" (Rosenberger, 2001, p. 84). However, that sense of fulfillment began to decline in the 1980s and on into the 1990s, and women began to assert that husbands should be more actively involved in child rearing. In 1992, 40 percent of married women endorsed the statement that women should take care of the home and men should focus on the workplace, but by 2002, only 27.5 percent expressed agreement with it (Hirao, 2007a). Somewhat more persistent was the view that the development of very young children would be severely compromised if their mothers worked outside the home, even though many experts – including government officials – labeled the idea a "myth" (Rice, 2001). Survey findings have fluctuated somewhat, perhaps an indication that perceptions are shifting. One recent national survey found that fully 83 percent of respondents believed that women should focus on child rearing while their children were under three years old (National Institute of Population and Social Security Research, 2003). In our own survey of 116 women, we found that 75 percent of the mothers either agreed or strongly agreed that mothers should stay at home with their children during the first three years of life.[2] Other researchers have found somewhat less support for this proposition. In a recent survey conducted by the Japan Institute of Labor (2003), 60 percent of the mothers surveyed agreed that children age three and under require their mother's constant presence to thrive. Similarly, a survey of 1,000 mothers of preschool-age children living in Tokyo found that 63 percent agreed that a mother's constant presence is important during the first three years (Benesse Educational Research Institute, 2006a).

Shifting Child-Rearing Practices During the Modern Period

During the twentieth century, as mothers were increasingly identified as the best primary caregiver for children, there were concomitant shifts in

---

[2]   Our findings may be slightly different from those of the national studies because our sample was recruited from preschools, which tend not to serve mothers who work full time. Also, our sample was restricted to women who have young children, whereas the others were tapping into a wider age range.

perceptions about what it takes to be a good mother. In particular, a growing emphasis was placed on the importance of maternal warmth as the ingredient most essential to successful child rearing. This is not to say, of course, that parental warmth is entirely a modern invention. Analysis of classical Japanese literature reveals examples of parental love as early as the eighth century (Yamamura, 1986). Evidence from diaries and memoirs of Japanese and non-Japanese observers at the turn of the nineteenth century suggests that many Japanese parents – including fathers – treated their children tenderly, particularly if they were boys (Uno, 1999). Even children who were expected to adopt the stoic behavior of a samurai in public were indulged by their parents in the privacy of their homes, according to Lafcadio Hearn, a European writer who first visited Japan in 1890, married a woman from a samurai family, and gained Japanese citizenship (King, 1984).

Parents may have always had an inclination to display warmth and affection to their children, but it was not always possible to do so, given the exigencies of life in the feudal and early modern period. As noted earlier, elders made decisions about children's lives to suit the interests of the *ie*, not based on the preferences of individual children or parents. This meant that upper-class women were sometimes forced to accept into the household their husbands' illegitimate children by concubines or household servants, and the biological mothers of such children sometimes had to relinquish them to be reared in the father's household by his wife (Mishima, 1941). Samurai women were expected to exhibit composure and self-discipline at all times, as Ishimoto (1935; 1984) suggested in this description of her mother, a samurai woman living in the late 1800s: "Strict with herself, and formal, she plays the part of a samurai's wife, majestically, as if in a dramatic performance. She rises earlier and retires later than anybody else in the family. She has never allowed herself to enjoy a lazy Sunday morning in bed, and the sickbed is the only place for her to rest. Nobody ever saw her sit in a relaxed manner: she is always erect, wearing her kimono tightly with her heavy sash folded on her back" (p. 9). Among working-class and poor families, poverty sometimes forced parents to overcome their attachment to their children and send them away to work in factories, private homes, geisha establishments, and even brothels (Ishigaki, 1940/2004).

The tension between parents' desire to indulge their children and social pressure to exercise emotional restraint toward them persisted into the 1940s and 1950s; it is illustrated in this excerpt from Dore's ethnography of Japanese families: "Overt expression of affection for children was permitted, however, though again to a smaller extent among the samurai than among the peasants or merchants. The samurai father, who preserved his aloofness, thereby strengthened his authority" (p. 107). Dore found that mothers tended to be warmer and more affectionate with their children than fathers, noting "a tendency in the traditional family for the enforcement of family control to be somewhat weakened by a contrary tendency for the mother to indulge every wish of her sons" (1958, p. 140).

The "professional housewife" of the 1960s and 1970s was expected to devote her energy exclusively to managing the home and providing a warm, supportive atmosphere for her husband and children. Lebra (1984) has argued that after the war, the tension women experienced between desiring closeness with their children and fulfilling the demands of the *ie* gave way. According to Lebra, this shift created an excessively strong focus on the mother–child bond: "The traditional mother thus embodied the conflict between the structural prescription for impersonal collective sharing of a child on the one hand, and the more 'natural' and yet equally culturally reinforced tie between mother and child, on the other, which forms the core of the mother's personal identity … The abolition of the legal status of the *ie*, together with the general decline of communal solidarity in postwar Japan, seems to have given rise to the increasingly exclusive nature of the mother–child bond" (p. 164).

The image of mother as primarily devoted to nurturing her children was further elaborated by academic writers during the postwar period. In 1973, psychiatrist Takeo Doi published a book in which he argued that giving and receiving deep, indulgent love formed the basis of all significant relationships in Japan. According to Doi, the experience of receiving this indulgent love (*amae*) first occurs during infancy, when a child basks happily in the warm care provided by the mother. Theoretically, in Doi's view, these reciprocal roles of provider and recipient of indulgent care are subsequently replicated in other relationships, including those of husband and wife and employer and employee. Noting the widespread acceptance of Doi's arguments within Japan, Borovoy (2005) argues that postwar Japan grew to be a "maternal society" in which motherhood "became a key metaphor for describing all Japanese social relationships" (p. 21). In this era, Japan was reconceptualized as a society "where social order is orchestrated and legitimized not through top-down commands but rather through intimate social relationships and shared understanding" and where there is a "possibility of harmonious human relationships that do not entail a curtailment of self-interest" (p. 23).

In today's Japan, the focus on *amae* manifests itself in the marital relationship as well as that of parent and child. Women are expected to pay scrupulous attention to their husbands and children, to the extent of managing their bodies, activities, possessions, and emotions. Anthropologists have catalogued the detailed list of services that wives are generally expected to provide to husbands, including setting out their clothes in the morning, helping them dress and undress, drawing their bath, lighting their cigarettes, changing the channel on the television, refreshing their drinks, and providing snacks and meals on demand (Borovoy, 2005; Lebra, 1984). Similarly, in caring for children, mothers should spare no effort – theoretically – to anticipate and meet their every physical and psychological need. Jolivet's analysis (1997) of recent advice books written for Japanese mothers by physicians and psychiatrists gives a sense of the intensity of these demands on mothers of infants. Among other things, they are instructed to make all baby food themselves, eschew disposable diapers, breastfeed on demand for a year, and maintain continuous physical contact with their infants. As we will see in subsequent chapters, these social expectations become a woman's framework for self-evaluation, although some women do contest them.

In summary, this historical overview suggests two major shifts in the nature of family life and parenting during the modern period. The first was a substantial structural change, as the extended household arrangement gave way to a nuclear family structure. Advocated by early reformers, who based their views on images of the Victorian family, the new nuclear family elevated women's status from laborers to primary caregivers and diminished the power of the older generation, particularly the mother-in-law. For a short time in the 1870s and 1880s, the term "good wife, wise mother" was used to connote the idea that women could balance an active role in civic society with a primary responsibility for child rearing – but that formulation gave way to an interpretation that emphasized the domestic over the productive function. The second change in the nature of child rearing occurred over the course of the twentieth century. Affective relations in the early modern period had been somewhat cool and distant, focusing on the need to restrain one's emotions and endure the inevitable hardships of life in a precarious world, but in the later modern period this notion shifted to the perception that children require intense attention from their mothers, particularly during the first three years of life, and the belief that warmth and responsiveness are the essential ingredients of good parenting.

In our research, we wanted to understand how these aspects of parenting and family life were understood by women in contemporary Japan. As I have indicated, survey findings suggest that many women – although not all – believe that children benefit from exclusive maternal care during the first three years of life, and many also endorse the view that mothers should be consistently warm and unfailingly responsive to their children. But surveys tend to emphasize the majority view and diminish that of the minority. They reveal little about the tensions and inconsistencies that lurk below the surface, nor do they illuminate why a person holds one view and not another. Anthropological investigations suggest, for example, that not all Japanese women share the sense that child rearing is a demanding project that requires all of a mother's attention. Indeed, when Hendry interviewed rural mothers during the early 1980s, they told her they did not use any particular methods of child rearing because they were too busy or "because the children learned 'naturally'" (1986, p. 72). Similarly, Kondo (1990) found that the working-class women living in Tokyo did not particularly pay attention to their children's educational achievement, nor did they believe it was their responsibility to do so. Accordingly, one of our goals was to learn more about women's images of the "ideal" mother. We wanted to find out when and where women were exposed to these images, how they evaluated them, and whether or not they served as a model for their own parenting. We were also interested in how women resolved the tensions and contradictions inherent in the older and newer discourses about mothering.

"Good Mothers" Watch Their Children from a Distance

In the first interview, we asked each mother to describe a person whom she thought of as a really good mother. Several respondents alluded to an old-fashioned, hard-working mother who seemed to represent the notion of a productive mother advocated by the Home Ministry in the early twentieth century. This type of mother was described as cheerful and fundamentally kind but also brisk and unsentimental toward her children. Chihiro, the industrial design engineer who longed for engagement in the world outside of child rearing, articulated her admiration of mothers who participated in child rearing without allowing it to engulf them. She believed that this type of mother was more likely to exist in "olden times," when women were busy with household tasks other than child rearing. Chihiro described the ideal mother as one "who did not blindly love her children or force her ideals on her children," who had a strong sense of herself, and who had neither the time nor the inclination to worry about small day-to-day problems involving her children.

Chihiro's ideas were echoed by Naoko, a mother of two boys, who admired women who could maintain their own identity and not become anxious about small, inconsequential problems in daily life:

An ideal mother is someone who looks at children from a long-term perspective – the type of mothers who have a good sense of themselves and their lifestyle.

I'm not referring to mothers who are preoccupied with their children, but like the mothers of the past, like working mothers, were raising children by having them look at the backs of those mothers. I think this kind of mother is good. Some mothers tend to focus only on trivial things with their children. I want to stop doing that.

Naoko believed that children of an earlier era, who learned from "looking at the mother's back," were more self-reliant and less spoiled than contemporary children, whose mothers focused more directly on their needs. She acknowledged that these old-fashioned mothers were not making a conscious choice to rear children this way; rather, they were simply too busy to be overly focused on their children. Mari, the mother of two, echoed Naoko's view that the differences in child rearing in the past resulted from the heavy responsibilities shouldered by hardworking rural parents: "People in the past weren't very meticulous about raising children because they had to work hard. Compared to them, we have plenty of time, ample time to think about our children."

Despite their admiration for this type of old-fashioned mother, our participants did not themselves take a casual or light-hearted approach to parenting. As I have already indicated, Chihiro threw herself into child rearing, even though she had a strong sense of losing her personal identity and sense of direction. Nor did she succeed in maintaining her own identity; rather, she was left with a strong but vague sense that she needed to find a direction other than staying at home. Mari, who also admired the brisk and busy mother of yore, was herself extremely focused on maximizing her son's development through intensive parenting. Eager to stimulate his language and literacy skills, she began speaking and reading to him when he was still in utero. After he was born, she reported checking out 80 books a week from two different libraries in order to meet her goal of exposing him to 10,000 books by the time he was three years old. Despite being attracted to a romanticized image of the traditional type of mother, Chihiro, Naoko, and Mari all believed that children in contemporary society would attain the skills and abilities needed to become successful adults only if their mothers were not highly involved in supporting their development.

There was one element of this "hands-off," parenting style that seemed to carry over to the child-rearing ideals and practices of a number of women in our sample: namely, the idea that a good mother knows how to stand on the sidelines and watch over a child without over-involvement in managing the child's behavior. The technique is known in Japanese by the word *mimamoru*, which conveys the idea of watching over and protecting a child.

In the ideal version of this interactive process, mother and child are alert to each other's moves (remember the idea of the child "watching the mother's back") but maintain enough distance that the mother is able to pursue her own activities and the child has opporunities to develop the skills needed to become mature and independent. According to several women in our sample, the value of the *mimamoru* strategy is that it allows the child to learn by experiencing the consequence of his or her own actions. They thought it fostered a more profound type of learning than that which resulted from direct teaching by the parent. In our sample, mothers who used this strategy hoped that by maintaining a watchful but distant presence, they were allowing their children to develop confidence in their own ability to find a solution to problems.

[handwritten margin note: can both have some independence]

Asako – the confident, soccer-playing mother – elaborated on the concept of *mimamoru* at several points during our conversations with her. She first used the term in talking about her son Kaito's fear that he might get sick if he had to finish all of his school lunch. Kaito wanted Asako to ask his teacher to excuse him from eating his entire lunch, but Asako wanted Kaito to resolve the problem himself. As she reflected on her child's difficulty in summoning the courage to approach his teacher, she emphasized the importance of being a reassuring presence, even as she allowed him to struggle with the problem:

When my child is struggling, or even when he has run up against a wall, my sitting next to him helps him calm down. It's not about me saying something in particular or doing something specific for him; rather what mothers, well, all mothers, have to do to provide a sense of security is to be there for them and he will be able to overcome the issue on his own. I really want to become a source of security (*anshin*). Even if I didn't do anything specific, just by being there, that alone could help him be at peace and continue to persevere.

Asako expected her son to become increasingly independent as an elementary school student but knew that she would continue to watch over him:

He is learning how to take care of himself in preschool. I can still be around him so I can help him whenever he needs help. But in elementary school you are on your own. All I can do is watch over him. You know, we have always been close to each other while he has been in preschool. If he runs into trouble, for instance, I am always there to help out. When he becomes an elementary school student, however, we will need a certain distance between us. That does not mean I am not willing to help him. I mean, just to watch over him is necessary.

Mothers who believed in the power of *mimamoru* tended to avoid actively teaching, lecturing, or scolding their children. Yasuko, the mother of three children, strongly believed that her children would gain confidence from making their own judgments about how to act. She acknowledged that it was difficult to find the right balance of distance and involvement:

Kids know how to solve their problems, you know. I will keep a distance from them so that they can do that. Even if you just want to watch over them, some parents will give their children various answers like, "See, you can avoid getting into a fight this way," or "You should not do it, because you will have a hard time." If I always decide for him, children will naturally get used to it. After hearing it every day, they will start to think, "I should do things this way because mom said so." I don't want my child to become like that. I think he should think, "Mom says I should do things this way, but I think it should be this way." He should make up his mind based on his own judgment, rather than on what I say. Ideally, he will be able to stick with his own decision no matter what I say. I will have to warn him only when he is obviously getting into trouble. Well, it is a difficult issue, you know. Depending on what he is facing, I will decide to what extent I should interfere with his decision. I want to be a good guide for him.

Mothers who advocated the use of *mimamoru* wanted to avoid being overly protective (*kahogo*). They perceived women who could not step back and watch their children when they were struggling to be gratifying their own needs rather than doing what was in the children's interest. Yuri related that she blamed herself for lacking the self-control to stand back and let her daughter grapple with small problems on her own:

overly
involved

Well, since I only have one child, I don't really have anywhere else to place my attention. I am really overprotective. Like, when she's eating, I pay attention to her chopsticks. I pay attention to everything that she does … Even when my child tries to button her shirt I cannot stand it, so I just do it for her.

Several mothers who tended to step in and "micromanage" said they were trying to avoid being criticized for their children's misbehavior. They described this "being afraid of other people's eyes" watching their children and noticing how they were behaving. For some mothers, it was tempting to step in quickly when a child was misbehaving so that the misbehavior would go unnoticed. Another reason mothers cited for active intervention was to avoid others perceiving them as being uncaring or uninvolved (*hōnin*). They worried that outsiders might mistake the strategic use of *mimamoru* for a simple failure to notice the problem and address it effectively.

Thus, many women wanted to engage in the practice of *mimamoru* but found it difficult because they feared being judged by others. In the past, when mothers were busy with many activities in addition to caring for their children, they simply did not have time to be constantly engaged with their children. But at the present time, the practice of *mimamoru* is a matter of individual choice rather than one of necessity, and mothers are thus more conscious of being evaluated if they do not employ it successfully.

"Good Mothers" Know How to Communicate with Their Children

A second element of good parenting that many mothers identified had to do with establishing good communication with one's child. In Japan, economy of expression has traditionally been viewed as characteristic of a mature, restrained individual. The value Japanese culture has placed on compressed, restrained communication is reflected in the arts, including the simple frame of traditional poetry, the stark beauty of calligraphy and brush painting, and the spare elegance of traditional architecture. In the pre-modern era, extensive conversation between husband and wife, or between parent and child, was not particularly expected or valued. As I have noted, at the turn of the twentieth century, Western-influenced educators and reformers began to promote the importance of frequent interaction among nuclear family members (Sand, 2003). They coined the term *ikka danran* (family circle) and encouraged nuclear family members to engage in conversation over dinner or during other moments of leisure.

What is the current thinking of mothers about the importance of verbal communication with their children? In research conducted over the past several decades, scholars have tested the hypothesis that Japanese women are less talkative with their children than are Western mothers. The findings indicate that Western mothers tend to focus more on verbal interaction and are more oriented to asking for and giving information, whereas Japanese mothers are more likely to interact using baby words and nonsense syllables (Fernald & Morikawa, 1993; Minami & McCabe, 1995; Murase, Dale, Ogura, Yamashita, & Mahieu, 2005). So, there is some evidence of persisting cultural patterns with respect to language interactions.

In the interviews with the 16 mothers, they identified the practice of fostering frequent and open communication as an important element of what it means to be a good parent. Miyuki, the good-natured mother of three who plied our research team with fried octopus, was one of many mothers who emphasized the importance of communication as a way of understanding her child's unique perspective. Since he was a quiet child, she often had to rely on her intuition to figure out when something was bothering him but she tried to get him to confirm whether her intuition was correct. For instance, she recounted that one morning her son became sad and tearful when his friends came to pick him up for school. Miyuki initially did not know why he was upset, but noticed that he was the only one wearing a hat. When he came home that afternoon, she made sure to ask him if he was upset about looking different than the other children, and he admitted that this was indeed the case.

Miyuki believed that she needed to understand each of her children as an individual in order to communicate with them. She felt that her experience as a preschool teacher had taught her that each child was unique:

I learned from my experience that each child has a distinct personality. My oldest child is a quick learner. But the second one isn't learning anything, even though I teach her repeatedly. The third one somehow learns, even though he is not motivated to do it. It is acceptable to me, because I have learned that kids are all different and that one has to respect the difference.

"Good Mothers" Teach Their Children Without Becoming Emotional

The third attribute of an ideal mother, according to many of the women in our sample, was the ability to shape a child's behavior and ideas by calmly reasoning with the child rather than nagging, yelling, or spanking. As we have already seen, many of them thought that children could learn better from circumstances rather than from direct intervention by their parents. Traditionally, a countervailing cultural model of child rearing placed a great deal of responsibility on the parent for directly shaping the child's behavior. Historical analysis by Hara and Minagawa (1996) reveals that, "[o]ne Tokugawa era belief that persists to some degree even today was *taikyo*, which refers to teaching and disciplining a child even before birth.... Japanese believed that a mother's thoughts, feelings, and actions during pregnancy were transmitted to the fetus and continued to influence a child's character, health, and abilities after birth" (p. 15). The notion of *taikyo* is still invoked by Japanese pediatricians, including a prominent pediatrician, author, and television star, Noboru Kobayashi, who has argued that the fetus experiences all its mother's emotions (Jolivet, 1997). Once the child is born, the concept of *taikyo* can then be extended to include the assumption of an active role in socializing the child. The mothers in our study were trying to strike the right balance between providing support as a child experiences the consequences of behavior and acting in a more overtly didactic manner.

As with the previous elements of a good mother that we have looked at, the goal here is to engage in these parenting practices without becoming overly emotional.

Junko, the spunky but low self-efficacy high school graduate, was one of several mothers who focused strongly on the parent's obligation to instill in their children a sense of propriety and obedience to social rules. As we see from the excerpt at the beginning of this chapter, Junko's focus was on getting her children to avoid bothering others. She believed that mothers should teach as well as model the behavior of not bothering others; an ideal mother, she said, was one who "doesn't do anything wrong, or who doesn't bother other people especially in a public place."

Although she advocated firmness in dealing with children, Junko believed that mothers should avoid power-assertive discipline techniques like harsh scolding or physical punishment. For her, the goal is to be "kind but not too kind." She particularly admired the parenting style of a friend who was able to scold her children calmly, without having "emotional waves." In fact, it was difficult for Junko to balance these competing goals. She repeatedly observed that she frequently found herself at a loss for the right words and actions to fulfill her goals and often relied on spanking and physical intimidation to control her children. In one interview, she acknowledged that others around her did not approve of her strict way of scolding her children but asserted that her methods were good for her children:

There are mothers who don't scold their children because they care about other people's eyes. Now many people talk about child abuse and when I scold my child a stranger comes to tell me, "You shouldn't abuse your child. Are you sure you are not abusing your child?" You cannot scold children if you care about that kind of eyes. I do scold my child and I do not care whether people see me like that.

But at another time she acknowledged that she reverted to corporal punishment as a last resort: "I cannot explain things well so I become loud and I slap their butts."

Other mothers shared Junko's view that mothers were responsible for teaching their children not to be bothersome toward others. For example, Mari said that she tried to teach her children moral values like decency (*reigi*) and "not bothering others." Masayo commented that she tried "to teach [her son] not to speak unkindly or to bother other people." Mothers who adhered to this more conservative line of thinking expressed concern about an approach that placed too much importance on the child's thoughts and feelings. Risa, a mother of three who had a high school education, commented on the importance of maintaining an appropriate balance between freedom and self-restraint:

Let the child do what he wants to do and listen to his opinions but at times maintain a sense of behaving appropriately given the situation. Recently people have been talking about children's freedoms and individuality, but I think that there is a thin line between selfishness and individuality or freedom. So the parent really has to see where it becomes selfishness and that evaluation is very difficult.

And, like Junko, many women emphasized the importance of being cheerful and kind at all times, and of not becoming emotional when disciplining a child. Masayo's view of an ideal mother was one who did not react just on the basis of being "emotional and moody." Mothers who could not control their emotions were viewed as immature and self-centered. As Yuri remarked about herself, "I am a type of woman who wants to be indulged, not indulge someone. I do not seem to be able to dedicate myself or contribute to someone else."

How Much Do Mothers Matter?

As the mothers in our study talked about what it takes to be a good mother, a second theme began to surface: how much influence does a mother – whether good or bad – actually have over her child's development? Some women addressed this issue directly, while others addressed it implicitly in talking about the importance of factors other than parenting that shape a child's developmental or academic trajectory. The answers to these questions have strong implications for mothers' choices about how to approach child rearing and for their sense of efficacy in affecting their children's character.

Some of the women we interviewed believed that their children's character was strongly influenced by factors that lay outside of parental control. These mothers tended to admire the old-fashioned kind of mother who paid little direct attention to her children. They believed in what Annette Lareau has called "the accomplishment of natural growth" (2003), meaning that children's development unfolds in a standard manner regardless of particular circumstances or types of adult intervention. Naoko was one of those who believed that development takes its own course. She described her son as a very dependent child but said, "I think children are like that so I am not worried about whether he is going to become independent. ... Children will grow as they do naturally." A similar comment came from Kayoko, who said that "even if parents leave their children alone or do not care for them, they just grow up anyway."

These mothers considered certain immutable factors such as gender and birth order to be powerful determinants, whose effects parents or other actors could not change. They saw gender as a particularly strong determinant of personality and behavior, boys being frequently seen as somewhat dependent at a young age, but ultimately expected to become more independent as they matured. Mothers commented on the paradox that boys, the "stronger sex," were nevertheless more weak-willed as children than were girls. A couple of mothers cited blood type as a determinant of personality. Junko, for instance, commented about her son, "He changes his mind all of a sudden, which is his character. You know, his blood type is 'B.'"

Some women believed that they had passed down certain personality characteristics to their children. For example, Hiromi thought that she had personality flaws which had contributed to her current social and emotional problems and she was concerned that her children would inherit these negative aspects of her personality. She frequently speculated about whether her daughter was showing signs of being similar to her. Hiromi's husband was also aware of a resemblance, and wondered what Hiromi herself had been like as a child. Hiromi commented on her husband's concerns: "When I started to think about which of our personalities my daughter has, my husband asked my mother what I was like when I was really small." Her concern was that nothing could be done to prevent her children from experiencing the same problems that had plagued her throughout her life: "I don't want them to have my personality. That's what was really worrying me after they were born.... But even if I am concerned, there is nothing that can be done about it."

A child's birth order was considered another strong determinant of children's behavior by many women. The role of the older child – particularly for girls – required more maturity than that of a subsequently born child, they thought. Older children were expected to give up their position of dependence when the new sibling was born. They therefore needed to exert self-control to manage their feelings, and were counted on to help the mother by not demanding her attention and by helping out to the best of their ability. For example, Miho noted that because her older daughter was just one year older than her sister, she had had to take the role of older sister at a very young age and has always been very focused and dependable. In contrast, the younger child in the family was frequently seen as being more dependent and childish. Children who had no siblings were also seen as more indulged. Yuri described her daughter in these terms:

She's very lively and hates losing. She's an only child right now. Yeah, she hates losing more than anything else.... Because she's an only child, I still indulge her. I'm also overprotective of her. So, I'm most worried that she will become too self-centered.

Mothers often commented on the interaction between birth order and gender. In the following passage, Chihiro speculated on whether her daughter's outgoing behavior was a function of personality, gender, or her position as the younger child:

She is the type who is loved by many people.... But she is the younger child. I think that might be why. Compared to my older child, even though boys and girls are different, their personalities are totally different. I wonder how they could be that different.

In contrast to the mothers who believed that various physiological forces necessarily limit the effects that parents could have on children's development, other mothers attributed a great deal of influence to environmental factors, especially the guidance of parents and teachers. The notion that parents can (and should) nurture their children's abilities and shape their character has been described by Lareau (2003) as a theory of "concerted cultivation." Sakura expressed her belief that parents exert a strong influence over their children's future:

Before they think about their future job, I want to expose them to various experiences. If I do that, the range of choices they will have will expand. After all, it is the responsibility of the parent to take care of their children.

While this group of environmentally oriented mothers viewed parents as the primary adults responsible for socializing children, they also cited the important influence of teachers. For example, Masayo believed that her son's growing self-confidence and persistence were the result of his interactions with a skilled teacher at a time when he was developmentally prepared to become mentally independent:

Something must have opened his eyes during this year. It's very different from the previous two years. Now, in the few times I've observed his class, I noticed that he's very, very persistent and diligent. I wonder if it is because he is getting along well with his teacher... Well, you know each kid has his own time to become mentally independent. In my son's case, it happened this year.

Asako, the confident, soccer-playing mother, also strongly believed that adults have the ability – and the moral responsibility – to shape children's character. In the following example, she talked about her view that coaches should teach young players about manners, with support from parents:

The team coach should teach kids those important manners. I frequently go to the soccer field to see what's going on, what the situation's like when they're practicing. It seems to me that the kids there are overprotected. The parents are right next to the kids ... the things that the kids should be doing themselves, the moms immediately say "OK!" and do it for them.

Conclusions

Several women in our study were strongly attracted to a romantic image of a certain type of hardworking mother who never had time to indulge her children but nevertheless protected them from harm. They mentioned television shows that featured mothers of this type, including a very popular television drama about a woman named Oshin that ran during the 1980s, when the mothers in our study were coming of age (Harvey, 1995; Jolivet, 1997). The character of Oshin is born into a poor farming family at the turn of the twentieth century and sent away at age seven to work as a babysitter and servant in another family. After undergoing many forms of mistreatment by the family, she marries but is treated cruelly by her mother-in-law. Eventually, she leaves her husband's family and manages to support her children on her own. To some of the women in our study, Oshin embodies the ideal woman from the early modern period, whose main characteristics of self-denial, self-restraint, and endurance are all put into play in the protection and support of her children. An "Oshin"-type mother projects a confident sense of self and a strong commitment to her children's welfare, a person who cares deeply for her children but does not indulge them.

The women in our study realized that times have changed, but some of them were nevertheless attracted to earlier ideas about parenting. When we asked them to specify the types of behavior that might be effective in raising a child well, the women drew from historical cultural models and sought to integrate them with contemporary ideas and standards. One historical notion that many participants emphasized was the importance of *mimamoru*, monitoring from afar but allowing the child to experience and learn from life experiences.

In previous work, I found a similar emphasis in my interviews with Japanese preschool directors (Holloway, 2000), who wanted to avoid imposing too many adult restrictions on children's activities. Along the same lines, other Western observers in the 1980s and 1990s observed many Japanese preschool teachers allowing children to get into fights with each other, handle dangerous materials (e.g., knives), and roam the school grounds out of sight of any adult (Lewis, 1995; Tobin, Wu, & Davidson, 1989). More recently, some of these practices have been abandoned, as parents and teachers become increasingly concerned about possible physical and psychological harm. But they still acknowledge the benefits of "natural" learning opportunities and hope to contrive experiences that provide these benefits without the inherent drawbacks (Tobin, Yeh, & Karasawa, 2009).

Other themes raised by our participants also show some continuity with earlier cultural models. The notion of warm engagement and even indulgence emerges in early accounts of parenting in the premodern period, but it existed in tension with household requirements that young mothers engage in household labor rather than child rearing and thus mothers then were less able to form an exclusive bond with a child. In contemporary times, mothers are expected to experience a "natural" and unequivocal flood of positive emotion toward their children and are discouraged from doing anything that would compete with devoting time and attention exclusively to child care. Thus, rather than experiencing a tension between the personal desire for intimacy with children and the social demand for labor other than parenting, contemporary mothers face a different internal tension as they seek to engage in warm and responsive parenting without stepping over the line into overprotection.

Another theme that reverberates through the historical record as well as into contemporary times is that of emotional self-regulation. The mothers in our study believed that they should avoid negative emotions, hoping to appear cheerful and kind under all circumstances and to remain calm when their children are misbehaving (see Rice, 2001 for similar findings). In the early modern period, Japanese women were raised "not only to not express, but *not even to become conscious of* potentially disruptive personal desires" (emphasis added, Dore, 1958, p. 140). But unlike the women of the early 1900s, contemporary mothers are the product of a more child-focused upbringing, and thus they are more likely to experience powerful emotions of sadness and anger in interacting with family members, which they nevertheless feel they should attempt to avoid expressing to their children.

Thus, echoes of historic models of parenting often surfaced in the comments of the contemporary women in our study, who were attempting to embody some of the more traditional characteristics of Japanese mothers. But the context of child rearing has changed radically, removing some of the structural factors that supported or necessitated certain types of parenting. These changes in family structure and economic demands make certain forms of parenting more difficult for contemporary mothers to achieve, or at least make their achievement more dependent on the individual efforts of the women themselves. Thus, in the absence of demanding work responsibilities or external pressure to remain aloof from their children, some contemporary mothers worry that they will indulge and overprotect their children, depriving them of the experience of resolving their own problems. And many repeatedly challenge the strong cultural imperative to maintain emotional self-control, as they give way to the frustration of daily interaction. In the next chapter, I examine how they evaluate their success in finding a reasonable solution to these parenting dilemmas.

4

Hansei: The Process of Self-Reflection

Parents are the ones who raise their children. I frequently refer back
to that notion. I don't have only the good ingredients needed to be a
parent; in fact, I think I have more of the bad ingredients. So I take in
this and that, reflect, and look back frequently. (Yasuko, high school
educated, high self-efficacy mother of three)

The words of Yasuko, quoted above, speak about the themes explored in
this chapter on self-reflection and perceptions of parenting efficacy. When
reflecting on her parenting, Yasuko used the term *hansei*, a complex concept
that refers to thinking carefully about something she has done, evaluating
whether she has performed well compared to an idealized image of correct
behavior, and pondering how she can improve in the future (Heine, Markus,
& Kitayama, 1999). The process of *hansei* is directed toward identifying one's
weaknesses rather than enumerating one's strengths, but not in a way that is
debilitating. Rather, after engaging in *hansei*, the individual is supposed to
approach new activities with renewed focus and a sense of vigor and confidence. According to Heine et al., "because any discrepancies from the ideal
are bound to be negative, Japanese self-perceptions tend to be critical and
self-effacing. Yet, this self-criticism is in service of future improvement and
achievement of the self" (1999, p. 771).

However, to Western observers familiar with the idea that self-confidence
is the key to high achievement, it may seem that focusing on one's weaknesses
would lead to low self-esteem, lack of confidence, and impaired performance
(Lewis, 1995). According to Bandura (1997), parents who have low self-efficacy – that is, those who focus on their incompetence and judge themselves
as incapable of doing whatever they think is important to being a good parent – are likely to appraise a child-rearing problem as a threat rather than
a positive challenge. They are also more likely to experience anxiety when
facing a difficult parenting situation and become preoccupied with failure.

These cognitive and emotional responses in turn prevent them from persevering when presented with difficult situations and make it difficult for them
to act in an authoritative and consistent manner toward their children.

In fact, as I have noted previously, researchers and media sources have
described a tendency of Japanese mothers to be more self-critical about their
own parenting than are mothers in other countries, sometimes to the point
of developing what is called "child-rearing neurosis." It would seem that this
degree of self-doubt would erode their effectiveness as parents, and indeed
some Japanese researchers believe that this is the case, citing mothers' lack
of confidence as a primary cause of inconsistent and incompetent parenting (Kazui, 1997; Ujie, 1997). Other observers tend to dismiss this compara-
tively low parenting self-efficacy as merely reflecting a Japanese tendency
to be modest and disavow one's accomplishments (Bornstein et al., 1998).
Furthermore, it seems logical to assume that if child-rearing neurosis were
truly a national epidemic, then Japanese parents would be the slackers of
the parenting world. And yet, empirical research suggests that as a general
rule Japanese mothers are sensitive and responsive in interactions with their
children and that most of them effectively support their children's work in
school (e.g., Hess et al., 1986; Holloway, 1988; Stevenson & Stigler, 1992). And
although debate rages in the Japanese media over whether Japanese children
are teetering on the brink of crisis, they tend to look good compared to their
counterparts in other societies. Japanese children have fewer mental health
problems, less likelihood of engaging in risk taking and antisocial behaviors, and less chance of dropping out of school (Crystal et al., 1994; Lewis,
1995).[1] On international tests of achievement, Japanese students have historically placed in the top tier (Gonzales et al., 2004; Stevenson & Stigler, 1992),
although they have dropped somewhat in recent years, as noted in Chapter
2 (Organisation for Economic Co-operation and Development Website,
2008).

What are the effects on contemporary Japanese women of contemplating
with such intensity their performance in the role of mother? Historically, the
practice of *hansei* may have provided a compelling motivational system that
underlay the accomplishments of Japanese people in many different domains.
But how does this discourse function in contemporary Japan? How can the
paradoxical finding of low parenting self-efficacy but effective parenting be
understood? Are these expressions of low confidence by Japanese mothers

---

[1] An exception to this generally positive pattern concerns adolescent suicide. The suicide rate
    of Japanese male youth aged 15 to 24 is twice as high as that of their American counterparts
    (Lester, 2003).

consistent with the traditional processes of self-evaluation outlined above, and do they ultimately result in a productive adjustment of thought, feeling, and action? One thing is clear: if effective parenting in Japan is a result of negative rather than positive judgments of efficacy, this would represent a major cultural difference in the dynamics of parenting between Japan and Western countries, given that high parenting self-efficacy has been conclusively and repeatedly linked to effective parenting in the United States and Europe (Coleman & Karraker, 1997; Oettingen, 1995).

Plural Meanings of *Hansei*

To understand the full meaning of *hansei* to the study participants, it may first be helpful to describe related concepts: the notion of role perfectionism. The Japanese have long been characterized as perfectionists when it comes to fulfilling their primary role, be it mother, employee, or student (White, 1995). In Japan, role expectations are particularly strong, and social approval is accorded to those who consistently act in accordance with their role. The culturally defined goal is not merely to attain adequate performance; rather, the individual is supposed to be strongly committed to work toward role perfection. Within this framework, role perfection is approached through "such things as the ability to endure trouble and pain, coolness in the face of threat, patience, dependability, persistence, self-reliance, and intense personal motivation – qualities we would associate with 'strong personal character'" (Rohlen, 1996, p. 69). In the process of *hansei*, role perfectionism inevitably leads to negative self-evaluation, since the individual always falls short of perfection. Indeed, perfection may be impossible to attain in any domain, but it is certainly most challenging in the complicated, messy arena of parenting, where there is no one model of how to succeed and where a parent has only partial control over the circumstances that might lead to relative success or failure.

The *hansei* process also involves the notion that there is a "best way" to approach any given task, a blueprint to guide one's actions as one strives to meet the goal of perfection. Articulation of a single correct approach to a task can be found in many traditional domains of art and crafts in Japan – whether it be making a *tatami* mat or creating a beautiful flower arrangement. Process and outcome sometimes fuse in the search for perfection – the perfect outcome is achieved by executing the component actions perfectly, as in the case of marital arts such as karate, which involve memorizing a precise sequence of moves that constitutes a single form, or *kata*. Hori calls this emphasis on learning a correct form "ritual formalism" and links it to the teaching of Zen Buddhism, with its focus on repetition, rote memorization, and behaving according to traditional prescription (1996, p. 21).

In contemporary Japanese society, mothers are often given very specific advice about how to engage in certain parenting activities. For example, parenting magazines offer detailed guidelines about such topics as how to enter a playground with one's child in a way that will gain acceptance from other mothers and their children. Although a woman can derive comfort from the idea of conforming to a clear blueprint, the danger is that she will come to believe that any deviation will have severe negative consequences. And if mothers evaluate themselves by their ability to follow a certain path, it is inevitable that many will find that they cannot measure up. Indeed, reliance on "how-to" manuals has been linked in Japan to "manual syndrome," in which these guides, with their blend of "performance perfectionism, a curriculum of conformity, and high demands," ultimately erode rather than build confidence as intended (White, 1995, p. 271).

Anxious Floundering Versus Calm Reflection

So far in this chapter I have been discussing self-evaluation and role perfectionism as a general cultural model that is commonly practiced by many Japanese mothers with regard to their own performance as a parent. As we delve more deeply into each woman's own personal thoughts about being a mother, we will begin to see differences in the way they engage in the process of *hansei*. During our interviews we became aware that some mothers seemed to reflect on parenting but not to the point of torturing themselves with obsessive rumination on every small detail about what they were doing. They explicitly avoided becoming overly preoccupied with self-evaluation. Miyuki, the cheerful homemaker and mother of three children, belonged in this group. She avoided wasting energy on worrying about whether or not she was doing everything well:

I didn't really have the mental energy to think about not being confident. I was just concentrating on being my kind of mother because that's good enough. It's true that I'm good at making cakes, but when I think about what I'm not confident in, I think that I'm not confident in anything. If you think like that, then you can't continue to be a mother.

One key element in Miyuki's ability to remain confident about her parenting is her rejection of the idea that there is a single recipe for being a good parent. Miyuki felt very strongly that she did not have to follow a single standard of behavior. She saw that if she avoided comparing herself to others, she would feel more confident and happy with her own style: "I think there are many kinds of mothers. I think it's pointless to say that this kind of mother is good or that kind is good. I think that I am myself and I've never thought about imitating other mothers."

Asako, the confident athlete, frequently engaged in *hansei*, but she realized that it was crucial not to second-guess her own decisions once she had committed to a course of action. She believed that if she were able to identify and hold on to her beliefs, then she would be able to move forward and not get bogged down in fruitless speculation about all possible alternatives:

I think that if you think about it deeply, if you keep on thinking and thinking about it, then wouldn't everyone end up thinking that it's incredibly difficult? But, as long as you hold onto your beliefs, and then when you reflect on such things you will think that it's going to be OK. But if you keep on thinking repeatedly about something, then you're going to start dwelling on questions like "What's going to happen? What should I do? What can I do?" But I think that if you can think, "This is what I think about the issue" and stick to your conclusions, then isn't that good enough?

The difference between pointless rumination and careful reflection is most clearly articulated by Yasuko, the mother of three whose comments about self-reflection were featured at the beginning of the chapter. In the following passage, she rejects that aspect of role perfectionism that leads to insecurity and argues for an alternative form of constructive self-questioning:

When I am in the middle of child rearing I always end up wondering if what I'm doing is truly OK. Well, first of all there's no such thing as doing something perfectly, so you will question yourself as to whether or not you're raising your children in the right way... People say that when parents are insecure (*fuan*) it will be transmitted to the child. But the type of insecurity I am talking about is not about, "Is this good? Is this bad? I don't know what to do" but it is more about questioning whether what you are doing for the child is good or not. This kind of doubting (*yuragi*) is something that I think parents should have.

This insight by Yasuko suggests that the practice of self-reflection can be done in a way that undermines a woman's sense of parenting efficacy, or it can be done in a way that spurs her to find new solutions to her problems. Women who were able to be self-doubting in the positive sense examined the results of a particular action they had taken, but they did not seem to make a global judgment about themselves as deficient parents. They felt in control of their actions and therefore had a sense that they could improve and experience better results in the future.

In contrast to confident mothers like Miyuki, Asako, and Yasuko, a second group of mothers went about the process of *hansei* in a way that exacerbated their anxiety and resulted in less effective action when problems arose. Yuri exemplifies someone who struggled with this issue. In spite of numerous accomplishments outside of the parenting role – she was a university graduate who had established a successful career as a musician – she had little confidence that she could be a good mother to her young daughter. With characteristic humor, Yuri could laugh at the irony of her predicament: she was worried about whether she was doing a good job of parenting, and she was also worried about the negative effect on her child of having a mother who was always worried. She simply couldn't believe that her own instincts and reasoning would lead to the right actions on behalf of her child. She thought that parenting "should be natural" but also believed that there was one right way to be effective or to attack a problem. She worried constantly that she would not be able to identify that single best solution.

Yuri's anxiety led her to seek advice from other people, but it was difficult for her to arrive at a reasonable course of action if she did not find consensus among her informants. To illustrate this predicament, she described how anxious she had become over the issue of breastfeeding when her daughter was an infant:

When she was born, I was really nervous. I read in a book that I should breast-feed and I was worrying about what would happen if I couldn't produce enough [milk]. So, I couldn't trust anyone, I couldn't trust anything except for books. I couldn't even trust my own parents! I just wanted to hear it with my ears. I went to a maternity class and there was a nurse visiting that class and she told me that I absolutely had to do this set of things. Even the hospital told me to do some specific thing regarding milk. But I couldn't even trust the hospital's advice because I truly believed that I didn't have enough milk ... I didn't know how to raise my child so that's probably why I was not acting very normal.

This example was one of many incidents in which Yuri's inability to trust her own parental instincts prevented her from taking a clear course of action.

In summary, I would argue that engaging in the process of *hansei* does not necessarily erode a mother's parenting self-efficacy and undermine her parenting effectiveness; nor, conversely, does it necessarily lead to more effective parenting. The effects of performing *hansei* depend on how it is done. Our data suggest that mothers who are able to avoid comparing themselves to an ideal model – recognizing that there are "many kinds of mother" – are more likely to use their self-reflection to identify options for constructive change. In addition, women who do not feel that they need to aim for perfection are better able to accept their imperfections and move on with confidence that they will try to do better next time. In contrast, mothers who were striving for perfection and those who believed that there was a single best way to approach a parenting situation were much more critical of their perceived parenting mistakes, and they seemed to have a difficult time knowing how to move forward rather than getting bogged down in self-doubt.

Mothers' Areas of High and Low Parenting Self-Efficacy

The comments about *hansei* that I have discussed so far should help to convince the reader that most of these mothers took the process very seriously. I now move to an examination of the results of the process of *hansei* as we look at the mothers' perceptions of their own strengths and weaknesses. In the first interview, we asked mothers to talk about areas of parenting in which they felt confident and areas in which they did not. Consistent with the norm of negative self-evaluation, most mothers had a hard time coming up with things that they felt confident about. Some preferred to mention things they were challenging themselves to do better rather than things they actually felt confident doing. For example, Kayoko, who was a very shy person, said that she was forcing herself to go out with her daughter: "I am trying to take her out in public and I'm trying to take her to a friend's house." Several women indicated that they were making a strong effort to suppress and control their emotions. Yuri mentioned that she was trying to tolerate her husband in order to give her daughter a happy home life, whereas Reiko and Hiromi indicated that they were trying to monitor and control their emotional outbursts toward their children.

Other women indicated that they were confident about their ability to perform simple and concrete activities; six mentioned cooking, sewing, or some other specific household activity, four mentioned being willing and able to play with their children, and one mentioned reading to her child (see Table 4.1 for excerpts from narratives of all 16 mothers). Even when describing something they were purportedly confident in doing, the women often qualified their assertions with caveats about their abilities. For example, when asked what aspect of parenting she felt most confident about, Junko replied that she was able to play at their level but hastened to indicate that this might not last for long:

TABLE 4.1. *Examples of Areas of Confidence in Parenting*

Beni	I don't know if it is something that I am good at but I like cooking and I am a good cook.
Yuri	I am trying to tolerate as much as possible … I am showing a good relationship with my husband in front of my child.
Kayoko	I am trying not to beat her as much as possible. I'm trying to scold verbally. I'm trying to take her out in public or I'm trying to take her to her friends' house.
Sakura	I like to cook and I haven't done serious cooking recently, but I used to like to sew, and I used to make sweets with my children.
Junko	I can play with my child the same way as they do.
Risa	My children are good at helping with housework … It's not for myself because I have to do them [the chores] all over again. But since they say they want to do it … I just say it's OK.
Naoko	I can play with my children. And I am trying to wait for them as long as possible.
Yasuko	The attitude I have to listen to my child as a mother; right now I think I am good at it.
Hiromi	Nothing. But for baton twirling, I do make their uniforms and I'm not good at it. Sometimes I have to buy the fabric again and again and I'm not good at it but I do my best.
Reiko	I am trying to control my emotions, and when I know that they are going in a strange way, I try to pause and take a breath, and get myself back, and try to interact with my children.
Mari	I guess I am confident with teaching discipline or decency, which is the basic knowledge [as a human]. I think that I am good at teaching such things.
Miho	I can make rice balls. I come to pick up my child [at school] twice a week. On that day I make a lot of rice balls and give all of them to everyone.
Miyuki	I am good at making cakes.
Masayo	I can read books to him. I do sports, play catch.
Asako	Compared to a normal mother I think I am very good at sports … So the things you can't do at home, I am doing well at those things, like outdoor activities.
Chihiro	I actively take my kids to different places so they can experience different things. I have lots of communication with the kids

If I know how to play games then I can communicate with my children better. I am not particularly good at them, but I like to play games and will play in the same way as my child … I don't know to what age I can do it. They may not want to do it anymore when they go to elementary school.

When we asked what they were not confident about, the women talked at greater length and, ironically, with more confidence (see Table 4.2 for

TABLE 4.2. *Examples of Areas of Low Confidence in Parenting*

Beni	Boys' emotions contain some things beyond my comprehension.
Yuri	I am not patient so you know children say the same things over and over and sometimes I have to listen to it and I'm not good at doing that. I say "I'm busy" and I just escape. And cooking. Or maybe I am not confident about anything.
Kayoko	Education. I am not smart so I don't think I can teach my children like other mothers.
Sakura	I'm not the kind of person who goes outside actively ... I wish I could be more open and outgoing. But it is difficult.
Junko	Well, I personally do not have confidence about child rearing ... I am not confident about letting them understand or listen to me.
Chihiro	I feel like I should be able to understand her [daughter's] feeling more ... I shouldn't look at her as an adult, but at her perspective as a child. I think I am restricting her, so I feel sorry for her.
Risa	It's hard to know how to bond (*sei shikatta*) with my child ... I scold my child too much ... I don't really like to read books to the children.
Naoko	I am not confident about making meals. I don't think much about nutrition. I don't know what to do about that.
Yasuko	I have worries about whether I can be adaptive. For example, you know the video games, there are various video games around now ... I wonder whether I should buy it for my child now or if I should keep telling my child that he doesn't need it based on my true belief.
Hiromi	I can't really listen to what my children say so I just talk and scold them but I can't really listen to my kids.
Reiko	I think that a parent's way of interacting with other parents, that kind of relationship influences the child. And I think it is really difficult.
Mari	I am completely incapable of organizing and housekeeping.
Miho	I do not think much and I am not worried much.
Miyuki	I feel that there is no perfect mother, so I think that I can be myself. I can be my kind of mother ... So I'm good at making cakes, but once I think about what I am not confident in, I think it is everything, and so if I think about it I cannot work as a mother anymore (*Hahaoya wo yatte ikenai*).
Masayo	It takes him [son] a lot of time to eat his vegetables and I lost confidence about his eating habits.
Asako	Yes, well, since I am an athlete I tend to want things to be black or white. And I am sometimes abrupt and I'm not as good with the details. Sometimes I compromise on little things within a bigger issue.

excerpts). Over the course of our interviews they identified three aspects of child rearing that presented the greatest challenge to them: (a) establishing good communication and a solid emotional connection with their child, (b) maintaining emotional self-control in disciplining their child, and (c) supporting their child's education. In the next section, I examine the challenges posed within each of these areas.

Difficulties in Establishing Good Communication and a Positive Emotional Connection

Some mothers worried because they didn't feel as close to their children as they thought they should feel. They described feelings of distance and detachment or mentioned disliking their children. They also worried whether they felt closer to one child than to another. And they described an inability to understand their children's feelings or to communicate with them.

Chihiro provides a strong example of someone who articulated all these worries. As I have indicated, Chihiro was one of the women who consistently criticized themselves for not being a good parent. She believed that she was not "mature" enough to be a parent, wondered aloud if she had the "qualifications" (*shikaku*) to be a parent, and stated on several occasions that she felt "sorry" for her children. Favoritism toward one child was a major theme in our discussions with Chihiro. She brought up the issue of feeling emotionally disconnected from her daughter (but close to her son) at several points during the four interviews. She repeatedly stated that she thought her son was cuter and more appealing than her daughter. She believed that the "natural" dynamic of mothers to prefer sons over daughters was more intense in her case, because her personality was more "boyish." She found it much easier to interact with her son, and she tended to ignore her daughter:

I'm probably nicer to my son because he's cute. Since I look at him as the opposite sex, he's cute ... Yeah, I think it's different [the way I treat them]. I understand him because my personality is more boyish. Boys are energetic and mobile, and I have to follow him. So, I end up paying attention to him. On the other hand, the younger one plays with little things, she looks like she's doing her own stuff, so I just tend to leave her alone.

Chihiro was also critical of herself for not being able to understand her children's point of view, particularly that of her daughter:

I don't feel as if I understand children's lives yet ... I feel that I need to try harder to understand where she's coming from. I need to pay attention to my children more. I feel that I shouldn't view her as an adult, but rather understand her from a child's perspective.

The same themes emerged in the narratives of other women. Several women, in addition to Chihiro, believed that they were too immature and self-centered to have a strong emotional connection to their children. For example, Reiko commented that she found child rearing challenging because she was not personally mature enough to pay close attention to her children: "I think it is my personality. I care about myself (*jibun mo kawaii*). I don't want to be bothered by children."

A couple of women shared Chihiro's preference for boys and felt guilty about their lack of warmth toward their daughters. For example, like Chihiro, Risa also felt closer to her son than her daughter and believed that something about his being a boy elicited her affectionate feelings. She had consulted with other mothers and with the director of her daughter's preschool for help with what she called her "difficulty with knowing how to bond with my child." She was trying to be more affectionate toward her daughter, scold her less often, and offer praise when she did something positive.

A couple of the women criticized themselves as having lacked "normal" feelings of motherly love when their children were infants. This feeling of emotional distance, or even aversion, to a new baby has been reported by Japanese mothers in government surveys as well (Hara & Minagawa, 1996). It is hard to know if the phenomenon is more common in Japan than in other countries, but it is nevertheless interesting to learn that some mothers report that they lack the feelings of motherly love that are widely described as "natural" in Japan (Jolivet, 1997). For example, Yasuko described herself as having been too young to focus on the needs of her first baby:

I think the main issue for me, as a mother, was that the love toward my child had not yet come flowing out. It was not flowing out from within me. Even though I had become a parent, in the middle of child rearing I think that it felt as if no matter what, I came first and the child second.

Hiromi was even more strongly convinced that her personal limitations prevented her from connecting with her children. Hiromi's early experiences as a child had left her with a great deal of anxiety about human relations, and as an adult she had a tendency to deal with this anxiety by shutting down emotionally and even regressing: "When I panic I become someone who is not like me. I can't think about my children and I become like a child."

Difficulties in Maintaining Emotional Self-Control

For many mothers, the issue of discipline presented great challenges. As we saw in their descriptions of the ideal mother, most women strongly believed that mothers should be kind and cheerful at all times. With respect to disciplinary interactions, the contemporary mothers we studied felt that the most effective form of discipline was to scold the child without showing emotion (often described by the terms *kanjōteki ni narazu ni, kanjō wo osaete,* or *reisei ni okoru*). In spite of this goal, they reported that they often failed to stay calm when their children misbehaved and ended up using punishments that were harsher than they had intended. Three of the four focal mothers – Miyuki, Junko, and Chihiro – identified this inability to control their emotions as a personal shortcoming.

Junko, in particular, was preoccupied with the issue of discipline and expressed a great deal of ambivalence about the importance of calmly reasoning with her children instead of hitting them out of anger. In the opening description of Junko in Chapter 2, I quoted her as saying in the first interview that her major flaw as a parent was that she did not know how to scold her children verbally the way that preschool teachers do, but instead she tended to lose her temper and slap her children. The fact that her father had been physically abusive toward her also made her aware that corporal punishment could get out of hand, and for that reason she drew the line at kicking her children, grabbing them by the shoulders, or hitting them on the back. However, over the course of the interviews, she went back and forth about whether expressing anger spontaneously (and physically) was acceptable, or even desirable. At one point, she strongly declared that it was her right to be firm, and even harsh, in disciplining her children, even if others would define it as abusive. She particularly distinguished hitting on the head versus on the child's behind, saying that she didn't get along with mothers who hold in their anger long enough to smack their children on the behind rather than just reaching out and cuffing them on the head.

For Miyuki, the issue was a bit different. Trained as a preschool teacher, she was usually able to reason with her children and believed that this was the best form of discipline. However, she admitted that it was not always possible for her to stay calm, and she didn't feel particularly guilty about her emotional outbursts:

I think I severely scold him and hurt him a lot.... but I don't really have the mental energy to think about these things when I'm scolding him. I don't have the time to think about whether or not what I say is going to hurt him or not.... My husband says it's verbal abuse (*kotoba no bōryoku*).

Difficulties in Supporting Children's Educational Achievement

When their children entered elementary school, most mothers reported becoming less worried about the issue of discipline, but some became increasingly concerned about their ability to support their child in terms of school. Some of them had increased the number of supplementary classes their children were taking and were worried about how to motivate their children to take on this extra work. They also worried about their ability to supervise their children's regular homework. They had questions about how to monitor what was going on in the classroom, and some worried about how to communicate with their child's teacher. These concerns were particularly intense among the mothers who had not liked school or who had not done well in it themselves (Yamamoto, 2001). These mothers were concerned that they did not know enough to help their children with their studies and they also feared that their children had inherited their lack of academic ability.

Among our focal mothers, Junko was the one who most often expressed a sense of inadequacy in terms of supporting her child's schooling. Junko had not enjoyed school as a child, and her descriptions of repeated failure suggested to us that she might have an undiagnosed learning disability: "Even though I did the work, I didn't really understand the content. I really didn't understand the meaning in my head." No one seemed to have found a way to support her in school, and she was barely able to complete her high school requirements. As I will describe in detail in Chapter 8, she was somewhat at a loss as to how to overcome her own educational disadvantage to support her children. She related making sporadic efforts to involve her son in educational activities at home, but said she tended to abandon these efforts when she ran into resistance from him. For example, like most Japanese mothers, she tried exposing him to the basic characters of the Japanese syllabary, but she stopped because she got the impression that he didn't like her to be teaching him.

Like Junko, Sakura was concerned that her own lack of schooling might prevent her from helping her children academically. In one interview, she compared herself unfavorably to the mother of her son's classmate:

There is a kid whose mom is very knowledgeable. This kid is an only child, so it seems like they have a lot of one-on-one conversations. This kid has an incredible knowledge base! So, somehow, when I'm looking at this child, I start wondering whether he's really the same age as my own child. When I look at this child, although I'm probably thinking too much, I wonder just for a bit if my son is going to succeed in school.

Another factor that affected the mothers' confidence in supporting their children academically was the nature of their emotional relationship. As we have already seen, mothers sometimes worried that they lacked a good emotional connection with their children, and felt somehow inadequate in their ways of interacting with them. Mothers who lacked a general sense of efficacy in connecting with their children tended to feel hampered in their efforts to support their children's academic work.

One mother who exemplified this pattern was Beni, mother of two sons and one daughter. Beni had an associate's degree from a junior college and felt confident in her intellectual ability. However, she did not feel successful in the area of discipline and often felt mystified by her sons. As the boys moved through elementary school, they began to experience academic problems that she was also unable to resolve. They failed to do their homework, couldn't keep track of their school materials, and received poor grades. She believed that her inability to help the boys overcome these academic challenges was related to her difficulties with discipline:

When my eldest child was a little kid, I'd smack his bottom and tell him to do something. His personality was the type that would listen to me and then do it. Yeah, when he was younger, I'd use physical punishment and other disciplinary actions. But, for some reason that I don't really understand, my second son, from a very young age, would refuse to do anything until he was convinced that he ought to do it. No matter what I tried, hitting him, or anything else, he would simply not do anything until he was convinced. So, like now, if I said, "You have to do your homework," he'd ask, "Why do I have to?" I'd have to explain everything and give him a lot of reasons. But even after he understands why, he still doesn't do his homework. So after going through this for so many years, recently I've been really stressed about what to do and how to handle the situation. Is physical punishment the best solution?

Beni was not able to work smoothly with her sons' teachers to resolve these problems. They frequently asked her to be more vigilant in monitoring her sons' behavior, but she was uncertain about her role in the matter and would have preferred to leave it up to the school:

I told his teacher that I knew it was bad that my child didn't study or didn't do his homework. But, I wanted the teacher to follow this, and the teacher would want me to follow that. So, even though I wanted to follow his advice, my child didn't seem to be motivated to study and I didn't want to force him. So, I was experiencing a major internal conflict.

In our final interview with Beni, she informed us that her older son, then in the eighth grade, had stopped attending class and rarely left the house (in Japanese, there is a term for children who do this, *hikikomori*). She was reluctant to leave him alone even though it was inconvenient for her to remain at home with him all the time. The circumstances were very stressful. Beni was unsure how to interpret her son's behavior and did not know how she should respond to it: "He is now in an ambiguous position. He wants us to be involved and yet he doesn't want us to be involved. It's really difficult to distinguish what he wants us to do."

Beni's comments suggest that she was a thoughtful person who was continually reflecting on what her responsibilities were to her children. But she seemed unable to intuit what her children needed from her and did not trust the advice of others. As a result, she felt paralyzed when it came to helping them do well in school. We will explore the connection between parenting self-efficacy and support for schooling more fully in Chapter 8.

Shifts in Mothers' Evaluation of Their Support for Children's Schooling

According to Bandura's theory of self-efficacy, how people evaluate their own capabilities does not shift significantly over time. They expect that their performance in the future will be similar to what it has been in similar settings in the past. And they tend to get fairly consistent information over time from other people about how well they are likely to do in certain situations. In addition, the theory holds that people tend to have a perceptual frame for interpreting the information about their abilities, and that they use that frame to eliminate information that might be at odds with their general self-perception. Thus, once Chihiro, for example, formed the belief that she was not able to understand her daughter's feelings, she would have been likely to ignore or discount the instances when she had actually done so. We were able to explore this idea in our survey data because we had included a similar parenting self-efficacy scale in each of the three surveys. As expected, we found that there was a high correlation from one survey to the next.[2] When we examined our interview data, we found that most of the women expressed a similar level of parenting self-efficacy as their children moved through preschool, first grade, and second grade. They witnessed their

---

[2] The correlation between successive assessments of parenting self-efficacy was .68 between the preschool and first grade surveys and .64 between the preschool and second grade survey. The correlation was .82 between the first grade and second grade survey.

children develop new competencies and acquire new interests but all within a familiar framework.

However, we found one important exception to this pattern, and that was in the area of academic achievement. We noticed that some mothers became increasingly less confident as their children moved from preschool into elementary school. It is not surprising that mothers' sense of efficacy in supporting their children's achievement changes during the period. Over the course of our interviews, mothers gained a lot of new information about their children's potential to do well in school. When the children were in preschool, mothers could only guess about their academic promise. By the fourth interview, the children were in second grade, their parents had gained a sense of how they were shaping up as students. If children began to have academic difficulties, mothers were forced to reassess their perceptions of their children and their aspirations for their future. In some cases, this also prompted a deep reflection on whether or not they had done the right things to help their children do well in school.

Examination of individual cases reveals that a number of factors some-times combined to dampen a mother's self-efficacy with regard to support of schooling. In the case of Mari, for instance, a decline in her parenting self-efficacy seemed to be associated with her son's decreasing academic performance and his growing resistance to her demands for achievement in many domains such as academics, sports, and music. Furthermore, as she experienced even less success with her younger daughter than with her son, she began to realize the limits of her control over her children's development.

A very active, strong-willed woman, Mari was determined to do every-thing in her power to raise her children well. At the first interview, she stood out as one of the most confident mothers in the sample. She expressed strong satisfaction with her son's development and explicitly said that she assessed her own competence by examining his level of development:

Well, I'm scared to say this about myself, but I think I am raising him to be a very good child. I believe that things are going perfectly right now. He is more reasonable than adults. If I am right, I think that I am good at directing my child. It's a very easy way of raising children.

However, she was becoming increasingly aware that her daughter, two years younger than her son, was neither a high achiever nor particularly well mannered. Again, Mari used the status of her child to evaluate her own per-formance as a parent, but with her daughter, the evidence was not positive:

Compared to Hiroyuki, Midori is not as well behaved. I often receive compliments about Hiroyuki. People tell me, "You have raised Hiroyuki well." But, people never say this sort of thing about Midori.

To explain the differences in "quality" between her son and daughter, she remarked that she had put less effort into developing her daughter's capabilities:

I worked hard and put lots of energy into the older child, and the younger one, because I put in so much energy to the older one, it was more like, okay, you come along, and when I realized, I found out that the younger one has nothing outstanding about her.

When Hiroyuki entered first grade, he did well but his grades were not perfect. Mari found this both unexpected and disappointing. She told us that she destroyed his first grade report cards so that in the future he would not find them and feel discouraged. She redoubled her efforts to stimulate his achievement, signing him up for many extracurricular activities. By the second grade, in addition to being enrolled in an after-school academic program, he was taking karate, kendo, piano, calligraphy, and tea ceremony classes. He was busy all day every day, including the weekends. He began resisting this heavy workload, but Mari was determined that he continue everything:

Since becoming a second grader, he started to frequently ask, "Why do I have to study," and he says that it's not fun, every day is really not fun. And, regarding studying, doing homework, and doing anything, he asks why he has to do all these things. He really makes his opinion heard. And I tell him that because it's something that you must do so you must do it, and I say it as if I will absolutely not lose the argument.

In spite of her determination to keep pushing him, she sometimes experienced doubts about whether she was doing the right thing. Her growing concern is evident in this comment: "Actually I do not know what we are doing now will lead to, and maybe it will end up being something bad. But I am a little bit worried about what will happen if they are being forced to do something they don't like to do every single day." With the passing of time, her perceptions had clearly changed regarding how easy it would be to create the brilliant child that she desired. As he began to perform at a slightly less than perfect level, she was faced with the limits of her own power and her parenting self-efficacy began to decline. This shift in perceptions was accentuated by her firm belief that her own success would be measured by his performance as evaluated by outsiders, and by the evidence that she was not really able to bring her daughter anywhere near the level of her son.

Other more subtle factors may also have contributed to this change in her sense of self-efficacy. Mari also appeared to be feeling increasingly frustrated with her husband's apparent unwillingness to spend time with the children. As we will see in Chapter 6, women whose husbands threw themselves actively into child rearing tended to feel more efficacious as parents. In a few cases, including that of Mari, when the couple's relationship began to deteriorate, there was a corresponding drop in the mother's parenting self-efficacy.

Conclusions

The emphasis placed on self-reflection (*hansei*) in Japan was evident in full force among the women in our sample. Most of them seemed to be engaged in frequent *hansei* about their parenting. Some, such as Chihiro, worried about not having sufficiently tender feelings about their children. Others, including Junko, worried about disciplining them too harshly. And some, also including Junko, worried about being unable to support their children's achievement in school.

Careful analysis of women's comments about the meaning and process of *hansei* revealed two different approaches. Certain mothers, including Asako, Miyuki, and Yasuko, seemed to have figured out how to be self-reflective without allowing self-doubts to undermine their parenting actions. These women also rejected the idea that there was one blueprint for being a parent. They were convinced that there were, as Miyuki put it, "many kinds of mother." They were not obsessed with role perfection. As Miyuki put it, "I was just concentrating on being my kind of mother because that's good enough." In contrast, other mothers were mired in anxious floundering and mental instability (*yuragi*), as Yasuko put it. They approached parenting as an activity with one "right" answer; when they were unable to identify the "correct" approach, they became panicky and self-recriminatory.

Western observers might be tempted to interpret Miyuki's form of *hansei* as "Westernized" because she seemed to reject the notion of role perfectionism and chose to follow her own ideas rather than to emulate a model. As I learned more about these elements of self-reflection, I came to think that Miyuki's approach is quite consistent with – and perhaps even a deeper interpretation and a more creative application of – Japanese cultural traditions. I would argue that the Miyuki's quest to be "my kind of mother" is consistent with Zen monk Victor Hori's description (1996) of how creativity can find its way into a ritualized activity:

Despite the ritualized form of monastery life, efficiency thus is very highly valued. And every cook is under great pressure to devise ever more efficient ways of work. Constantly he is scrutinizing every step of his actions, asking is it faster to reverse the order of these two jobs, can I use the residual heat from this fire for some other task, can I get a better cut if I hold the blade of my knife this way, and so on. Although "what" he is required to do is prescribed for him, the cook subjects every detail of "how" he does the task to minute examination in a constant search for improvement. (p. 30)

Hori concludes that "necessity is the mother of invention, but in a Japanese Zen monastery, maintaining ritual form is the unexpected father of insight" (pp. 30–31). Applying this idea to the case of Miyuki, I would argue that she started from a general cultural schema about what it took to be a good parent but within that form she was able to creatively improvise and move beyond, in order to figure out how to be "my kind of mother."

In this chapter, I have described *hansei* as a matter of personal introspection and self-evaluation. This limited description of *hansei* must be broadened to include the role of criticism by others. In the Zen tradition, peers and superiors are expected to provide criticism intended to help the individual understand and analyze his or her behavior. Monks are sanctioned not only by the senior monk, but also by their peers, in a process that Hori calls "mutual polishing":

Long after initiation is over, monks continue to constantly admonish, warn, reprimand, and lecture each other ... "The seam of your robe is crooked. Fix it! ... Your attitude is wrong. Be grateful when someone corrects you! No running away!" (Hori, 1996, p. 33)

Somewhat paradoxically, it is through this process of mutual polishing that a feeling of commitment and trust is said to emerge in a community. When the elements of self-reflection, challenge, endurance, and effort are in balance, the individual and the group can function in harmony. The individual is exerting strong self-discipline to contribute through his or her role-related activities to the welfare of the group. The individual can trust that others will, for their part, try their utmost to hold up their side of the bargain. Rohlen (1996) underscores the demands this system places on the individual:

The interdependent nature of society generates duties and obligations that make the diligent performance of every role important. This is a basic assumption taught as a fact of life. The necessity of responsibility to one's social role follow from this fact... When such social realities are underlined, individual differences are ignored or treated as unimportant. (p. 71)

Whether in the context of workplace, school, or family, the process of *hansei* is mediated by social interaction as group members stimulate each other to think through the good and bad points of a day's activities. For example, elementary schools often set aside time at the end of the school day for the children to reflect on their behavior and to set goals for the future. Lewis (1995) identifies *hansei* as a cornerstone of the Japanese educational system: "*Hansei* undergirds discipline, group formation, efforts to foster the 'whole child's' development, and academic learning as well. Whatever the subject matter, reflection seemed to be a part of learning" (p. 170). *Hansei* is also a component of some forms of Japanese psychotherapy that discourage clients from blaming others for their problems and encourage them to focus on their own shortcomings (Lebra, 1986; Murase, 1986). In the context of therapy, people who practice *hansei* become more grateful for the care they have received by others and develop a renewed sense of confidence regarding future activities.

How does the process of "mutual polishing" play itself out in the domain of parenting? As we have seen in this chapter, the women in this study experienced significant concern about the most fundamental aspects of parenting. They doubted their ability to communicate with their children and sometimes even questioned their basic emotional commitment to them. They felt unable to suppress their emotions and present a calm and cheerful demeanor to their children. And they worried that they were not going to be able to support their children's achievement in school. How did they communicate these self-doubts to those around them, and what sort of response did they receive? While much of parenting is performed in private, without witnesses or judges, parents can and do endure criticism or gain support from family members and friends in their immediate context as well as from more distal sources including professionals and members of the media.

As I have already noted, Japanese mothers tend to receive a lot of public criticism (Holloway, 2000). Does this type of criticism spur individual commitment on the part of parents and a feeling of trust, as it is supposed to do in the process of *hansei*, or does it undermine the confidence and enjoyment that mothers might otherwise feel in the role of parent? Some observers doubt whether the criticism of mothers is constructive or helpful in the least. For instance, psychologist Miyuki Kazui (1997) has argued that Japanese women's anxiety about child rearing is a result of comments "conveyed by in-laws, insensitive husbands, or other mothers who criticized women's child rearing methods, or by professionals' comments in the media." She has called for an end to this practice: "In my opinion, it is time for those who foster the old image of the Japanese 'good mothers' to understand that they are the problem and that they are not offering a solution" (p. 494).

A sleepy monk who is nodding off during a meditation session may derive benefit when his fellow monk smacks him in reproof. But to what extent does criticism assist Japanese women in becoming more confident and effective parents in the twenty-first century? In subsequent chapters, we will look at the role of "mutual polishing" when we examine the role of support and criticism by a host of actors – parents, in-laws, friends, and spouses – on mothers' perceptions of themselves and on their ability to find effective ways of parenting their young children.

PART III

5

Memories of Childhood

When my first child was born, I was scared because I hated children and that may be because I myself wasn't treated like a child.... So I can't really think that children are cute. Sometimes, I suddenly feel that they are nothing more than a responsibility. (Hiromi, high school educated, high self-efficacy mother of two children)

For a pilot study that preceded the research reported in this book, Kazuko Behrens and I interviewed 40 mothers in Sapporo about their lives as mothers, wives, and workers. We asked the women a number of questions about their childhood experiences and their early relationships with their parents. We were intrigued with the possibility of exploring these issues but didn't know if they would be willing to divulge personal feelings about sensitive matters in a brief interview. To our surprise, these questions elicited long and often emotional responses, to the point that Kazuko began bringing tissues in case anyone started crying during the interview. Even as grown women, with children of their own, these mothers still experienced raw emotions about the way that they had been treated by their own parents and most did not hesitate to share them with us.

In addition to their candor and emotionality, we were also surprised by how negative and even bitter some of the women were about their early childhood experiences. Many women described their own mothers as frightening, strict, and controlling (see Holloway & Behrens, 2002). This dark portrait of their early years was particularly surprising to us because the research literature on early socialization in Japan available to us at that time emphasized the gentle, indirect strategies used by Japanese mothers to manipulate children into behaving well (e.g., Conroy, Hess, Azuma, & Kashiwagi, 1980). Furthermore, we were well aware of work of Takeo Doi and others who highlighted the tender, indulgent treatment by Japanese mothers of their infants.

When I started designing the current project, I wanted to follow up on the findings from the pilot study, and I was eager to explore possible connections between the women's early experiences and their later parenting self-efficacy. Research in the United States and other Western countries strongly indicates that children who experience their parents as responsive and trustworthy are more likely to develop a positive view of others and see themselves as worthy relationship partners (Bowlby, 1973; Bugental & Shennum, 1984; Grusec, Hastings, & Mammone, 1994; Main, Kaplan, & Cassidy, 1985). As children mature, these early representations serve as templates to guide their appraisal of and response to others. Mothers who have come to terms with their own childhood experiences – be they negative or positive – tend to feel more efficacious, and less helpless and out of control than those who continue to distort the events of the past or deny that they occurred (Cohn, Cowan, Cowan, & Pearson, 1992; Coleman & Karraker, 1997; Deutsch, Ruble, Fleming, Brooks-Gunn, & Stangor, 1988; George & Solomon, 1999; Grusec, Hastings, & Mammone, 1994; Williams et al., 1987). We wanted to see whether similar dynamics would emerge in Japan.

Accordingly, in the first survey of the present study, administered when the children were in preschool, we asked participating mothers to indicate how often they had felt protected (*mimamoru*) and understood (*kimochi wo rikai shite iru*) as children by their own mother and father. We were then able to examine whether mothers who felt more protected and understood by their parents in turn experienced higher parenting self-efficacy than those who perceived their parents as more distant or harsh. Indeed, we found a strong relationship. In fact, the memory of being protected and understood by one's parents was a stronger predictor of women's current judgments of parenting self-efficacy than were their perceptions of any current source of support, including that by husbands, mothers, or friends (details reported in Holloway, Suzuki, Yamamoto, & Behrens, 2005; Suzuki, in press).

This significant quantitative association prompted us to obtain more information on women's early childhood experiences. We wanted to understand *how* and *why* their perception of being cared for as children was connected to their sense of parenting efficacy. We opened up a discussion on this topic in our first interview with these mothers: we asked them to describe their childhood and tell us what their parents had been like when they were growing up. We followed up on the topic in the second interview, much of which was devoted to the women's adolescence and early adulthood. The interviews once again proved to be illuminating and charged with emotion, with the women speaking candidly about their experiences.

TABLE 5.1. *Women's Descriptions of Their Own Parents*
(Ranked According to Parenting Self-Efficacy)

Name	Parenting Self-Efficacy Score	Parent	Description of Parent during Mother's Childhood
Asako	5.8	Mom	Very strict and "clear on what's good and what's bad"; "very wonderful mother."
		Dad	"In his own world"; "hardly ever around the house and hardly ever attentive to us."
Mari	5.4	Mom	"A god" whom Mari never saw relax, eat, or sleep.
		Dad	"Extremely frightening"; abusive; didn't listen to her.
Masayo	5.4	Mom	Very strict and competitive; pushed Masayo to do her best.
		Dad	Very strict and "traditional"; didn't want Masayo to go to college.
Yasuko	5.1	Mom	Kind but busy with seven children; should have been "a little more strict" and involved with schooling.
		Dad	Quiet, but Yasuko felt he could help her if she needed; sensed his underlying love.
Miho	4.6	Mom	Sweet to younger siblings but strict toward Miho and older sister; easygoing: "She didn't think about things in depth."
		Dad	"Very talkative"; Miho often spent time with him at shop but he didn't give advice about her future.
Miyuki	4.3	Mom	Very hardworking and kind; treated Miyuki better than her older sister.
		Dad	No interest in children: "In hindsight it's like he isn't my father."
Sakura	4.3	Mom	Sakura "really, really liked" her; mother worked hard but still made clothing by hand.
		Dad	He was ill and often at home so Sakura spent lots of time with him; he "liked children."
Risa	4.2	Mom	Very strict but played with them and took them everywhere. Risa was favorite child. "I love my mother a lot and want to be like her."
		Dad	"He drank a lot. He wasn't violent, but he said the same thing over and over. He didn't talk a lot if he wasn't drinking, but he was scary."
Naoko	4.0	Mom	Worked hard; "She was very permissive – just let us do what we wanted"; "I didn't hate my mother or ... love her too much."

(continued)

TABLE 5.1. *(continued)*

Name	Parenting Self-Efficacy Score	Parent	Description of Parent during Mother's Childhood
Reiko	3.9	Dad	"Usually he was a kind and funny guy"; "I had a more friend-like relationship with my father." Felt distant from both parents; "I didn't talk much to them."
		Mom	Reiko believes she and mother are similar; Reiko has "good image of her in childhood."
Hiromi	3.8	Dad	He was around a lot; got along well when Reiko was little but not as adolescent.
		Mom	Hardworking, strict, and frightening; "never bought anything for me, for example toys or anything."
Junko	3.8	Dad	Violent, alcoholic; "He is strange. I haven't liked him since I was little. I don't want to think of him as my father."
		Mom	Serious; Junko didn't get along with her; admired but didn't like her.
Kayoko	3.6	Dad	Strict and used very harsh physical discipline, but Junko was a "daddy's girl" and they liked joking around together.
		Mom	"I didn't talk to my mother much. I remember that when I talked to her I quarreled with her."
Yuri	3.6	Dad	"He liked to drink a lot and when he drank he became violent." "I didn't have a good relationship with him . . . I didn't talk to him much."
		Mom	Kind; "She always laughed and had the capacity to protect the children"; "I was a mommy's girl."
Chihiro	3.4	Dad	Silent; parents "fought a lot and I really have bad memories about him."
		Mom	Stood up for Chihiro when she was bullied in elementary school.
Beni	3.3	Dad	Got along well; "I might have been a daddy's little girl."
		Mom	Worked hard; Beni "wanted to do *amae*" but felt mother wouldn't accept it.
		Dad	Didn't know "how to interact with children"; almost no relationship.

Note: Parenting self-efficacy score was obtained during first survey, administered when focal child was in preschool. Possible scores ranged from 1 to 6.

Frightening Fathers and Silent Fathers

The traditional Japanese father of the premodern era has been described as akin to a force of nature, his ascribed power reflected in a proverb warning that one should fear "earthquakes, thunder, fire, and fathers" (Shwalb, Imaizumi, & Nakazawa, 1987). Did real-life fathers live up to this ferocious image? In all likelihood they did not. Wagatsuma (1978) points out that while the cultural ideal may have been to maintain a rather formal distance between father and children, it is clear that many fathers were personally inclined to form warm emotional bonds with their children (see Sugimoto, 1927, for an example). Azuma (1986) also argues that there has never been a strong father figure in Japanese families; according to him, the notion of a strongly patriarchal family was "accepted as *tatemae*" – that is, it was officially accepted – whereas in reality, the majority of people rejected the idea of men as strongly powerful (pp. 6–7).

In any case, the image of the strong father, head of the *ie*, was appropriated by government officials in the early years of the modern state, who sought to connect the notion of the father as head of the household with that of the emperor as head of the nation. These politicians hoped that by enforcing the absolute authority of the father, they could also reinforce the allegiance of the citizen to the emperor, whose newly restored status was badly in need of legitimization. The following passage by Yatsuka Hozumi, a conservative writing in the 1890s, emphasizes the absolute power of the father (cited in Ito, 2008, p. 24):

When children are young, the father is clearly superior both in terms of intellect and physical strength. This is usually the case, no matter who the father is. It is the most clearly discernible standard by which superiority and inferiority are naturally divided. That is to say that the standard has to do with a relationship of power, and that power is the logic involved in issuing a command and compelling obedience. I believe that this is where the relationship of command and obedience is taught and where it grows. Thus the veneration of parents is a veneration of power.

In contrast to this idealized image of powerful fathers from the past, contemporary Japanese fathers are most often characterized as shadowy figures who are "marginal" or "peripheral" members of the nuclear family. Allison (1994) has written that most women believe that "life operates fully and smoothly without the father around, so long as he provides the necessary financial support" (p. 109). Iwao (1993) has argued that men's relationship to their children is even weaker than their relationship with their wives:

"A mother regards her bond with the children as stronger than the bond with her husband while the husband regards his bond with his wife as stronger than that with his children" (pp. 135–136).

In our interviews, we saw glimpses of both types of father. Nearly half the women described their own fathers as powerful, and even explosive. These women typically used the term *kowai*, which means scary or frightening, to describe their fathers. Four women – Hiromi, Kayoko, Junko, and Mari – grew up in fear of physical violence (see Table 5.1 for a description of each woman's recollections of her parents). Mari described her father in these terms:

My father was an extremely frightening father. Extremely frightening. Really, I don't think there could be a more frightening father.... Regarding his ways of discipline, it was beyond discipline or even common sense. For instance, if we didn't greet someone the right way or did anything incorrectly the first time around, he'd correct us. But if we ever repeated the same mistake, he'd spank us. By the second or third time, for example, if we didn't put away our things he'd spank us without saying anything. And actually, after spanking us, he'd destroy and then throw out the scissors or toys that we hadn't put back. The stuff would be destroyed beyond repair ... If I fought with my brother or sister we were punished by our father. He would hit us here using a rubber belt. After being hit, our skin would have welts.

In a later interview, Mari returned to this topic, describing how her father had been raised in an era when parents were stricter, in part because they were working too hard to pay close attention to their children and their emotions:

In my father's generation a lot of people lived in poverty. It was a time when parents could not be concerned about their kids as much as we do now. In fact, I heard that the parents could not pay attention to their kids. Instead, the older siblings would take care of their younger sisters and brothers. My father used to tell us over and over how fortunate we were, in the sense that we were taken care of. My father would be very strict when we were being just a little self-centered. He was really strict. I think that he was strict on us because his own father was strict on him ... I heard that he would hang my father upside down. If my father misbehaved just a little bit, he would tie him up with a rope and hang him upside down over the tree branch. Well, my father did the same thing to me.

The mothers had different evaluations and interpretations of the harsh treatment they received from their fathers. Some women felt little affection for their fathers and had never really forgiven them, while others described having a positive relationship with their father in spite of the eruptions of violence. Those who thought that their father was attempting to teach them something were more forgiving than the ones who thought their father was simply violent or out of control. For example, Mari had decided that her father was well intentioned, and she forgave him for being so abusive:

I think he did those things because he wanted us to be well-mannered and self-disciplined. At that time, although I didn't really see the reasons behind his actions, I now think that it was really good for me. After I became an adult, I could finally understand [my father].

In a later interview, Mari commented that she and her siblings were well behaved as a result of their father's strict discipline techniques:

I think that it is really good for kids to be raised by strict parents.... they can understand a person's pain, they will show respect to their elders and their teachers. And they will understand hierarchical relations (*jōge-kankei*) and know how to act appropriately.

Women with a benign interpretation of their fathers' strict or detached behavior tended to say that they had only realized as adults that their fathers were motivated by a loving impulse. Risa was one of those who had "really hated" her father because he was so frightening when he was drunk. As an adult, she came to realize that he had "loved the family environment." She said that her views about him started changing after she moved away from home:

I went to a private high school and lived in a boarding house during that time. After I left for high school, I started to like my father. I hadn't really hated to spend time with him or thought that he was dirty. I just disliked him because he was frightening and always nagging. But eventually, I realized that he really cared about me.

Other women did not believe that their fathers' violent behavior was motivated by any positive intention. They saw their fathers as frustrated by a hard life or a bad marriage, or as simply lacking self-control, and noted that their rages were often fueled by alcohol. Typical of this perspective was Hiromi, who noted: "My parents didn't get along with each other, and my father was drunk and he was really violent when he was drunk." Similarly,

Kayoko said that she never really formed a relationship with her father: "He liked to drink a lot and when he drank he became violent.... I didn't have a good relationship with him."

A second group of women described their fathers as emotionally detached from the family and uninterested in their children, more along the lines of the stereotypical image of contemporary fathers as marginal members of the family. The women who experienced this sort of treatment tended not to attribute it to any sort of positive intention. Most tended to blame their fathers for being too self-indulgent or self-involved to form an emotional connection with their children. For example, Beni thought that her father's lack of involvement stemmed from his own upbringing and personality, as well as from his volatile relationship with Beni's mother:

You know my father was born in a wealthy family. My father and his brother each had their own nanny, and when they got up in the morning the nanny took off their pajamas and changed their clothing for them.... When my father angered his parents, or at least when he upset his father, he was spanked. He was brought up in a military way. So, that's why my father doesn't know how to interact with children. He doesn't know how to play with children. Even when he brought us to an amusement park, he wouldn't know what to do.... So, when talking about my childhood, I don't have any memories of playing with him.... When I was really young, he was like the typical back-in-the-day Japanese guy. He played around at night; he played around with women. To him, this was just how things were supposed to be. So, when he came home around midnight, he didn't care if the house was littered with toys. As long as there was somewhere he could sleep, then that was good enough for him.

It was difficult for the women who had never as children felt close to their fathers to form a positive relationship in their adult years. Beni had never been able to kindle a warm connection to her father, in spite of an attempt he made to bridge the gap between them:

When I was 32, one day, my father suddenly apologized to me. He said: "I gave you hardship when you were a child." It was just one sentence, but for some reason it made me really happy to hear him say that. I hated my father. Well, I couldn't really express that, but when I realized that he had reflected on his behavior, it made me happy.

In spite of her father's desire for rapprochement, Beni did not care to interact with her parents, even though they lived close by. She said: "if my parents are not hospitalized or nothing serious has happened, unless I bump into them on the street, I just see them once a month."

A third group of women described their fathers in a way that was consistent with the image of Japanese men as somewhat marginal, but not because they were emotionally detached or egocentric; rather, they were hardworking, traditional men who were not demonstrative but cared about their children in their own quiet way. For example, Yasuko, one of seven children who grew up in a rural area, noted that her father was very reserved but managed nevertheless to convey warm feelings toward his children through simple acts of kindness:

Because it was my father, there was a certain distance between us. When I say distance, I mean it was the old days. Then, parents were always busy, and so it wasn't like they could always give attention to kids. So our relationship wasn't like we were always having conversations or always talking to each other, but I always thought he could understand me if I needed to talk with him. And my dad would only say the minimum but within those few words, I could perceive a deeper meaning. For example if I was taking a nap, he wouldn't gently place a towel over me, he'd kind of toss it over me so my stomach wouldn't get too cold. That's the kind of parent he was. So even though he was strict, I could sense his kindness.

Growing Up with a Warm, Involved Father

Chihiro was the only one of the mothers we interviewed who seemed to have experienced consistent emotional support and enjoyable interactions with her father. An only child, she described herself as a "daddy's girl." Throughout her childhood, her father supported her educational aspirations. Her parents didn't directly pressure her to study, but were happy when she did well enough to be accepted to a four-year university. Her father was actively involved in her college application process. He vetoed her initial dream of becoming an architect, arguing that it was an unsuitable profession for a woman, and stipulated that she could attend college only if she lived at home. Although she was frustrated with her father's intervention at the time, she came to think he had been correct in restricting her to a local college. She intended to follow the same model with her own children, reasoning that boys needed to move away and experience hardship in order to become mentally and physically tough, whereas girls should be brought up in a more sheltered and protected environment.

Chihiro was also the only woman in the sample who appeared to have maintained a close relationship with her father in her adulthood. She was also the only one living with her father during the time of the interviews. Apparently, he continued to act as a benevolent but somewhat controlling force in her life. When she and her husband decided to live with her parents, the younger couple was inclined to build a house with a separate "in-law unit." However, Chihiro's father ignored their preferences and elected to build a house in which the whole family could live together. In spite of feeling somewhat dominated by her father, she reported enjoying their living arrangement and felt that having her parents around made the house more cheerful. Her father gave her advice about her volunteer work at the schools, and he was also encouraging her to run for a position in the local government.

No other woman portrayed her adult relationship with her father in such a positive manner. However, a number of women described some positive elements, so it is possible to get a sense of what sort of connection they were seeking and what they found to be supportive and enjoyable. A couple of mothers said they enjoyed joking around with their fathers or saw themselves as having a relationship that was somewhat like that of a friend. Junko provided one example of this. On the one hand, her father was very strict and controlling, particularly at mealtime. He would become enraged if Junko didn't eat all of her food or if she wasn't sitting up correctly at the table. At these times he would sometimes punch or hit her, and she occasionally had to flee the apartment to avoid being seriously hurt. However, they sometimes had a good time together: "But usually he was really fun. We were like comedians together and we joked around a lot."

Early Relationships with Mothers: Support and Protection

The women in our study almost all described their mothers as very hardworking. Their mothers were part of the generation of Japanese born in the late 1930s and early 1940s, who struggled to overcome the privation following the end of the Second World War. Virtually all the women we interviewed acknowledged that their mothers had experienced many hardships. Most of the women in this older generation had worked outside the home as shopkeepers, wage laborers, or farmers. Only a few were able to stay at home with their children, and some faced the demands of caring for as many as seven children. About half of the women we interviewed believed that their mothers' many responsibilities had made them unable to provide guidance when their children needed it. For example, Naoko used the term *hōnin* to describe her mother, a term that connotes permissive parenting bordering on neglect:

She was working hard. She was running a family business. So, she wouldn't focus on trivial things. She wouldn't even say things like "You should study" or "Go do something." She didn't say anything about the trivial matters. She was really permissive (*hōnin*) – she just let us do anything we wanted.

Some of our participants also felt that they had to suppress their own feelings and needs when they were children because their mothers were too overwhelmed with work to pay attention to them. Beni grew up wanting more attention and coddling from her mother but never asked for it, because she had the feeling that she "should not say things that were self-centered."

In contrast, others remembered that their mothers had somehow made time for them in spite of working hard, having difficult husbands, or being busy rearing large numbers of children. These young women revered their own mothers for their ability to remain focused and dedicated to their children in spite of the obstacles. For example, Asako described how her mother managed to instill in her children a strong sense of right and wrong, despite living in factory housing where many inhabitants were morally lax. Sakura mentioned that her mother sewed her children's clothing by hand even though she worked full time. Even Yasuko, who believed that her busy parents were somewhat too permissive, acknowledged that they were able to convey important values about education to her and her siblings:

But not once did they tell me to do homework. Well, I guess I should say that they were too busy working to have the time to tell me I should do my homework. They let me do whatever I wanted to do and gave me no restrictions. They thought we should study as much as we wanted, and they did not mind getting into debt to send us to universities.

Several women mentioned that they appreciated how their own mothers had protected them from their fathers. As we have seen, most of the women in the study found their fathers to be somewhat frightening and prone to physical violence. Some of them described how their mothers tried to buffer and protect their children from their fathers' anger. For example, even though Junko and her mother did not get along very well, Junko acknowledged that her mother tried to protect her: "My father was just slapping and punching, and if it was too extreme, my mother tried to stop it." Mari appreciated how hard it was for her mother to oppose her abusive spouse:

My mother was incredibly gentle. She was the exact opposite of my father. He would get extremely angry and punish us severely. But my mother never spanked us, not even once. She always protected me.... My father was also very strict with my mother. I think my mother was really scared of him. But she is a very traditional person and would never go against her husband. She obeyed him and told us to obey him as well.

In addition to describing how their mothers protected them from their fathers' violent tempers, several of the women described how their mothers advocated for them, particularly when their fathers were limiting their opportunities due to gender-based assumptions about appropriate behavior for girls. For example, Masayo talked about the difference between her mother and father concerning her aspirations to go to college. Her father wanted her to grow up as a traditional girl and discouraged her from studying:

Anyhow, my father only expected me to act feminine, just like the average girl. That meant being docile and obedient. He told me to not become a pretentious woman. But my mother was a bit different. My mother told me to never lose. Well, she never directly stated that, but I could sense it, I knew what she was implying – losing is unacceptable.

Masayo's mother felt she could not actively oppose her husband's wishes, but when he died unexpectedly during Masayo's high school years, she became openly supportive of Masayo's educational goals.

Asako's mother also provided support that shaped Asako's life in crucial ways. When Asako developed a passion for soccer as a young girl, her father discouraged her from pursuing it because he did not believe that girls should become seriously engaged in sports. Asako's mother decided to support her desire to play soccer despite her husband's objections and despite criticism from others in their community and concerns about her daughter's health:

My father would say, "You can't [play soccer] because you are a girl." This sort of thinking was common back then. In my generation girls hardly ever played soccer.... But my mother, even on very cold nights, would put on a big coat and watch me as I was jogging outside. She would say, "After all, since you are a girl, it's not too safe." She would watch over me. But my father, on the other hand, did not look out for me in that way.

Some of the women acknowledged that their mothers faced a difficult dilemma if they tried to oppose a demanding or unfair spouse. Some wives were able to manage their husbands so skillfully that they were able to get their way without openly resisting them while others were more confrontational and provoked angry retaliation. The women in our study were grateful to their mothers for their willingness to engage in these risky acts of advocacy.

Growing Up and Coming to Terms with Early Experiences

As noted earlier, the survey data showed a strong association between women's perceptions of having been cared for in a warm manner and their sense of parenting self-efficacy but our questions did not distinguish between the care of mothers and that of fathers. In these qualitative data, we were able to learn that women's relationship with their own mothers was the crucial determinant of parenting self-efficacy, as Table 5.1 reveals.

Furthermore, most of the higher efficacy mothers felt that over time they had gained a better perspective on why their parents acted as they did. They tended to believe that factors beyond their parents' control – including poverty, tradition, and large family size – were at least partly to blame for any problems they had experienced. The birth of their own children was often a turning point when our participants began to feel a sense of understanding and compassion for their parents. Some of the higher efficacy mothers tried to be analytical about their experiences and draw useful lessons from them, even the negative ones. For example, Mari, who experienced much harsh discipline from her father, said she was trying to avoid treating her children the same way:

I am trying not to spank my children without asking them the reason [behind their actions]. Because I was really hurt by my father never listening to the reason why I did something when I was a child; I wanted to make sure that the same thing never happened to my children.

In contrast, the lower efficacy mothers tended to characterize their early relationships with their own mothers as having been distant or full of conflict. Chihiro was the lone exception; although she reported having a positive relationship with both parents (both in her childhood and at the present time), she expressed little confidence in her parenting ability. Unlike the higher efficacy mothers, who seemed to have moved beyond some of their early disappointments, the lower self-efficacy mothers continued to struggle with feelings of resentment toward parents who had been unwilling or unable to provide the basic attention, love, and protection that these women had sought when they were younger.

For example, Beni described her mother as a "selfish old woman" who still expected Beni to suppress her own feelings and defer to her mother's needs. Her irritation was intensified by the sense that her mother's demands could no longer be justified by the excuse of working hard:

My mother asks to be indulged a lot. She'll say, "Bring this over for me, bring that over for me." But after I bring it over, she'll say that it's not what she wanted and tell me to go back and fetch what she had requested. It's obviously something that doesn't need to be taken care of right away, yet she still demands that it be done immediately.

Of all the women, Hiromi most clearly articulated how her early experiences affected her confidence as a parent. Her father was an alcoholic, and her mother had disappeared when Hiromi was in middle school. Hiromi believed that her difficult childhood had affected her ability to relax and enjoy spending time with other people:

It had been difficult for me to adjust to a life where a person is there in the morning and comes home at night. Well, this is a normal life but for me it wasn't normal. That's why I actually prefer spending time alone.... I would sometimes feel really unsettled by the presence of my child and my husband.

As the brief quotation at the beginning of this chapter illustrates, Hiromi strongly believed that her difficult childhood had impaired her ability to connect emotionally with her children. However, she also saw some possibility of changing with the support of other people. Over the course of the interviews, Hiromi spoke at several points of having learned from others – particularly her husband – about human relations and what constitutes a normal family life:

Well, because my husband accepts me entirely at home, I now feel like I want to become a normal person for my husband and for my children.... After all, I guess it's important that I listen to my children [just like my husband does to me] at home.

Hiromi's sense of vulnerability stemming from her childhood experiences framed her expectations about other close relationships. Because she was such a reflective person, she was able to articulate how her mistrust of others accounted for her responses to her husband and children. In addition to her own acumen, the sheer intensity of her early experiences may have served to highlight in a very strong manner how early memories can affect later perceptions. Her story suggests that women can overcome the negative assumptions about themselves that result from their early experience. In her case, it was her husband who helped her re-evaluate these debilitating assumptions. We will return to this topic in Chapter 6, which deals extensively with spousal support.

Conclusions

Digging into the these women's narratives about their early childhood, we can see that their interpretations of the reasons for their parents' actions – more than the actions themselves – were the key to their emotional response. Mothers who perceived their parents as trying to implement a child-rearing philosophy – however extreme it may have been – were more likely to emerge from a difficult family situation with a sense of self-efficacy than those who viewed their parents as too self-centered or self-indulgent to be consistent and nurturing.

Many studies conducted in the United States and Europe have found that children who form a secure bond with their parents are more likely as adults to see themselves as worthy of others' regard and to view others as trustworthy (Bowlby, 1973; Main, Kaplan & Cassidy, 1985). In these studies, as in ours, there is an emphasis on the individual's interpretation of early experiences. The cognitive framework guiding the appraisal of early events is often more important in determining subsequent relationships than the objective nature of the experiences. Recently Kazuko Behrens found evidence that Japanese mothers who have come to terms with their own childhood experiences – positive or negative – are more likely to have children who in turn can rely on their mothers as a secure base in uncertain situations (Behrens, Hesse, & Main, 2007).

The women in our study tended to describe their parents in one of three ways. First there were those who characterized their mothers or fathers as hardworking, quiet parents who did not necessarily say much, but whose love and caring took the form of watchful supervision (*mimamoru*) and were demonstrated indirectly through such actions as covering a sleeping child (Yasuko's father) or standing in the cold watching a daughter run laps in the dark (Asako's mother). Although our participants believed that these parents were well intentioned, they felt that they were sometimes unable to provide needed supervision and were sometimes overly permissive (*hōnin*). In Chapter 3, we saw that some women still believed that this type of traditional parent embodied the ideal.

A second type of parent was very strict and strongly enforced social conventions such as politeness, posture, and table manners. This was the opposite of *hōnin* parenting. Such parents, most of whom were fathers, tended to rely on corporal punishment and made little attempt to reason with a child or understand the child's motives and intentions. These men did not shy away from conflict, nor did they hesitate to impose their will strongly on their wives and children. Women who grew up with this type of parent saw them as remnants of an earlier era and recognized that their parents may have been trying to imbue them with moral characteristics that were socially valued. They appreciated the attempt and even saw how such strict treatment may have prevented them from becoming lazy or self-indulgent. But most women saw this view as being too harsh and out of step with the times.

A third type of parent was communicative and supportive. For the most part, those described in this way were mothers. Chihiro's father was the only man to fit this profile. This type of parent enjoyed frequent and extensive conversations with the child and attempted to support the child's goals and desires unless they seemed inappropriate. Some of our respondents described this type of parent as being like a friend, but always keeping the child's interests uppermost in mind. Most of the mothers aspired to be this type of parent with their own children.

The women's depiction of the strict type of parent is particularly striking, because it provides a much different perspective than the one that is usually depicted in Western writing on the Japanese family, the mild-mannered salary man. These fathers, however, were more akin to the frightening and powerful father of Japanese proverb. Furthermore, this description of the father does not square with the frequently cited claim that close relationships in Japan are characterized by "symbiotic harmony," in which conflict is minimized at all costs: "In Japan, if an intimate complains directly, it probably signals the end of the relationship.... Conflict is not readily accepted; rather, cohesion, mind reading and cherishing of the relationship are stressed" (Rothbaum, Pott, Azuma, Miyake, & Weisz, 2000, p. 1135). This characterization would have come as a surprise to Mari's mother, as she pondered how to prevent her husband from suspending her daughter upside down from a tree for quarreling with her brother.

One important question is whether these men were enacting a culturally sanctioned form of parenting or whether they were an example of people who failed to conform to widely accepted values about the role of father. When we asked Mari and Junko how others in the community might have evaluated their fathers' actions, they maintained that their father's behavior fell within the spectrum of normal parenting for the time. In spite of the dire conditions faced by Mari, Junko, and Hiromi when they were growing up, their family problems were apparently undetected by outsiders or were viewed as a personal family matter. The women described their mothers as their sole protectors; rarely, if ever, did teachers or other professionals provide them with support or protection. The narratives suggest the painful cost of living in a community where women and children could not speak out publicly and receive help when they were mistreated.

There is no way for me to determine how representative these women's experiences are of family dynamics in Japan. My purpose here is to expose some of the themes that emerged, not to assess their prevalence. In any case, until recently, there has been little public focus in Japan on the topic of child and spousal abuse. Government agencies are beginning to collect data on such issues, but definitions of abuse vary from one jurisdiction to the next, making it hard to aggregate. Private as well as public organizations are also developing policies and programs to address the problem of family violence (Goodman, 2006; Shoji, 2005). Novels and memoirs have also brought attention to the plight of Japanese women and children who are caught in abusive relationships (e.g., Mori, 1993, 1995; Ozeki, 1998). Similarly, the issue of alcoholism – clearly implicated in the family dynamics described in this chapter – has historically been accepted as a family matter and often left untreated; however, it too is now being given more attention by health-care professionals and the government (Borovoy, 2005).

One fundamental issue that poses a serious challenge to all of these reforms is the power differential between men and women, which remains quite wide in Japan. The strong value placed on the role of mother is in turn connected to women's social power vis-à-vis men, because it precludes them from attaining parity in the domains of education and employment. To the extent that women are less highly educated and more financially dependent on men, they and their children remain relatively vulnerable to maltreatment. These and other issues will be explored in the next chapter, which focuses on the marital relationship.

6

Husbands: Crucial Partners or Peripheral Strangers?

> My husband is not like one of those fathers who work too hard and do not even care about their kids. . . . He does everything. I cannot think of anything else he should do as a father. He takes Kaito [their son] with him everywhere he goes. (Asako, high school educated, high self-efficacy mother of two)

> Before we were married, I was thinking we could probably share the housework. But I gave up on that eventually. He stopped helping me, knowing I would do everything. . . . He does not do a thing, even if I ask. That's why I have come to expect nothing from him. (Junko, high school educated, low self-efficacy mother of two)

The diary of Makiko Nakano, the wife of a pharmacist living in Kyoto, provides a fascinating glimpse of married life in 1910, when the modern family structure was taking shape in Japan (Nakano, 1995). In her diary, Makiko describes the challenges of being a young wife who must learn the ways of a new household. Married for four years, she portrays herself as a novice who has yet to learn how to be a good household manager. Her well-intentioned efforts sometimes meet with criticism from her husband and mother-in-law, leaving her feeling hurt and disappointed, but she always tries to learn from her mistakes. In one passage from the diary she describes an incident in  which she attempts to prepare a special dish – frozen tofu – for her husband. She writes of her surprise when he tells her that the dish was inedible: "Contrary to my expectation of praise and appreciation, I got nothing but criticism. . . . I was very disappointed, but recognized that I was at fault. I bought more tofu this morning and will try again tonight, in hopes that this time he will approve my efforts" (p. 82).

Young wives like Makiko had little status in the household, particularly prior to giving birth to a child. As the frozen tofu fiasco illustrates, Makiko sought the approval of her husband and considered herself subordinate to him. Her role in the household and the nature of her relations with her husband and his mother reflect the transitional nature of the Japanese family in the early twentieth century. At the time the diary was written, the *ie* had been inscribed as the officially recognized family structure. Under the *ie* structure, the head of the household (usually a man) was in a position of unquestionable authority; however, to the extent that Japanese family patterns reflected Confucian ethical notions, wives could theoretically expect benevolence and the cultivation of harmony on the part of more powerful family members (Wagatsuma, 1978).

Indeed, Makiko describes her mother-in-law as a benevolent woman who, contrary to many accounts portraying mothers-in-law as cruel taskmasters, seems to have treated Makiko in a firm but kind manner. Makiko's mother-in-law may have pitied Makiko because the younger woman's own mother had died several months earlier. She seems to have been a forward-looking woman who was training Makiko not only to perpetuate the household traditions but also to learn new skills and engage in activities that were in keeping with the changing times.

Although the Nakano family adhered to the traditional norms of the *ie* in certain ways, there were also signs that Makiko's relationship with her husband was more than just an arrangement of financial expedience. As exposure to Western ideas and institutions intensified during the time that Makiko was writing, educators and reformers urged citizens to redefine the family as a unit anchored by the husband and wife relationship (Sand, 2003). This new form of family had its own name – *katei* – to convey the notion of an intimate domestic space governed by sentiment and to distinguish it from the *ie* structure (Ito, 2008; White, 2002). While records from 1912 indicate that only 3 percent of marriages were characterized as love matches (Fuess, 2004), there was a growing expectation that warmth and intimacy should characterize the relations between husband and wife. A new word for love – *ai* – came into use during the late 1800s to reflect the experience of romantic feelings within a monogamous, heterosexual domestic context. The term *ai* displaced the word *iro*, formerly used to refer to male feelings of attachment, which had, in addition to an emotional component, a strong connotation of sexual relations including "male-male relations…and the possibility of multiple sexual partners" (Ito, 2008, p. 100).

Indeed, it is possible to see in the frozen tofu episode signs that Makiko feels genuine affection for her husband. In her diary, she describes nursing him day and night through an illness that preceded the making of the tofu. Relieved when he finally started feeling better, she hit on the idea of making frozen tofu as a special treat, a small celebration of his recovery.

Not only was Makiko fond of her husband, but she clearly expected to be treated with kindness and consideration in return. At points in her diary, she notes with indignation when her husband fails to take her feelings into account. For example, she describes frequently having to wait up past midnight for him to return from an evening out with friends. She was expected to let him in the house, serve a late-night snack, and assist with his bath. Although she accepts these tasks as part of a wife's responsibility, she criticizes him for not acknowledging her sacrifice:

It seems to me that he has acquired a bad habit lately of staying too late when he visits the Matsuis' house ... I am equally cold and sleepy waiting up late at night. If I lie down, I always go to sleep without knowing when he comes home, and that leads to leaving him standing at the door for as long as a half-hour [waiting for someone to let him in]. If only he would come home by midnight, I would have no problem. He should realize that I am frightened to stay up all alone at night. (p. 209)

While Makiko seems to be relatively happy on the whole, there are signs in her diary that she is not content to be relegated to the role of *shufu*, or professional housewife, even if this status represented an elevation compared to that experienced by most women in the older version of the *ie*. For example, throughout her diary, Makiko writes about a desire to participate more fully in the rich cultural life enjoyed by her husband and his male friends. Makiko is restricted to occasional visits with her relatives and childhood friends, whereas her husband spends a great deal of time attending art exhibits, going to the theater and musical events, and dining in the company of friends. She occasionally attends a cultural event with a friend, but only after asking permission from her husband and his mother. When her husband chides her for neglecting her household duties to go to the theater, Makiko's quiet grumbling to her diary signals a significant crack in the *ie* system, which was built on the assumption of women's unquestioned and willing subordination to the household head (Ito, 2008).

This hybrid family structure – in which new assumptions of domestic life were grafted onto a facsimile of the older *ie* – persisted during the several decades in which Japan focused on building its military strength and engaging in empire-building activities. Japanese family life again changed radically in the postwar years, when the size and composition of the household, the timing of major family events, and the nature of family roles all underwent significant change and reinterpretation (Hendry, 1981; Uno, 1991; White, 2002; Yoshizumi, 1995). During their seven years of occupying Japan, American forces drew up a new constitution that reformed many of the laws related to the family. The *ie* structure was abolished in favor of the nuclear family, with the married couple as its anchor. Parental permission to marry was no longer required for individuals over the age of 20. In this period the custom of arranged marriages became less common, and young people came increasingly to expect romantic and sexual compatibility as the basis for marriage. The percentage of so-called love marriages gradually rose from 3 percent in 1912 to over 20 percent in the 1950s, eventually exceeding the percentage of arranged marriages in the 1960s (Fuess, 2004).

made marriage based on love, but made it harder to get a divorce

These behavioral shifts were accompanied by changes in societal laws and conventions regarding marriage and divorce (Fuess, 2004). In the early modern period, it was easy for men as well as women to sue for divorce, and Japan had one of the highest rates of divorce in the world. But criticism from the West prompted Japanese government officials to pass new legislation making it more difficult for couples to divorce. A particularly stringent law promulgated in 1952 stipulated that a spouse who was at fault (e.g., for adultery) could not obtain a divorce over the objections of a legally innocent spouse. This law effectively provided a guarantee of lifetime marriage – and thus of financial support – to any legally innocent spouse. The law not only resulted in a sharp drop in the divorce rate but also contributed to the final transformation of the "good wife and wise mother" from a person who balanced household responsibilities, civic engagement, and employment to a "professional housewife" devoted entirely to household chores and child rearing.

but then changed it, why?

Twenty-five years later, the Supreme Court reversed its 1952 decision, making it possible for a guilty party to obtain a divorce from a legally innocent spouse. The divorce rate began to rise during the subsequent decades, moving from a low of 0.75 in the 1950s, up to 1.6 in 1995, and then to 2.3 in 2001 (Tsuya & Bumpass, 2004). By comparison, the crude divorce rate in Ireland, Italy, and Spain was under 1.0 in 2001, while the United States was on the high end, at 4.0. Custody in Japan is awarded "in the child's best interest," which results in the mother's taking custody in the vast majority of cases. However, current law makes little provision for spousal support or for child support by the noncustodial parent, making the financial outcome of divorce highly disadvantageous for women (Fuess, 2004). As we will see later in this chapter, women who are unhappily married have to think carefully about the financial implications of ending the marriage.

women can keep children, but had financially

Other social changes further shaped the transformation of women's role in the home during the postwar years. As the Japanese economy shifted increasingly toward industrial and corporate enterprises, gender roles became more rigid. Work demands kept husbands away from home for long hours. Wives were increasingly expected to maintain the home, handle family finances, and care for the children. With educational credentials the criterion by which status was measured in the corporate workplace, mothers were strongly expected to devote themselves to supporting their children's trajectory through the school system, thereby reducing their opportunities for long-term or high-level participation in the labor force (Allison, 1991, 1996; Yamamoto, 2001). Women's household duties also increased during the twentieth century as family life became increasingly associated with materialism and consumption (Sand, 2003; White, 2002).

During the 1960s and 1970s, the role of mother was seen as paramount for women (Hendry, 1981; Schooler & Smith, 1978), but those who came of age during the 1980s also held high expectations about emotional fulfillment in the role of wife (Iwao, 1993; Rosenberger, 2001; Shwalb, Nakawaza, Yamamoto, & Hyun, 2004). There is some disagreement in the scholarly literature about the degree of contemporary women's satisfaction with the quality of their marriages. Some scholars argue that most Japanese women have low but attainable expectations concerning married life and are just as satisfied with their husbands as are their counterparts in Western countries (Iwao, 1993; Mori, 1997). Others find evidence that men's behavior has not kept pace with the changes in women's expectations, leading to considerable dissatisfaction (Borovoy, 2005; Condon, 1985). For example, a comparison of unmarried women and men in Japan and in the United States conducted in the mid-1990s found that Japanese women expressed a far less favorable attitude toward the benefits of marriage than young American women did (Tsuya, Mason, & Bumpass, 2004).

[In fact, during the period between 1993 and 2003, Japanese men began doing slightly more housework and providing slightly more child care, primarily on the weekends.] However, many women continued to feel dissatisfied with their husbands' involvement in these activities. National surveys conducted between 1993 and 1998 found a rise in the number of married Japanese women who were dissatisfied with the level of husband involvement in the family, despite a slight increase in men's overall participation during the five-year period (National Institute of Population and Social Security Research, 2000). A follow-up survey by the same organization found a very slight increase between 1998 and 2003 in women's satisfaction with their husbands' involvement in housework and child rearing and a large decrease in their expectations concerning husbands' involvement (National Institute of Population and Social Security Research, 2006).

Survey evidence also suggests that women's employment status has little effect on the distribution of household work between husbands and wives.

A time-use study that looked at workplace as well as household labor found that women who were unemployed spent 37.6 hours per week on household tasks, while their husbands spent 49.1 hours working on the job and in the home. Women who were employed spent nearly twice as much time (73.1 hours) on the combination of work and household tasks as unemployed women whereas working women's husbands devoted only 51.4 hours to such tasks, just two hours more per week than the husbands of unemployed women (Tsuya & Bumpass, 2004). This basic picture does not change, even among women who are graduates of elite universities like Tokyo University (Stroeber & Chan, 2001).

The amount of time that Japanese men spend with their children is very limited compared to that spent by men in other countries. An international survey conducted in 2005 revealed that Japanese fathers report spending an average of 3.3 hours per day with their children aged four to six, lower than fathers in Thailand (5.7 hours), the United States (4.4), France (3.6), and Sweden (4.5) (National Women's Education Center, Japan, 2005). Only in Korea did fathers report spending less time with their children (2.7). The discrepancy between hours spent by fathers and hours spent by mothers (averaged across all ages from birth to age 12) was higher in Japan (4.5) than in Korea (4.3), Thailand (1.2), United States (2.5), France (1.9), and Sweden (1.2). The gap in paternal involvement between Japan and other Asian countries is particularly interesting, given the similarities in cultural heritage and rate of economic development. A second study that compared fathers' family involvement in five Asian cities also found relatively low rates of involvement in Japan. Fathers in Tokyo tended to return home much later than did fathers in Seoul, Beijing, Shanghai, and Taipei. Tokyo fathers were the least involved in housework and the least involved in child care (with the exception of bathing their children). For example, just 26.8 percent of fathers in Tokyo reported playing with their children on a daily basis, as opposed to 41.2 percent in Seoul, 54.2 in Beijing, 44.4 percent in Shanghai, and 48.5 percent in Taipei (Benesse, 2006a; see also Benesse, 2006b).

A detailed survey analyzed by Ishii-Kuntz (1994) reveals differences in the type of activities that Japanese and American fathers engaged in with their children aged 10 to 15 years old. Japanese fathers were less likely than American fathers to talk with their children on a daily basis, eat dinner with their children, assist with homework, and engage in sports or other recreational activities. Significantly, these differences could not be attributed primarily to employment demands on the Japanese fathers. On the weekends, Japanese and American fathers were equally likely to engage in employment-related activities, but Japanese men were far more likely to spend their

[handwritten margin note: when men were free spent time for themselves vs. w/ their children]

weekends engaged in adult leisure activities like golf or *pachinko* (Japanese pinball), whereas American men were more engaged in housework or interacting with their children.

If the sheer number of hours on the job does not explain the low participation rate of Japanese fathers, what other factors might contribute to this pattern? On one hand, surveys indicate that Japanese men themselves purport to value the paternal role above all other roles and view themselves as more committed to being a parent than their own fathers were (Shwalb, Kawai, Shoj, & Tsunetsugu, 1997). But some scholars have argued that workplace conditions foster a cultural definition of masculinity that emphasizes and intensifies nonparticipation in home life, to the point that Japanese men "consider their absence from home due to work demands an important factor contributing to their masculinities" (Ishii-Kuntz, 2003, p. 199). Exploring the demands on men for after-hours socializing, Allison (1994) argues that the intent of corporate sponsorship of these activities is to expand the realm of work and define it as a masculine domain, whereas the home becomes defined as exclusively and "naturally" feminine (p. 199). She also points out that as the realm of family becomes increasingly estranged from that of work, men are increasingly willing to commit more strongly to the workplace: "When a family is not pulling him home, the demands a company can make on his time and energies become greater and are more easily accepted" (p. 199). These strong structural pressures have proven to be more powerful than the demands of Japanese women or the government's anemic attempts to encourage men to participate in family life (Ishii-Kuntz, 2008).

[handwritten margin note: think they are committed parents, but not really]

Another way in which the workplace contributes to paternal noninvolvement is through the corporate practice of transferring workers to a new region on a periodic basis (*tanshin funin*). Rather than uproot their children and disrupt their schooling, families often opt for the wife and children remaining in one place while the husband moves alone. Current estimates are that approximately 3.7 percent of families are of this type, about three times the percentage in the United States (Bassani, 2007; Hamada, 1997; Tanaka & Nakazawa, 2005).

Can men's lack of involvement also be attributed to the actions of women themselves? Research in the United States has explored the extent to which mothers may consciously or unconsciously block their husbands' involvement in child care in order to preserve their own identity, a phenomenon known as "maternal gate keeping" (McBride et al., 2005). Something similar may be operating in Japan as well. Although surveys indicate that women are dissatisfied with their husbands' contribution to family life, many women continue to believe that women should be responsible for housework and child care, even if they are employed. A report compiled by the Japanese Prime Minister's Office (2000) cited a 1997 public opinion survey in which adults were asked whether they agreed that "women may work but that housework and child rearing should be properly attended to [by them]." Women expressed agreement or general agreement with this statement whether they were working full time (81.1 percent), part time (85.2 percent), or not employed (83.2 percent). The views of the women were quite similar to those of their husbands on this issue. Indeed, Japanese women are more conservative when it comes to gender-role expectations than are their counterparts in other developed countries. A comparative study conducted by the National Women's Education Center Japan (2005) found that women in Japan and Korea were much more likely to expect their husbands to prioritize work over child rearing than were their peers in Thailand, the United States, France, and Sweden. In view of the changing structure of the family and marriage over the last century, and the lack of social validation for alternative identities to that of mother, it is perhaps not surprising to find inconsistencies and a lack of consensus among Japanese women as well as men.

Next, I turn to our data to explore in more detail women's views about their husbands, including what wives expect from husbands and what women feel they have actually received in terms of support. Also of interest is learning how they react when their husbands fail to live up to their expectations and how their husbands' actions serve to either boost or undermine their sense of parenting efficacy. The survey data, described in the next section, get us started on this topic by providing an overview of the types of activities that men were involved in (according to their wives) as well as offering a snapshot of the women's subjective impressions of their husbands and their marriages.

Contemporary Fathers' Involvement in Family Activities

To obtain an overview of the balance of household responsibilities among the 116 families in our survey sample, we asked the women to indicate how often their husbands undertook each of 22 activities pertaining to housework, child care, relations with extended family and friends, and marital communication. Husbands reportedly spent almost no time on household chores like doing the laundry, cooking, and taking out the garbage. However, their wives rated them as relatively more involved in the lives of their children, often playing and talking with them.

To learn more about how the women evaluated the nature of support that their husbands were providing, we asked them to select five activities that they considered the most important sources of support. They ranked most highly activities that involved interacting with their children and providing emotional support to their wives. The most frequently nominated item was "talk with my child," ranked in the top five by 83 percent of the mothers, along with "play with my child" (54 percent), "make time for the two of us" (55 percent), and "listen to me" (49 percent). In contrast, items referring to housework received few nominations. For example, none of the mothers put "do the laundry" in the top five, and only seven mothers put "cook, wash the dishes" in the top five. Given that relatively few of the participants were employed in full-time work, it is perhaps not surprising that they did not expect their husbands to take on a great deal of housework. However, given these men's role as primary breadwinners, we were surprised to learn that only 38 percent of the women accorded high importance to their husband's ability to contribute financially to support a comfortable lifestyle for the family.

Another indication that mothers accepted the gendered division of labor in their families emerged from a series of questions that asked the women to rate how satisfied they were with ten aspects of their marriage. The women seemed to be somewhat more satisfied with the ways the couple had allocated roles and responsibilities in the marriage than they were with their actual relationship with their husband. For instance, while 61 percent were happy with the division of marital responsibilities, only 47 percent said they liked their husband's personality, and only 45 percent said they liked the way they and their husband expressed affection and related sexually.

Having obtained a sense of what it was that they expected from their husbands, we then attempted to gain a sense of the psychological effects of husband support. Our findings showed that women who perceived their husbands as more supportive were less likely to be depressed. We also found that women who reported more positive relationships with their husbands also experienced less stress with regard to their parenting, which in turn led to higher perceptions of parenting self-efficacy (Suzuki, in press). In other words, the effect of husband support on wives' confidence in their parenting abilities seemed due to the way in which it reduced mothers' feeling of stress.

The findings from the survey suggested that, far from being peripheral members of the family unit, fathers played a powerful role through the emotional support they gave their wives. These findings prompted further questions. Specifically, we wanted to know more about what these marriages felt like to the women themselves, what made them happy and what made them feel frustrated. We wanted to see examples of how husbands' emotional support served to lower women's rate of depression and sense of stress, and how it boosted their parenting self-efficacy. We also wanted to learn more about the reasons the women gave for why their husbands were – or were not – involved in family life.

Perspectives on Marriage: Anger and Disillusionment

Our analysis of the narratives and the survey responses provided by the 16 women we interviewed suggests that seven women, including Chihiro and Junko, assessed their marriage primarily in negative terms. In contrast, four of the women, including Asako and Miyuki, were consistently positive regarding their husbands. And five were neither overwhelmingly negative nor positive. Of these five, two women were initially positive about their husbands but reported becoming increasingly disillusioned and negative over the course of the data collection period. First, I examine the perceptions of the wives who were strongly critical of their husbands, beginning with Junko.

Junko, the young working-class woman whose early childhood was marred by an abusive father and a difficult experience in school, met her husband when she was 19. After dating for four years, they decided to get married over the objection of her parents. As Junko put it, "They had no choice because we decided to do so." Junko became pregnant immediately after the wedding and was thus quickly initiated into the new roles of wife and mother.

Throughout the three years we were in contact with Junko, she struggled to find some emotional balance in the context of a deeply unsatisfying marriage. Her negative perceptions of the relationship emerged during an interview in which we asked her to draw a pie chart indicating the share of time that she devoted, respectively, to the roles of wife, mother, worker, friend and job/hobbies/other activities. Junko began by setting aside three quarters of the circle for the role of mother. Dividing the remaining quarter into three equal slices, she allocated one slice for worker and one for hobbies, remarking that if she didn't take that much time for her work and other activities, she would not be able to stay emotionally balanced and would become very stressed. The third slice she further divided into two pieces, one was for being a friend and the other for being a wife. Contemplating the thin sliver she had allocated to the role of wife, she jokingly mused that she would like to "erase" it entirely.

One source of Junko's dissatisfaction was her husband's unwillingness to do any work around the house. During the first interview, Junko reported that she held a part-time job and performed all the housework and child care with no help from her husband, despite the fact that his workday rarely exceeded six hours. When they first got married, she expected that he would help around the house, but that proved to be an unattainable dream. As she notes in the quote featured at the beginning of this chapter, she had given up all hope that he would contribute anything to the household other than his paycheck.

Second, Junko was dissatisfied with her husband's way of interacting with their children. Her ideal image of a father was "someone who won't say anything about the normal, trivial (*komakai*) things, but will get angry when necessary." In reality, her husband was reluctant to resolve problems, and showed little interest in interacting with his children:

I wish he would take our kids out more often. He doesn't really do that nowadays. After he comes home, he's the type that just lies around and doesn't do anything but watch TV. Even now, I tell him, "Take them outside and play with them." ... My husband does nothing at home but eat meals, you know.

A third problem was that he rarely acknowledged her contribution to the family, nor did he show an interest in her or her feelings. She frequently characterized him as an immature and self-centered individual. He became particularly critical and argumentative when he had been drinking, a pattern reminiscent of Junko's father. One time he surprised her by acknowledging that he was less considerate of her than their five-year-old son was. He even admitted to her that he realized that he never took the time to find out how she was feeling, even when he could see that she looked a little tired.

During their ten-year marriage, Junko adopted a variety of ways to cope with her husband's lack of involvement and affection. She initially put up with his criticisms and lack of engagement, but eventually decided that "it was ridiculous to keep my mouth shut" and started "talking back to him." This strategy resulted in fierce arguments that frightened their children. In our fourth interview, she confided that rather than confronting her husband actively, she now simply avoided him as much as possible. She expressed relief that he had begun working longer hours, because "family life is more comfortable without him here." There was less work for her to do when he was not around, and she added, "It's not like the children want something from their father or anything." On his days off she tried to leave the house – doing errands with the children or going out with a friend – so that she would not have to spend time with him.

The other women who shared Junko's negative assessment of married life raised similar issues about their husbands' lack of involvement. Not one of them reported receiving instrumental help around the home from their husbands. Mari described herself as having three children – one of whom was her husband – and said that he was so lazy and passive that he didn't even brush his teeth without being told. Reiko, who was employed part time, characterized her marriage as very turbulent because of her husband's refusal to help her at all with housework and child rearing. Her husband believed that wives should take a job only if they had sufficient time and energy for it after taking care of household tasks. She expressed particular resentment at the fact that, rather than helping her, he spent a great deal of time playing basketball and drinking with his friends.

Another thing these unhappy women all shared was the perception that their husbands paid little attention to their children. Beni said that although she had never really cared deeply for her husband, she had originally held certain expectations about what he would be like as a father:

I had an image of the ideal father. I wanted my husband to play with our kids. But I found out that my husband is not good at it because he is shy. I had wanted him to be like other young fathers who take their kids to the park. But, considering his personality, I'm thinking he can't really be like that. Nowadays, I just want him to try a little harder [as a father].

Beni's low estimation of her husband's parenting skills persisted through the three years of our study. She expressed considerable distress when her husband appeared unable to address their sons' serious social and academic difficulties in elementary school. Even when the older son stopped attending school and sequestered himself in his room, Beni's husband reportedly did not try to spend time with him or figure out how to help him resolve his problems.

The women in troubled marriages reported that their husbands rarely expressed affection toward them, nor did these men show an interest in trying to establish better communication. In the first interview, Yuri expressed some hope that she could persuade her husband to pay attention to her, but by the fourth interview she had given up: "The more I say, you know, it's useless. When he says 'whatever!' I get very sad, so I just stop saying anything.... His words, I just hate it so much, so I don't say anything anymore." Her sense of sadness and isolation was echoed by Beni, who noted that she usually felt worse rather than better after attempting to confide in her husband: "The more I talk, this may sound strange, but I feel a gap [forming] between us. And, sometimes I get depressed."

In the literature on Japanese men, it is common to note that heavy work demands, semi-mandatory after-hours socializing, and long commute times constitute structural impediments to full participation in family life, or work to shape a male identity that is estranged from involvement in family life (Allison, 1994; Ishii-Kuntz, Makino, Kato, & Tsuchiya, 2004). But it was clear from these narratives that the women themselves faulted their husbands personally rather than attributing their lack of involvement to workplace demands. Mothers attributed their husbands' disappointing performance as husbands and fathers to such character flaws as laziness, dependency, and egotism, not to job-related pressure. For example, Junko made it clear that her husband had plenty of time to participate in household chores and slightingly compared her husband's light work schedule to that of a preschool child – leave at 9, home by 3. Other women pointed out that their husbands claimed they had no time for their children but were somehow able to engage in leisure pursuits like *pachinko*. Even women whose husbands actually did work long hours were not always sympathetic. For instance, Mari's husband, an executive in a large, successful company, did work long hours. Nonetheless, Mari expected him to participate in housework and wanted him to interact more frequently with their two children during his time off. She was convinced that if he reset his priorities and became more organized at work he would have sufficient time to spend with her and the children.

It is well known in psychology that the reasons a person gives to explain a particular outcome are likely to affect the person's emotional response to that outcome. If a wife attributes her husband's lack of family involvement to his having an unfair boss who piles on the overtime, she may feel disappointed but is unlikely to feel angry with him. But if she attributes his lack of involvement to his personal preference for playing basketball or to a personality flaw such as egocentrism, the wife is likely to become very angry. The seven wives in unhappy marriages were definitely angry. Some reportedly tried to suppress this anger in the presence of their families. For example, Yasuko hoped she would develop a more charitable attitude toward her husband's childlike qualities by telling herself that she was "raising" him as well as her children. However, this strategy was only partially successful: "I try to keep my eyes on my husband as well as my kids ... but I can't stop getting into fights with him." Chihiro also practiced an attitude of emotional detachment and tried to avoid contact with her husband, citing the aphorism, "the best thing is for the husband to be healthy and not at home."

Several women chose not to suppress their feelings and instigated strenuous resistance on certain issues. Mari, for instance, was engaged in a sustained battle with her husband over what she perceived to be his choice to prioritize work over family. Since he was not living up to his family obligations in her view, she no longer felt she needed to help him take care of his personal possessions: "I guess it's because my husband isn't doing what he is supposed to do, what he should do as a father, so it all came about from me thinking, he should do whatever is related to work by himself." She was willing to wash his shirts but not to iron them, and so "in the morning he irons as if his life depended on it." She concluded that, "If he became a husband who pleases his wife, then I'd iron for him every day."

Why Stay in an Unhappy Marriage?

The primary reason that women gave for remaining in a deeply unsatisfying marriage was to ensure adequate financial support for themselves and their children. Yuri was particularly explicit in discussing the role of money in her relationship with her husband. According to Yuri, her husband was rarely at home and had lost all fond feelings toward her and their daughter. Despite his emotional estrangement, he continued to provide financially for the family. Yuri was an accomplished musician but had been laid off from her job when she became visibly pregnant. She had taken on a number of part-time jobs to supplement the family income, but acknowledged that she was unable to make enough to support herself and her daughter. She was determined to give her daughter access to enrichment classes and after-school lessons, and she herself enjoyed shopping and going out with friends. Without her husband's income she would not be able to maintain a middle-class lifestyle, so she tried to put up with the loneliness of an empty marriage:

So I will endure as long as I can ... that is, if I have more income [from him] I can endure longer. It's because I don't have my own income. If I had an income, this is bad, but I'd feel bad for him (laughs). *Interviewer: You mean you would get divorced?* Yeah, I guess so, although I would keep him around as my daughter's father.... But he is not really fulfilling that role, so I really don't need him.

There was one woman, Kayoko, whose husband was not able to meet her minimal expectations with regard to any of the criteria by which wives judged their husbands. Kayoko's parents had arranged her marriage to a man who turned out to be very unsuitable as a husband and father. According to Kayoko, he was not able to make a good living and was not willing to be involved in family life. He did not attend the children's school events and was unwilling to do even the simplest household tasks, like changing a light bulb. Kayoko described him as quick tempered and said that he tended to become very angry, particularly when he had been drinking. She explained that he sometimes punished her for some perceived failure on her part by withdrawing into a silence that lasted for days. She said that she was "more afraid of him" when he was silent than when he was openly angry: "I just can't stand not to talk. I can stand it for one or two days but not any longer. I used to apologize to him. Now ... I try to be careful not to say something that would make him angry." In spite of these difficulties, Kayoko did not appear to have any intention of leaving her husband. She had attended school only through middle school and was very shy. This reality, plus the knowledge that even well-educated women face significant hurdles when they try to re-enter the job market after taking time off to rear their children, gave her little hope of being economically self-sufficient.

Ingredients of a Satisfactory Marriage

As I have noted, there were four women who seemed satisfied, even happy, with married life. They described their husbands as being involved in activities with the children. They also felt that they could confide in their husbands and perceived their husbands as sympathetic to their problems and able to provide good advice when necessary. Of all the women we spoke with, Asako seemed to feel the greatest degree of support from her husband. In describing her early years, Asako told us that she was never a typical Japanese woman and her parents had worried that she would never find a man interested in marrying her. She had always been athletic, and as she became increasingly involved in soccer, she conformed less and less to stereotypical notions of a Japanese woman. However, a stroke of luck came in the form of a blind date with a man who – to her surprise and delight – shared her passion for soccer. After a brief courtship they married, and their mutual love of sports became a foundation of their marriage:

I sometimes wonder if it is OK for me to be involved in playing soccer to this degree. But I am always counted as a member of the team. I go out to play soccer because my husband is very understanding. Most important, this is what I really like. We play [soccer] together. That is why we can get along well.

In addition to sharing her love of soccer, Asako said, her husband greatly enjoyed interacting with children. She knew of his love for children even before they married because he was always eager to spend time with his young nieces and nephews. When their son was born, he took advantage of every opportunity to be with him. Laughing, Asako said that sometimes it felt lonely on the weekends "because he takes our son with him wherever he goes!" In addition to taking his son on errands and to the park, he took the boy to the racetrack or they watched horse racing on television together. As a toddler, Kaito learned the colors by watching the races with his father. Asako's husband also tried to find activities that that would complement and extend his son's interests. During the period when Kaito was interested in trains, the pair took train rides around the city for fun, and Kaito learned to identify numbers and characters by reading the train schedules and deciphering the signs posted at each station.

Other than sometimes feeling a bit left out when they were gone for a long time, Asako did not seem seriously threatened by her husband's active involvement with Kaito. She cast herself in the role of facilitating the relationship rather than acting as a gatekeeper. She remarked that she thought it was only fair for her to give them the opportunity to form a deep relationship, saying "Since I had an intimate relationship with Kaito when I was breastfeeding him, I just thought that I should let my husband bathe with Kaito [so they can also have that kind of relationship]." Furthermore, the three of them often did things together, including working out at the sports club they belonged to and attending soccer games. And when their second son was born, the couple found new ways to be together, including going for long drives in their new car.

Asako attributed her husband's active involvement in parenting to his interests and personality, and noted that his relatively undemanding and predictable work schedule allowed him to be home by 6 o'clock every evening. She also noted that she was capable of asserting her own views and could assume that her husband would listen to and respect her. It may be that Asako learned this lesson from her mother, who had earlier supported Asako's unconventional interest in sports in spite of criticism from Asako's father. When her husband proposed that they move in with his parents early in their marriage, Asako's mother counseled her to communicate clearly to him:

My mother's point was that my husband should not take it for granted that I was willing to live with his parents. Rather, he should know that I made up my mind to do so even though I knew that I was going to go through some problems. Therefore, he would have to keep his ears open to what I was saying to him. Otherwise, I would get very stressed out. [My mother thought that] if my husband could not be supportive and listen to me, then I should not live with his parents.

While Asako's assertiveness with her husband, her involvement in sports, and her comfort with sharing the parenting of their sons may sound less "traditional" and more Western, her ideas about marriage are part of a larger philosophy of human relations that is consistent with Buddhism, of which she is an active practitioner. On repeated occasions she stressed her view that it was important for everyone to be empathic and caring regardless of their gender and social status: "I think having good relationships with other people and having a kind heart (*yasashisa*) are the most important things." Her husband was also a strongly religious person; the relationship between Asako and her husband may be particularly successful because they share a system of beliefs and practices that give a sense of meaning and purpose to their lives.

The case of Miyuki, another woman who described her marriage as a happy one, is somewhat different from Asako's because Miyuki placed more emphasis on the wife's obligation to accommodate the needs, demands, and activities of her husband. As I have tried to show, Miyuki embodied the warmth and sweetness of a traditional housewife, but was sometimes able to act with grit and tenacity, whether it was setting out to make a huge meal for visiting researchers from the United States or, as we will see in subsequent chapters, demanding that her child's teacher attend properly to a pressing problem rather than sweeping it under the rug.

We heard little evidence of self-determination in her description of the beginning of her married life. Miyuki seemed to have drifted somewhat passively into a relationship with the man who was to become her husband. She met him on a blind date that had been initially set up for her sister. When her sister became ill shortly before the date, Miyuki was sent as a substitute and found that she enjoyed the company of this young man, who was somewhat awkward and combative even on this first date. They dated steadily for several years, but she described herself as "almost indifferent" at the time she accepted her husband's proposal.

Although she was employed before they were married, she decided to quit and devote herself to being a full-time mother and housewife, because he expected her to care for him from head to toe. She told us that she realized this on their first date, when she jokingly remarked that his socks were inside out and he retorted that it was his mother's fault for not preparing them correctly. At that point, Miyuki realized that after they got married, it would be her fault if his socks were inside out, and she knew that she would never be able to hold down a job and satisfy this demanding man.

For the most part, after nearly 15 years of marriage and the birth of three children, she reported a great deal of satisfaction with married life. She definitely thought that he fulfilled her expectations concerning the children: "He teaches the kids many things, such as the computer, basketball, and rollerblading." She described occasionally becoming impatient because he slept so much in his spare time, but unlike Junko, Miyuki was able to get her husband to do what she wanted: "When I judge that he has had enough sleep, I wake him up. I say, 'Take the [kids] out to play somewhere, get some exercise.' So, I wake him up and then he'll take the kids out for about an hour."

In spite of her husband's demanding nature, Miyuki believed that she benefited greatly from his counsel and support. On several occasions, she described her strategy for getting his attention, which basically involved forcefully demanding that he listen to her:

I told him, "When I am desperate, I will cry out for your help. I am not the type of woman who remains quiet."... I will ask for help before I go crazy. We all have limitations, you know. I needed him to understand that.

At various points, Miyuki described her husband as being sympathetic with her stress over a difficult problem. In one instance, when she was being criticized and attacked by his mother, he asked her to "please just endure" this bad treatment, but also said that he could see why she would be upset about it. Miyuki was one of the few mothers we spoke with who strongly believed that her husband's opinions about child rearing were helpful: "I rely on my husband. He covers my weaknesses like that, which I think is great in terms of our child-rearing experience. He looks like he is not listening to me, but he actually does listen to me. I think he is great."

The other two women who seemed satisfied with their marriages, Hiromi and Risa, shared certain elements in common with Miyuki and Asako. None of these women strongly favored an egalitarian relationship in which both members of the couple partake equally in work and household responsibilities, but they expected their husbands to show respect for their contribution to the family and consideration for their feelings. Hiromi in particular relied heavily on her husband to help her stay calm and optimistic about her ability to resolve small daily problems. One example that Hiromi gave of her husband's tenderness occurred around the time when she was expecting their first child. One night she was unable to sleep because of her anxiety about the impending birth and had a feeling of discomfort and heaviness in her legs. She said that her husband, with "utmost care and kindness," let her put her legs on him even though it probably made him quite uncomfortable. His simple action helped her calm down because it made her realize that he would be there to understand and take care of her after their baby was born.

While Asako's husband stands out as being exceptionally involved in parenting, other fathers in this group of happily married couples typically spent some time with their children in the evenings, bathing together, playing, or watching television. Hiromi said that her husband was involved in the PTA, participated in the neighborhood children's association, bathed with her children, and talked with her about "everything" concerning their care. Hiromi and Risa also enjoyed spending leisure time with their husbands. Both women said they socialized with other couples on the weekends, usually getting together at someone's house to play cards and drink beer.

These husbands were even willing to become slightly involved in housework. Hiromi reported that her husband took care of his own clothes and packed whatever he needed for work or for playing baseball, his hobby. Risa reported that her husband began getting himself dressed two mornings a week after she took a job. She acknowledged that her husband worked long hours whereas she was working part time, and she did not expect him to take on a lot of household tasks.

In terms of a quantitative assessment of how much they did, these husbands may seem to be far from equal partners in family life. When it came to involvement with their children, only Asako's husband seemed to be deeply engaged in more than brief playful interactions for limited periods at night and on the weekends. And these husbands' engagement in household tasks is significantly below that which might be expected by many Western wives, regardless of whether the wife is employed. But relative to the other husbands in the sample, they were much more active and, more important, they came closer to the expectations of their wives.

Husband's Support and Wife's Parenting Self-Efficacy

As I noted earlier, the survey findings for the full sample of 116 women showed that wives who received more support from their husbands were less likely to feel depressed. This pattern was borne out among the small group of mothers we interviewed as well. The four women who expressed satisfaction with their marriage had depression scores that were one-third as severe as the seven mothers who expressed a lack of satisfaction with their marriages. And when we examined the parenting self-efficacy scores of the 16 mothers, we found that most of the women who rated themselves as highly efficacious

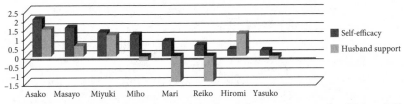

FIGURE 6.1. Parenting Self-Efficacy and Husband Support Ratings for Higher Self-Efficacy Mothers.
Note: Item values were standardized to create equivalent metric.

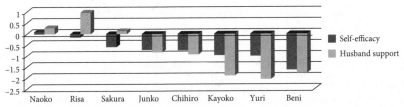

FIGURE 6.2. Parenting Self-Efficacy and Husband Support Ratings for Lower Self-Efficacy Mothers.
Note: Item values were standardized to create equivalent metric.

mothers were more satisfied with the support they received from their husbands. The self-efficacy scores of these mothers are displayed in Figure 6.1, along with their ratings of satisfaction with their husbands. In Figure 6.2, the self-efficacy scores of the least efficacious women are depicted along with their husband-satisfaction ratings.

These graphs reveal three notable exceptions to an otherwise clear relation: Mari, Reiko, and Hiromi. Mari and Reiko, both of whom had highly disputatious marriages, were initially found to be generally efficacious as mothers (although Mari became significantly less efficacious over time, as documented in Chapter 4). Examination of the narratives of Mari and Reiko revealed that each had a strong social support network outside of her marriage. Mari was highly interested in educational issues and since the birth of her first child had read widely about child development. She had strong ties to a company that produces educational materials and gives classes. In addition to reading their materials, attending seminars, and enrolling her children in their classes, she also personally consulted with an educational researcher at the company about her children's progress on a biweekly basis. This advice enabled her to feel confident with regard to child rearing when her son was in preschool, even though her husband was unavailable for consultation and, according to her, rarely interacted with the children.

Reiko derived emotional and instrumental support from two sources outside her marriage. She was a good friend of the director of her children's cram school. This woman was available for her to consult with concerning their educational progress but also provided guidance concerning developmental issues. Additionally, Reiko was part of a strong network of women at work. These women, and the work environment in general, not only contributed to her personal growth but also provided support and information to her as a parent. She reported that they were particularly helpful in enabling her to become firmer and more decisive in disciplining her children.

The opposite pattern can be noted in the case of Hiromi, a mother who scored low in parenting self-efficacy in spite of having a very supporting and involved husband. Hiromi's level of confidence was relatively stable across the three-year time span, as was her perception of support from her husband. As noted previously, Hiromi herself expressed the view that her husband played an important role in helping her control her anxiety about parenting. The traumatic conditions of Hiromi's early childhood, described in Chapter 5, appear to have shaped her responses to current situations to an extent that could not be completely mitigated by the support of her husband and friends. Although Hiromi had psychological scars, she had been able to find a husband who could help her build, piece by piece, an idea of "normal" family life.

Conclusions

A Japanese friend once showed me a kimono that had belonged to her grandmother. Marked with a subtle pattern of soft grays, the fabric was attractive but not showy. My friend told me that her grandmother had received the kimono from her husband when they were newlyweds. The special significance of the gift became apparent when my friend folded back the front panel of the kimono to show me the pearl-colored lining where, with a few simple brushstrokes, the young husband had painted a pair of cranes. This lovely expression of his hope for a long and happy life together could be seen and appreciated only by his new wife, and was hidden from the rest of the world. As we listened to the women in our study describe their husbands, we caught glimpses of similarly tender moments. Women appreciated their husbands for taking a child to the park, giving advice on how to respond to a critical mother-in-law, or tolerating the weight of heavy legs under the futon cover.

The women in our larger survey sample indicated that they placed little importance on their husbands' willingness to help with housework or take care of their own personal belongings. What they most wanted was for their husbands to fulfill the role of father – playing and talking with the children, and discussing their future. Women also wanted to receive emotional support from them, and hoped that their husbands would at least pause for a moment after work to inquire about their day. In the surveys, they placed relatively little importance on the husband's financial support, although in interviews they indicated a growing awareness of the costs of extra lessons and classes, and hence the need for husbands to maintain a good income. Overall, our findings are consistent with the work by David Shwalb and his colleagues (1997), who found that mothers were most likely to name the provision of emotional support as the most important component of fathering.

When we listened carefully to the four mothers who most consistently described themselves as happy with their husbands, we learned that these women felt that their husbands were trying to interact with them and their children, within the limits of their own personalities and the demands of their jobs. While Miyuki indicated a substantial degree of subordination to her husband, she was nevertheless confident that if she really needed something from him, she would be able to ask for it and he would respond. The other women portrayed themselves and their husbands as having a more reciprocal relationship. This is not to say that they perceived the roles of husband and wife as equal or overlapping, but rather that both members of the couple believed that the contributions of husband as well as wife were equally important and should be similarly respected.

For the seven couples that were unhappy, the issues of contention – laziness, immaturity, and emotional detachment – were hardly exotic. The survey revealed that women were particularly dissatisfied with their husbands' personality, rather than with the distribution of work or any other aspect of their married life. However, I find it particularly striking that the wives found personal fault with their husbands for failing to live up to their responsibilities rather than attributing their inadequacies to workplace obligations, long commute times, or any other structural constraints. The sharp, personal nature of their critique echoes the findings in Karen Kelskey's (2001) historical analysis, in which she describes Japanese women's long-lasting critique of Japanese men, and their concomitant idealization of Western men.

I wonder if this phenomenon is not part of a general cultural tendency to engage in personal critique rather than to contemplate larger societal factors that structure and valorize particular roles and responsibilities for each gender. In Chapter 4, I introduced the notion of "mutual polishing," which refers to the practice of criticizing others with the goal of helping them reflect on and improve their performance. Underlying the use of "polishing" is the belief that success or failure as a mother (or a Zen monk!) is largely a function of the effort one puts into fulfilling the requirements of the role. In other words, the stance puts the emphasis on individual gumption rather than on external impediments. Thus, in the case of a man's performance in the role of father or husband, success would be thought to hinge on whether or not he was, as Mari put it, setting the right priorities and working hard to achieve them. It would be interesting to learn more about the perspectives of the men themselves; the research literature is strikingly devoid of studies that elicit the views of Japanese fathers.

In spite of their anger and disappointment, only one of the 16 women that we interviewed appeared to have seriously contemplated divorce. While recent surveys suggest that young Japanese women are more accepting of divorce than are their older counterparts (Bumpass & Choe, 2004; Choe, Bumpass, & Tsuya, 2004), the women in our sample who were deeply unhappy with their husbands appeared to be putting up with the difficulties by stifling their own emotions, avoiding contact with their husbands, and spending time with friends or at work. They occasionally lost their self-control and erupted in anger, but none of them seemed to be systematically engaged in an attempt to change the relationship dynamics. No one mentioned getting professional help and no one indicated that her husband was sincerely motivated to improve the relationship.

These coping strategies may have saved the marriage in the formal sense, but at what psychological cost to these women? Some writers argue that there are few costs and many benefits to the typical Japanese marriage. They contend that Japanese women accept the peripheral role of their husbands in the family system and experience in their marriages a refreshing absence of emotional demands. For example, Rothbaum and his colleagues (2000) contrast what they call the Japanese orientation toward "symbiotic harmony" with the American pursuit of "generative tension." Drawing from Iwao (1993), they argue that Japanese couples have the luxury of taking each other for granted: "Japanese relationships are symbiotically harmonious because they are based on assurance – the knowledge that role-prescribed behaviors, social networks, and societal values ensure continuity. Loyalty-based love, which is unconditional, permanent, and grounded in compassion, is emphasized" (Rothbaum et al., 2000, p. 1135). According to Rothbaum and his colleagues, Japanese spouses feel little need to communicate verbally, to express appreciation to each other, or to "work on" their relationship, because they view it as permanent and unassailable.

But my sense is that what appears to be acceptance by women of a "separate spheres" type of marital arrangement is often a silence expressive of resignation, depression, or even fear. The narratives vividly convey Beni's deep sense of isolation after a conversation with her husband or Kyoko's worry that her husband will again erupt in anger and then subject her to days of the silent treatment. As the women in our study illustrate, Japanese marriages endure for many reasons, but the experience of those who remain in the difficult ones is often anything but harmonious. The deep silence that Rothbaum and colleagues attribute to culturally sanctioned "mental telepathy" between husband and wife may just as easily indicate indifference or an attempt to squelch feelings of anger or despair through sheer force of will. As Yuri remarked about her attempts to cope with her bad marriage, "every day is *gaman* (endurance) day."

Clearly, Rothbaum's image of Japanese marriages is at best a statement of a cultural ideal rather than a description of reality (although he does not portray it as such). However, based on our data, I do not believe that it represents a cultural ideal for contemporary wives, at least in this particular generation. The women who had happy marriages valued their ability to confide in their husbands. In contrast to Rothbaum's image of married life, they were glad when their husbands explicitly expressed appreciation for them and when they were not taken for granted. They eagerly accepted a kind of active partnership in which they took major responsibility for the house and children but also received some instrumental help as well as advice from their husbands. Even sweet-tempered Miyuki knew how to obtain what she needed from her husband. I would argue that these interviews reveal the successful Japanese marriage to be far less exotic – that is, less culturally bounded – than the prototypical relationship based on an idealized vision of "symbiotic harmony."

PART IV

7

Shitsuke: The Art of Child Rearing

If he doesn't listen to me, I sometimes slap his butt. I tell him, "OK, I am going to expose your butt and I will let other people look." So if there is a woman or girl around, he would get really embarrassed ... I sometimes care about other people's eyes, though. I usually scold them when I go shopping. But when I am with friends I do not scold my child enough, because I care about what my friends think. (Junko, high school educated, low self-efficacy mother of two)

I don't know what I should say ... I don't know what words I should use ...When I scold her, she becomes really sullen and she cries easily. So, sometimes, I really don't know what to say. At those times, I just leave her alone ... I become sad. When I think about what I can say to this child, I become sad. She doesn't understand what her parent is saying ... At times, I get stressed over figuring out what I should be doing. (Kayoko, middle school educated, low self-efficacy mother of two)

Raising a child is not an easy task. In Junko's comments about discipline, quoted above, she alternated between defending her use of corporal punishment and criticizing herself for not being skillful in her discipline methods. Kayoko's comments reflect her considerable anxiety about how to communicate with her daughter. She wanted her daughter to understand the need for good behavior but often found herself unable to explain things clearly and felt like a failure when her daughter reacted with tears. These are just two examples of the many problems that the women in our study faced in their everyday interactions with their children.

In this chapter, my first goal is to examine the topic of early socialization in perspective by looking from a historical perspective at the nature of childhood and the goals of child rearing. With this background, I then turn to the narratives of the 16 mothers to learn what their aspirations are for their children. In general, the data indicate substantial continuity across historical time in terms of mothers' aspirations that their children learn to become empathic, compassionate adults who do not cause trouble for others and have the skills to make their way in the world.

My second goal is to describe these mothers' ideas about how to nurture the competencies that will enable their children to develop into exemplary adults. Of particular concern to them was how to promote a balance between dependence and independence on the part of their children and how to help their children understand how to behave appropriately in social situations. I will discuss the difficulties that mothers faced in accomplishing these objectives and show that those who were confident in their child-rearing ability were able to select a reasonable course of action and stick with it, while those who were less confident found themselves struggling to find an approach they could follow with consistency.

My third and final goal in the chapter is to examine the role of the extended family and friends in supporting these mothers' child-rearing efforts. As we saw in Chapter 6, some women perceived their husbands as more involved and supportive, and felt much more efficacious than those whose husbands were felt to be distant or uncooperative. Similarly, extended family members and friends offered variable levels of support, at times helpful to mothers who faced child-rearing challenges and at other times augmenting the stress and anxiety occasioned by such challenges.

Historical Perspectives on *Shitsuke*

The term for childhood socialization in Japanese is *shitsuke*, which refers to inculcating good manners and teaching correct behavior. To provide a sense of the traditional meaning of the term, anthropologist Joy Hendry quotes a dictionary of Japanese folklore, which defines *shitsuke* as "the putting into the body of a child the arts of living and good manners in order to create one grown-up person" (1986, p. 11). The historical record mentions expert advice on child rearing in texts obtained from China as early as the seventh century. Manuscripts from the 1600s onward show that Japanese writers built on the ideas of Chinese teachers and philosophers, adapting them to the norms of the indigenous Japanese people (Kojima, 1996). Western thinking on child rearing percolated into Japan from the middle of the nineteenth century onward and Japanese thinkers and reformers have adapted and appropriated elements of it on such topics as the influence of caregivers on personality and intellectual development, the danger of overstimulation and overprotection, and the need to adjust the timing of parental actions to the child's emerging skills.

A persistent theme emphasized in the early Japanese writing on *shitsuke* is that children are inherently good (Kojima, 1986; Yamamura, 1986). Chinese Confucian writers emphasized children's basic moral rectitude and argued that in order to develop into worthy adults, children required kindness and nurturance from caregivers, rather than strict discipline. Japanese thinkers took the notion of children's purity even further by forcefully contrasting the "noble spirit" of the child with the "worthlessness" of the parent (Yamamura, 1986). In this regard, Western religious thought (e.g., Calvinism), with its emphasis on original sin and the consequent capacity for moral depravity, apparently had little impact on Japanese thinking about children.

Another way in which Japanese beliefs during the premodern period may be distinguished from those promulgated in the West concerns the notion of childhood as a separate stage of life from adulthood. Yamamura (1986) argues that in contrast to medieval Europe, where childhood was not viewed as being distinctly different from adulthood, Japan has always differentiated children from adults and believed that they should be "gradually led to adulthood through a series of socially systemized stages, established on the basis of age" (p. 30). For the premodern Japanese, the most important transition came at age six; at that time the child was first recognized as an independent human being and member of the community. Prior to the seventh birthday, children were considered to be "among the gods" and therefore worthy of particular respect (see Chen, 1996, for a different interpretation of this historical literature). By age 15, children of all social classes were perceived as adults and were expected to take on domestic and work responsibilities accordingly (Hara & Minagawa, 1996).

A final theme that emerges in early Japanese writing about the nature of children is that they were viewed as essentially similar to each other at birth in terms of moral attributes and intellectual abilities. In contrast to early Western ideas about the powerful effects of a child's inborn character traits, Japanese writers believed that an adult's successes and failures in life were attributable to that individual's own efforts, which were in turn seen as being affected by the conditions of the child's upbringing (Kojima, 1986). This perception is echoed by contemporary writers who see persistence and effort as the key to achievement and view parents as largely responsible for fostering their children's diligence (Holloway, 1988).

With regard to the goals of child rearing, two general themes were prominently discussed in much of the writing from the premodern period. First, children were supposed to be socialized to understand and value harmonious human relationships. And second, they were expected to recognize the importance of "knowing one's role, accepting one's place in society, and working hard at one's assigned task" (Kojima, 1986, p. 43). The goals for children's development have differed, and continue to differ, somewhat by gender, with girls expected to be more submissive and restrained than boys (Dore, 1958). The requirements of successful adulthood also varied by social class, with different expectations pegged to the occupational options available to a member of a particular class.

In order to inculcate the values of social harmony and personal diligence, adults were advised above all to form a strong personal connection between parent and child. Early writers use the word *shin* to indicate "kinlike closeness and affection" that is mutual, humane, and flexible (Kojima, 1986, p. 46). Thus parents were discouraged from using harsh or abusive language and were advised not to show anger or impatience toward their children. As we saw in Chapter 3, the concept of *amae* – which refers to a pleasurable feeling of being dependent on and indulged by another person – is frequently cited as a strong feature of Japanese child rearing (Doi, 1973/2002). As Hara and Minagawa (1996) argue, based on a review of the literature on Japanese child rearing, "Westerners associated maturity with becoming an independent individual, while Japanese assumed that a mature person knows when, how, and on whom to be dependent or not be dependent" (p. 11). [1]

In the context of this supportive relationship, children were thought to learn best through observation rather than by being subjected to behavioral control by adults (Kojima, 1986). Children were viewed as autonomous individuals who could not easily be controlled from the outside, and hence the goal of socialization was to change the child's understanding rather than the child's behavior. Experts in the premodern period therefore urged parents to use mild forms of management and to eschew corporal punishment. The danger of overprotection and indulgence was always lurking; many writers emphasized the importance of exposing children to mild deprivation and hardship. Such experiences would help children develop the ability to endure difficulties encountered during adulthood (Kojima, 1986).

During the postwar period, the lives of children changed in important ways. When the *ie* structure was abolished and the nuclear family became the norm, extended family members were increasingly excluded from child-rearing responsibilities. And as children spent increasingly long hours at school and fathers spent increasingly long hours in distant office buildings, there were fewer opportunities for interaction between father and child.

---

[1]   As we will see, Japanese adults also value autonomy and expect children to develop the skills to operate effectively and reliably on their own (Hendry, 1986). This is a major goal of preschool education (Holloway, 2000).

Mothers, conversely, were excluded from activities other than those connected to the home. The result of these changes was that mothers became the only consistent source of *shitsuke* in the lives of young children.

In general, parents continued to focus on helping their children attain the social skills needed for successful engagement with one's social roles. Interview and survey data obtained in the early 1980s suggest that mothers of preschool-aged children were focused on teaching their children everyday social routines (*reigi sahō*), including greeting others appropriately, maintaining good posture, developing polite table manners, and taking care of possessions (Hendry, 1986). In addition to these behavioral routines, mothers were attempting to foster certain moral qualities in their children: thinking of others, being kind, avoiding causing trouble, and persevering in difficult situations. Some mothers also emphasized the ability to express one's own ideas, desires, and feelings clearly. Corroborating evidence of the emphasis on social skills came from a comparative study of Japanese and American mothers with preschool-aged children conducted in the late 1970s. The researchers found that compared to their American counterparts, Japanese mothers emphasized earlier development of skills related to maintaining good relations with others, including emotional maturity, self-control, and basic courtesy (Hess, Kashiwagi, Azuma, Price, & Dickson, 1980).

Both prewar and postwar accounts focus on gaining a child's understanding of the reasons for doing something, as opposed to merely obtaining the child's behavioral compliance. Drawing from surveys conducted in the 1950s and 1960s, Lanham and Garrick (1996) found that "Japanese responses continued to stress the importance of *wakaraseru* (having the child understand), implying that compliance without a willing desire on the part of the child was of little or no value" (p. 104). These authors connected the notion of *wakaraseru* to a belief in the essential goodness of human nature. If a parent believes that a child's nature is basically good, she will be likely to assume that the child misbehaves because he or she has not yet learned right from wrong or does not yet understand the proper way to act in a given situation. Generally speaking, mothers hope for a child to be *sunao*, a term that connotes whole-hearted compliance, rather than mere submissiveness, to adult authority (White & LeVine, 1986).

A final theme in some discussions of child-rearing goals is the notion that parents should raise children who are not eccentric or extreme in any way. For example, Hendry (1986) found that some mothers valued the notion of being ordinary or average (*jūninnami*). Others criticized that goal, identifying it as an outdated Japanese cultural model. As we will see in Chapter 8, the idea of being average appeared in our data in relation to academic and professional achievement. The notion that many mothers were aiming for average achievement is at odds with the stereotype of the Japanese as pushing their children to be ultra-high achieving. What I argue in this chapter and the next is that while many Japanese mothers hoped that their children would be average, they perceived this relatively modest aspiration as being quite difficult to accomplish.

What Is a Good Child? The Enduring Focus on Social Responsiveness

In order to understand the thoughts and feelings of the women in our study, we first turn to the views of the 16 mothers about their goals for their children. We asked them to describe their children and enumerate their strong and weak points, and also inquired about their hopes for their children in the future. Their responses indicated a very strong emphasis on learning to value human relationships and becoming skillful at interacting with others. The quality that mothers most often sought in their child – whether a girl or a boy – was that of basic kindness (*yasashisa*). Mothers hoped their child would be empathic (*omoiyari*), sensitive (*sensai*), and polite (*reigi tadashii*). They also emphasized the importance of learning how to avoid bothering others (*meiwaku kakenai yōni*). They expressed pride and pleasure when their children showed signs of attending to the effects of their behavior on other people.

For example, Asako, the high-efficacy mother who was a star soccer player, emphasized the importance of helping her son learn to care about others. Asako highlighted the practical benefits of developing good relations with others as well as the moral aspects:

After all, it is important to have caring relationships with people (*hito to no fureai*). If that is the case, then it would be very scary if he becomes a person who didn't think of anything else but himself. So, even while he's doing something he likes, I think that the most important thing is to be able to consider the people around you, to consider other people. Above all, [being considerate] is the most important. I think that if people don't have good relationships with others, it's impossible to continue doing anything. Yeah, I think that you can't accomplish anything by yourself. Things get done when people get together and work on one thing together.

Junko, the low self-efficacy but spunky young mother of two, also placed a strong emphasis on her child's learning to become a socially competent person. Compared to Asako, who tended to focus more on psychological attitudes like empathy, Junko tended to focus more on learning behavioral routines and on not bothering others:

It is much better for my children to know about how to act. I feel like teaching them because I know how to be decent and polite. I have always been conscious about my kids being noisy in public ... I scold them when they do that. I've always been conscious of my kids bothering others.

Contrary to the stereotypical images of Japanese society as being "collectivistic," these mothers did not want their children to overly conform to group norms. Rather, they hoped their children would be able to balance social sensitivity with the ability to be independent. They sometimes used the term *maipēsu*, a loan word from the English term "my pace," to describe children who were able to formulate their own plans and were not excessively influenced by the actions of others. Junko repeatedly described her son as someone who was *maipēsu*, but expressed some ambivalence about whether this attribute was entirely good:

He is kind and likes older people...We have a grandmother who is old and weak. She is in an old people's home. He really doesn't know her but when he saw her for the first time he went close to her.... I thought he was really kind. But on the other hand sometimes I would say he is a bit cold. I don't know if I would say cold but he is *maipēsu*. I think it has good parts as well as bad. They are connected to each other.

Mothers also expressed admiration for children who were lively, upbeat, and even a bit rowdy. When Asako's son was in preschool, she worried about his being somewhat timid and cautious. He preferred quiet activities like reading and playing the piano to sports. He tended to focus exclusively on one or two areas of interest rather than jumping into many different activities. She was particularly eager that he be willing to try different athletic activities, since her family was so involved in soccer, and she was worried that he was not more open to new experiences. During the second interview she reported her joy upon hearing him say that he liked taking classes at their sports club: "He must have found that there were many things he could enjoy. I was very happy. I could not believe my ears."

Some attributes that mothers valued were connected to the gender of the child. The concern that mothers felt about shyness, anxiety, and passivity was stronger for boys than for girls. As Miyuki said about her son, "For a boy he is a little bit too quiet." She also described him initially as "a little bit emotionally weak for a boy" and worried that "even if he is bullied he cannot fight back." In subsequent interviews she was happy because he had become boisterous and was more steady and determined in his interactions with others.

In contrast, mothers tended to expect their girls to be quieter and more compliant, and some of them placed less importance on their academic achievement. For example, Miyuki believed that it was important for her girls to be cute and lovable, but, though she did push them to do well in school, she placed less importance on their achievement than on that of her son. Comparing her two daughters, she viewed one as smart but not so cute, and the other as cute but not so smart. She was sometimes frustrated with the relatively low academic achievement of her "less smart" daughter, but she told her husband that this daughter might ultimately have a better life than Mio, the smarter daughter, because "girls who are not that intelligent are adored," whereas "an intelligent and talented person like Mio will not find a husband."

Chihiro, a high-achieving woman, strongly believed that a child's personality and behavior were determined by gender. Despite the fact that she herself had challenged stereotypical gender expectations by obtaining a bachelor's degree and working as a professional, she believed that girls and boys were fundamentally different and should be encouraged to develop skills and attitudes consistent with gender stereotypes. In describing what she thought her daughter would need to learn in order to do well in school, Chihiro struggled to describe how a girl should learn to express herself without being overly forceful:

I guess it's to be patient, above all. Instead of being self-centered, being able to get along with other people is important. Yeah, everyone is a part of a class, so you can't just push whatever you want to do.... You need to try and to listen to other ideas and opinions ... and not to express yourself so much ... I guess it's OK to express yourself but you need to take the time and place into consideration when you do ... Then I guess you will naturally learn to be patient or to express your opinion in any appropriate manner. Actually, it is difficult to do.

Accepting a Child's Need for Dependence While Encouraging Autonomy

The notion of *amae* (dependence and reception of indulgence) has received attention in the Japanese child-rearing literature. As I noted previously, *amae* is viewed as a relationship dynamic that underlies the mother–child relationship and forms the template on which other dyadic relationships are based, including the relation between employer and employee and between teacher and student (Behrens, 2004). In our study, we were curious to learn what mothers expected of their children in terms of dependence and how they responded to their children's desire for indulgence as well as their desire for independence. We also sought to understand the association between the *amae* relationship and the challenges that mothers faced in disciplining their children appropriately.

We spoke with all 116 mothers about their perceptions of *amae* in the first interview. When we directly asked them how satisfied they were with the extent to which their child expressed *amae* toward them, 69 percent said they were satisfied, 22 percent said they wished their child expressed *amae* more, and 9 percent wished their child would express *amae* less often. These mothers expected their five-year-old children to express a need to be indulged at this age, but did not always think the children were doing so in appropriate ways or quantities, or at appropriate times. Most indicated that their children were more likely to want *amae* when they felt tired or distressed. In that sense, the mothers saw *amae* as fulfilling a reassuring, comforting function. Only 17 percent of mothers mentioned that their child wanted *amae* to express their closeness or joyful feelings. Not surprisingly, since *amae* seemed to come into play when their child was feeling vulnerable, they noticed their child wanting *amae* more often at bedtime or when the child was tired. These might also be the times when mothers were most available and most ready to be indulgent.

Most mothers viewed *amae* as a phenomenon that was likely to decrease as the child matured. When we asked them to describe times when they did not want their child to express *amae*, mothers cited instances when it was not convenient for them to indulge their child's need for attention, such as when the mother was tired or busy, and instances when they believed the child needed to exert more self-control and maturity, such as when they were in public. Mothers tended to welcome a child's desire for *amae* if the child really felt lonely or frightened, or just to express a positive feeling of connection. In general, then, we got the impression from these responses that mothers generally viewed *amae* as a natural phenomenon that was not particularly problematic or difficult to deal with.

The more detailed narratives of our 16 mothers provide further evidence that mothers of children at this age acknowledge and accept their children's need for dependency up to a point. On the one hand, no one reported discouraging their children entirely from expressing *amae* or viewed it as a pathological need. On the other hand, they were all aware of feeling that there were times when *amae* was not appropriate and when they did not accept it. Asako provided a thoughtful account of the changing function of *amae* in a young child's development:

I think the expression of *amae* changes over time ... I think the *amae* of small children includes communication. It's like being very intimate or being needy towards parents. But when the child enters kindergarten or elementary school, it is time for the child to discipline their *amae*. If the parent didn't do anything about it, it wouldn't be good for the child. Then when the child grew up, *amae* would become a kind of expectation that others would do things for him even though he could do them himself. That's why I think the word *amae* can mean so many things depending on the time or occasion. That's why I think there are both good *amae* and bad *amae* depending on the child.

In the first interview, when her son was still in preschool, Asako was worried that he was too dependent. She didn't refuse his overtures, however, but started limiting them to situations within the privacy of their home. She acknowledged that even this degree of indulgence may be seen by others as too much:

He does *amae* a lot. When he remembers something at preschool that makes him feel anxious he comes clinging to me at home.... When I want to give him *amae* I play with him. I am a mother but I want to do it when we are playing together. I might say babyish things to him and play with him, and he might say babyish things and play with me. At times like this we – including my husband – play things that if other people saw us they might think it's not good. But I think times like that, it's OK for him to do a lot of *amae*. When I don't want him to do *amae* is when he should overcome an issue by himself. I think that when he can confront the anxiety he has, I would like to have him overcome it by himself.

Junko also tried to permit some *amae* at home but not in public:

When it's time to sleep, I allow him to do *amae*. It's better to go to sleep feeling relieved rather than being angry at the end of the day. So at those times, even when he comes close to me, instead of saying "You are already a first grader and are grown up," I have more physical contact with him, patting him and telling him he's a good boy and that he's really adorable. In front of people ... when he has to be proper I actually think that I don't want him to do *amae*. It's for the sake of appearances, because I thought the others would say something if the kids weren't being good.

The distinction that Junko is making is part of a general Japanese tendency to strongly contrast official appearance and hidden reality. As articulated by Sugimoto (2003), Japanese people strongly distinguish between "the façade, which is normatively proper and correct, and the actuality, which may be publicly unacceptable but adopted privately or among outsiders" (p. 28). In the Japanese language there are several pairs of terms that refer to this distinction; for our purposes the most important one is the distinction between *soto* (outside or exterior) and *uchi* (inside or interior). Individuals are expected to show certain types of behavior to the outside world, while engaging in other types of behavior in the privacy of their own home. People indicate their awareness that public behavior is evaluated by referring to the watchful eyes of the *seken*, that is, imagined community members who perceive and evaluate the behavior of others. The women in our study often mentioned behaving with greater restraint in public because they were mindful of the eyes of others. Mothers were particularly sensitive to the appropriateness of expressing *amae* in private settings only, as in this statement by Miyuki:

At preschool I don't want him to say, "Hold me." It's embarrassing. At home it's OK, but you know when I go to preschool to pick him up and he takes my hand and wants me to hold him, it's embarrassing. So I say, "No, no, no, not at preschool." There are other people's eyes and he is going to elementary school next year.

Another important theme, which Junko articulated in her thoughts about *amae*, is the notion that it is not only the *child* who may want to be dependent on the mother but also the *mother* who may enjoy caring for and indulging a dependent child. She sometimes wanted him to do more *amae*, she said, but he often preferred to be with his friends: "I miss him sometimes. I want him to be close to me. But I know it's difficult because children leave parents gradually." She started to feel a desire for a third child when she realized that her son and daughter were becoming more interested in spending time with their friends: "You know, when my children do not want to cuddle with me, when they refuse me, that's when I think, I really want to have another child who will cuddle with me." Junko's desires to provide *amae* were based on her own needs rather than those of her children, and she tried to restrain herself from expressing those needs. Like most of the women in our sample, she believed that her children's desire for independence was normal and inevitable.

Chihiro also noted the role of her own feelings in the provision of *amae*, specifically her strong attachment to her son and her lack of warm feelings for her daughter. She acknowledged that this differential affected her willingness to indulge the dependent feelings of her daughter:

I have two children, and the boy is more lovable to me. I think that other people say the same thing. I don't know if it is because of his gender, but somehow boys are more lovable. For my daughter, I see her with the feeling of being the same gender as her, and scold her with that feeling. So I am more mean or strict to my daughter. When my son goes to play with other children and only my daughter is with me, I pay attention to her. She stays closer to me than usual. You know, something like "skinship" [close physical contact]. So I want to do that more. But usually I am not really with her.

Most of the mothers believed that their emotional connection with their children formed the foundation for their attempts to discipline and educate them. As we will see, mothers who had trouble making an emotional connection also tended to have difficulty figuring out how to get them to understand the importance of behaving properly.

What Disciplinary Strategies Do Mother Use?

Most of the 116 mothers reported using multiple strategies to deal with misbehavior when their children were six years old. The most common strategies involved scolding the child (mentioned by almost all the women) and explaining why a behavior was harmful and what the right way to act was (mentioned by almost half the women). Spanking or some form of corporal punishment was mentioned by about one-third of the mothers. Other forms of discipline, including threats and isolating the child, were mentioned by less than 15 percent of the women.

We also explored whether mothers' general sense of efficacy in rearing their children was related to the way they engaged in *shitsuke*. As we see in Figure 7.1, we found that mothers with a general sense of parenting self-confidence were more likely to believe that they could react to misbehavior consistently regardless of their own mood, were more able to be flexible in disciplinary situations, and ultimately felt their disciplinary efforts were more effective. There was no difference between higher and lower self-efficacy mothers with regard to whether they thought their child's behavior improved subsequent to being disciplined, whether they believed they understood the child's feelings, or whether they gave in to avoid the trouble of scolding or to avoid the child's unpleasant reaction (there was, however, a trend in the direction of more confident mothers perceiving themselves as more effective in all these situations). Thus, the area of discipline where mothers' behavior (as they perceived it) seemed to be the most strongly affected by their sense of parenting efficacy was their ability to regulate their emotions and react with flexibility, rather than their ability to actually engage in an act of discipline.

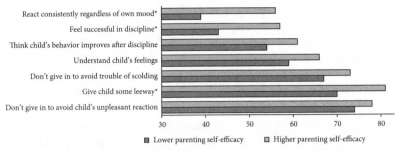

FIGURE 7.1. Mothers' Report of Disciplinary Effectiveness for Mothers Varying in Parenting Self-Efficacy (Significant Differences Indicated by Asterisk).

These survey findings prompt a number of questions about *how* and *why* parenting self-efficacy is linked to disciplinary effectiveness. What goes through the mind of the confident mother when she encounters a child who refuses to clean up her toys? Why is she more able to respond calmly and consistently than someone who starts with a sense that she will not be able to manage the situation? And conversely, what are the thoughts and emotions of a less confident mother as she formulates a response to her child's whining or refusal to get to bed on time? We turn to the interview data for enlightenment on these questions.

Helping a Child Understand the Reasons for Behaving Well

As I outlined at the beginning of the chapter, Japanese parents believe that the goal of good discipline is to help children understand why something should be done, not just to attain their behavioral compliance. Most of the mothers endorsed the notion that it is important to foster a child's understanding and positive attitude toward compliance. Asako, for instance, mentioned several incidents that provided her with the opportunity to impress upon her son the importance of having consideration for others. She described one time when her son came home from preschool and told her that a child in his class had wet his pants. Asako explained how she used the incident to teach him something about having empathy for others:

I said, "It was nice of you to tell me what happened, but don't you think you would feel bad if you were being talked about like that? Since that kid may have had a stomachache or something and that could be why it happened. But instead of saying things like, 'He wet his pants!' it is more important to say things like, 'How do you feel?' or 'Are you OK?'" So that's what I tried to tell him. Although he may not have understood at that moment, I told him that if he didn't want other people to do something to him, he shouldn't do it to others ... Well, so I told him that he should never do things like that, which I don't know if he was convinced of or understood well, but these are the things that I need to keep telling him. Yeah, I think he will understand one day, so I will keep telling him.

In contrast, as noted earlier, Junko put more emphasis than Asako did on observing conventional manners, and she also used corporal punishment at times. She was ambivalent about the value of corporal punishment and sometimes criticized herself for not being able to "explain to my child in a nice way like the preschool teachers do ...," but at other times she defended corporal punishment as old-fashioned but effective. She declared that she preferred to smack her children on the head sometimes, and noted that she did not "get along with the mothers who hit their kids on the butt instead of on the head," saying "I don't know if the mothers these days would agree, but I think that it is not the way to do *shitsuke*."

In spite of her views of corporal punishment, she still spoke about wanting to be sure that her child had understood the point of behaving well:

I usually scold him strictly. Many people say I look like someone who doesn't scold their children, but I do scold them ... I really don't think I am good at scolding because I usually react as soon as my child has done something wrong. So I only think that my scolding was successful when my child does the thing I told him to do. It is easy to understand my children, but it is hard to understand if what I have said has really been understood.

Junko and many other mothers distinguished between the ideal of achieving understanding and the reality of obtaining compliance. Mari was one mother who spoke frankly about the fact that sometimes she just insisted on compliance:

When I understand his feelings, and he says "Yes, that's right," that's when I think that he understands what I am saying. I try to take as much time as possible for him to understand what I am telling him ... But when he is in trouble, I sometimes force him to do what I am telling him.

In order to attain the goal of having a child understand the right behavior, most of the mothers initially relied on verbal methods rather than corporal punishment. The verbal technique of choice was scolding – which usually consists of pointing out the wrong behavior, focusing the child on the feelings of those who were hurt or inconvenienced by the action, and asking the child to think about how to behave better. The strategies they felt were the most effective were those that involved being calm and cool-headed. However, it was not always possible for mothers to control their anger. All the mothers admitted that when they were tired or very busy, or when the misbehavior persisted in spite of their attempts to resolve it with calm words, their emotions boiled over and they exploded in anger. Most of the mothers viewed these explosions as counterproductive, as in the following account from Risa, who made the connection between her emotions and her child's understanding:

When I think about something, I try to say it in a way she'll understand. I use my hands and I try to explain. But when I am emotional and upset, I guess nothing remains in Shiori's head, in terms of [what I am] scolding about.... When I am like, "BAAHH!" [description of herself exploding], Shiori just gets scared, and thinks, "I have to apologize, I have to answer," and she says she is sorry ... It's miserable for her. I mean she is just being a little annoying, but I have such a big reaction.

Asako illustrated the typical progression of discipline strategies in describing a problem she frequently experienced when she asked her son to clear away his toys before dinner. She said she usually started by telling him calmly that he should clean up. He would often refuse, saying that he wanted to continue playing with the toys after dinner. From that point on, her behavior often escalated to more coercive techniques as she became more frustrated:

The first time I can say it very calmly but when he responds like that, I start thinking, "No, that's not what you are supposed to say." But then if he responds again with excuses, I become upset and say with a very loud voice, "No, you clean up!" Then he cleans up in a sullen manner. I can't tell if he is convinced or not. Actually, there is one more step in between. I tell him if he doesn't clean up, I will get rid of the toys. Then he cleans up, because he doesn't want that to happen. In the end, I yell at him, "Father is going to come home. Hurry up and clean up!" It's really loud, and it's in Osaka dialect.

Miyuki also described herself, like Junko, as a "hard" scolder. She was always trying to keep her temper under control, but said that her husband and children frequently remarked on how much she scolded, and compared her to a devil with horns when she was mad: "I scold him [my son] a lot. It would be embarrassing if other people listened to me. My husband said he was surprised that I scold that much, and I scold in a high voice and my children say, 'You have horns,' and so you get an idea of how much I scold them."

Most of the women reported that after losing their tempers, they tried to reflect on what had happened. Some engaged in self-recrimination, but others did not seem too worried about their failure to meet the goal of scolding without emotion. Miyuki viewed her tendency to boil over as inevitable, given how much time she spent with her three lively young children:

I think I severely scold him and hurt him a lot.... but I don't really have the mental energy to think about these things when I'm scolding him. I don't have the time to think about whether or not what I say is going to hurt him or not.... My husband says it's verbal abuse (*kotoba no bōryoku*). But, for me, I'm with them 365 days, every day, so I feel that I have to scold that much, because otherwise they won't listen to me. I clearly tell him that it's not abuse.

Asako, also a relatively high-efficacy mother, noted that she sometimes reviewed her behavior and concluded that she had been too emotional due to stress, but she didn't berate herself for this lapse of self-control:

I sometimes think maybe I was too upset or maybe I was too emotional.... I guess I tend to become more emotional when I am stressed out ... Later on, I would get upset, and then after I calmed down I often reflected on it. Later on I would think, "Oh, this or that happened." Especially, I reflect on it in bed and I think, "Oh, maybe I was a little overly emotional." Things like that, when I reflect on that day, it's usually when I'm in bed."

Who Helps? The Role of Husbands, Parents, In-Laws, and Friends

As we saw in Chapter 6, the women in our study varied in their perceptions of their husbands' willingness and ability to interact and communicate with their children. Not surprisingly, husbands who were generally more available to participate in family life tended to play an important role in providing *shitsuke*. For example, Asako and her husband had developed a strategy to buffer their son from the negative effects of her emotional outbursts. She reported always trying "to leave him a way to escape" from her and her anger. If her husband was home, he was careful not to take sides in the altercation so that her son could seek comfort from him. If her husband was not at home at the time of a disciplinary incident, her son was allowed to call one of his grandmothers and ask if he could come over for a brief visit.

Miyuki, another high-efficacy mother with a good marriage, mentioned a similar strategy used by her and her husband:

I wanted him [her husband] to stand by our kids when I was very mad at them. When I get too emotional with my kids, I want him to calm down the situation … And when my husband is irritated and lets his stress out on her kids, I am the one to stand by my kids … My kids have someone to protect them from anything like that. If they are with their grandmother, they hide themselves behind her.

She had nothing but praise for her husband, who offset her difficult relations with their oldest daughter by developing an independent relationship with her:

When Mio was very little, it was so hard for me to deal with her by myself.… My husband said that it was because she was smart. In fact, she asked me about many things. I suppose it was even harder for me because I treated her in a girlish way. However, my husband treated her as if she were a boy. And she very much liked that. According to my husband, I get along better with my other daughter because she is girlish. I know that I should be flexible depending on whom I deal with. But I can't. So I am dependent on my husband. He covers my weaknesses like that, which is a great thing about our child-rearing experience.

The women whose husbands did not participate in child rearing had to create a disciplinary system on their own. In some cases, their husbands actively contributed to the difficulty of disciplining the children because of their own immaturity, as noted by Chihiro: "You know how some men stay somewhat like kids forever? So they compete with their own sons … Japanese men don't know their sons are children. So if a son destroys something of the father's, the father gets so mad … It is between two equals, like a boys' fight, you know." She also described her husband as passive and lazy, and said that his attempts to tell the children to stop lying around playing video games were not effective because he himself was lying around watching television. Like Chihiro, Junko felt that she carried the full burden of disciplining her children. Her husband was picky and evaluative toward the children but tended merely to criticize them without offering any solutions.

As we saw from the historical accounts of family life, in Japan mothers-in-law have traditionally played a strong role in providing advice and support regarding child rearing. In contemporary times, one would expect that women's own mothers would play a role as well, since young wives do not sever ties with their own mothers as they were required to do in the past. Our data suggest that women sometimes perceived their own mothers as helpful and drew upon them for emotional support as well as advice and information about child rearing. However, they usually felt that their mothers-in-law were too critical (see also Imamura, 1987). Asako provides a clear example of this pattern. As we saw in Chapter 5, she grew up feeling close to her mother, who supported her unusual passion for soccer. Her mother was supportive during the early days of her marriage as well, counseling her to indicate clearly to her new husband that she was making a big sacrifice by moving in with her in-laws. The time spent with the in-laws did indeed become challenging once their son was born:

I have been feeling much better since we moved out of my parents-in-law's place. They can no longer watch me all day long.... You know, my mother-in-law is too direct when she is talking to us. She does not care how her words are perceived by other people. And I often think about what she has said to me to try to figure out what she actually meant to say. She sometimes hurts my feelings by the way she talks.

Characteristically, Asako tended to look on the positive side, appreciating the help that her relatives could provide. But she noted that relatives were also a source of stress:

My mother lives so close that I could probably see her house from my door, and my mother-in-law lives a bicycle ride away. I am surrounded by relatives. And since my family all lives close together they have been very helpful. In a time like now when there are so many nuclear families, having these relatives around can also be a source of stress, I think. To have your relatives around you and not just your immediate family can be stressful, too, but I experience the things that people in the past experienced.

Miyuki was also obligated to endure regular contact with a demanding and critical mother-in-law. When she became pregnant, she had the unsettling sensation that the baby she was carrying belonged not to her but to her mother-in-law:

In Japan, the relationship between a mother-in-law and daughter-in-law affects many things. Your kids are not necessarily your kids. A mother-in-law interferes with your child rearing to a great degree. They have many suggestions about child rearing from their own experiences. My mother-in-law did not like the way I changed diapers and said, "You should not do it like that. You should do it like this, or the baby's leg will become dislocated." I really wanted to make her remember that I had teaching experience in a preschool … Even though my in-laws live in a separate home, they interfere in our lives to a great degree … The two styles conflict with each other sometimes, but overall my in-laws' style is more dominant. It is often said that contemporary families are more individual. But their lives are greatly affected by their in-laws … Once you have a kid, your in-laws never leave you alone.

Miyuki felt fortunate that she could at least vent her feelings of frustration by talking with her husband, who sympathized with her but urged her to endure his mother as much as she could. Miyuki tried hard to be a good daughter-in-law and rarely confronted or contradicted her mother-in-law. In contrast, Junko had to endure the criticisms of a harsh mother-in-law without the benefit of a sympathetic husband. True to her feisty nature, she eventually gave up on trying to stifle her annoyance:

What my mother-in-law says is very discouraging. She sticks her nose in my kids' lives. She once told me, "He should learn something else instead of English. Why don't you put him in a sports club?"… I hate it when she acts like the decision-maker. I used to be able to pretend that I agreed with her. But at some point, I decided to be honest with my feelings. Ever since, I've been very clear about my views.

Chihiro is the only one of the 16 mothers in our sample to live with her parents. She was particularly close to her father, as we noted in Chapter 6. Her parents served the same function as a "safe harbor" for her children that Asako's mother and mother-in-law did. Chihiro said, "Grandpa and Grandma are, after all, sweet. I think it is good that there is a place to escape to when you are scolded." Chihiro's parents were generally supportive of her but sometimes criticized her *shitsuke*, causing her to become stressed and react emotionally to her children:

When I get scolded like that, I get mad and scold our children. Well, you can't help it since we're all human.… Though I try not to do that, I'll get mad at a child for a little thing.

Chihiro distinguished her parents' criticism from that of an in-law, saying that she tended to ignore criticism from "a blood relation." Indeed, for her, the best coping strategy seemed to be trying not to dwell on things that upset her, and she rarely confided in her parents or her friends: "I don't really ask much, even if I have something on my mind. I felt that it doesn't help to complain about things. So I really don't talk about them."

For many of the women in our sample, friends provided another important source of support. Many told us that hearing other women describe the problems they were having with their children reassured them. As Junko put it, "When I find out while chatting that my friends' kids are the same way as my kids, I can get rid of that anxiety.... I think it is important for mothers to make sure that nothing is unusual with their kids. We need to feel relieved about it." Similarly, Sakura said: "I'm always alone raising the children, so sometimes I don't understand things that happen to me. That's why when I see that other people's situation is similar to mine, I feel relieved. It's like, when I find out that my kids aren't oddballs, I feel happier!"

In addition to reassuring the mothers that their problems were not unique, friends also provided them with information and advice about child rearing. Asako, a strongly religious woman, met once a week with other women from her religious group to discuss their faith and anything else that was on their minds. She felt that she could trust them to help her whenever she needed it. Junko, too, had a network of friends she saw on a regular basis. One particular friend provided a much-needed sounding board for her many questions and concerns about child rearing:

People's advice sometimes sounds like preaching to me. Mrs. Kashiwagi is not like that, though. She's always been encouraging about my son. "He will be fine," she says. Then I usually tell her, "I don't think so. Really." I say so because of my worries for my son. Or else, I probably don't expect much of my son. I can be very honest and humble when I am with Mrs. Kashiwagi.

Miyuki, because of her training as a preschool teacher, tended to be in a position of dispensing rather than receiving support and advice:

There have been many friends who were very impressed by my stories. You know my experiences as a preschool teacher have greatly helped me. I am often asked for advice from other mothers because of that. They think I know more about child rearing, you know.

Some of the women kept their relationships light, preferring just to go out and do things together without confiding deeply in their friends. Chihiro was one who took this path. She enjoyed working with other women on school events and also made friends through her involvement in classes and lessons. But she rarely revealed her problems, because she was too concerned about being evaluated by others:

I feel more embarrassed about talking to others about things. I don't want them to say, "Oh, does that happen to your family?" I guess I like to look cool. I don't like to tell people much. I don't want to tell unnecessary things, so I tell them what I can tell. I just agree with them.

Asako also expressed the need for caution in interactions with mothers who were casual friends:

Sometimes I don't agree with other mothers' "common sense" which is different from mine.... Some mothers have a big mouth, you know. They will talk nicely to someone, but then badmouth that same person to someone else.... I feel that I need to be cautious when interacting with people like that.

Conclusions

Parents face new challenges every day as their children grow and develop. In Japan as elsewhere, parents have few reliable signposts to suggest whether they are doing the right thing. The effects of their actions are often difficult to discern, at least in the short run. In any case, the success of any one parenting action depends on the history of interactions among family members, on the particulars of a given situation, as well as on the personal characteristics of the individuals involved. In this complex and ambiguous situation, it is clearly important for parents to have some sense of confidence that they are capable of identifying a reasonable course of action. Mothers who lack confidence may actually have the skills to be effective parents, but their sense of uncertainty prevents them from putting these skills into play. In the absence of parenting self-confidence, a parent is likely to pass by opportunities for action or zigzag from one approach to the next. When a particularly challenging situation arises, a mother who lacks confidence may find it hard to persevere in a planned course of action. And parents who are flooded with anxiety and self-doubt may find it difficult to focus on their child rather than being preoccupied with their own emotions. Thus, effective parenting is more likely to happen when mothers have a strong sense of their own efficacy.

In this chapter, I began by examining mothers' goals for their children and looking at how they have evolved over time. In spite of the many structural and economic changes that have occurred in modern Japan, there has been considerable stability in the preferred approach to early childhood socialization (Hendry, 1986; Lanham & Garrick, 1996; Peak, 1991; White, 2001). On the whole, the women in this study wanted their children to develop the characteristics of kindness and empathy toward others. They also expected their children to learn how to interact harmoniously with others, and they focused strongly on helping their children learn not to bother other people.

In one sense, these goals are very modest. In general, the mothers did not want a child to develop outstanding qualities, but rather to develop the everyday human characteristics that would enable them to co-exist with others. Some specifically even mentioned "averageness" as a goal for their children. We will see a similar pattern in the next chapter with regard to children's achievement and eventual professional attainment. Most mothers hoped simply that their children would become solid, average citizens.

Yet, while their goals seem modest, these mothers set very high standards for their own behavior vis-à-vis the child. They were trying to implement a set of behaviors that required a great deal of attention to the child's mood and developmental state, great sensitivity in figuring out how to respond to the child, and much self-control to maintain a calm and reasoned stance with regard to discipline. Above all, they defined the success of their endeavors not on the actual behavior that children exhibited, but on their internalization – understanding – of the norms that motivated the behavioral objectives. If a child obeyed in body but not in heart, mothers felt that their *shitsuke* had not been successful. They did not want to dampen their child's enthusiasm, energy, and openness to experience, but rather to harness it and direct it toward its mature expression as an adult member of society.

We saw that most women acknowledged their children's desire for connection and dependence but gently encouraged them to become independent in certain situations. They wanted their children to derive a sense of security from the mother's presence, but not to rely self-indulgently on their mothers to do things that they could already do on their own. They began enforcing situational compliance by refusing to acknowledge their children's dependency bids in public, while still accepting them in private. The more efficacious mothers, Asako and Miyuki, felt fairly confident that this process was going well. The less efficacious mothers expressed more concern. Chihiro repeatedly expressed her sense of emotional distance from her daughter and worried that she could not understand or communicate effectively with her. Junko, too, perceived a distance between her and her son, but she attributed it to his naturally developing orientation toward peers rather than parents.

Like Japanese mothers in previous decades, the women in our study wanted to help their children understand the right way to behave and thought that the best way to do so was through calm and persistent persuasion. They desired to avoid emotional outbursts and did not want to impose their wills strongly on the children or use harsh punishments. What our study highlights more strongly than previous work is how hard it is for many mothers to remain calm in the face of repeated misbehavior by their children. The mothers observed several decades ago by Hendry (1986) gave her the impression that mothers' "ability to maintain a pleasant example" was the rule rather than the exception. She remarked of a mother who lived in a nearby apartment that she "never heard the mother raise her voice, either to an often quite miserable baby or to her mischievous four-year-old" (p. 100). In contrast to this peaceful image, the women in our sample spoke of "exploding" at their children at the end of a long day, ignoring them when they were busy, even flying into a rage when they were upset.

The latter portion of the chapter examined the ways in which husbands, extended family members, and friends were able – or unable – to support the women as they attempted to engage in these complex child-rearing actions. The popular press in Japan frequently attributes contemporary parenting problems to the fact that mothers and mothers-in-law are not on hand to support and teach young mothers about parenting. A more sophisticated analysis is provided by Susan Vogel (1996), who writes about the effects of consolidating the socialization function into the single figure of the mother, rather than distributing it across the extended household. She argues that in the past, mothers were able to rely on other family members and members of the community to reinforce the requirement for mature self-regulated behavior. In contemporary Japan, Vogel maintains, few actors other than the mother and teacher are involved in children's lives on a regular basis, making it incumbent on mothers to be the primary disciplinarian as well as the provider of indulgence.

Our interviews revealed that many women still believed that it was best for *shitsuke* to be distributed across several family members. Each person in the setting – husband, mother, mother-in-law, and friend – had the potential to provide emotional and instrumental support. Our analyses have consistently suggested that the husband is the most important actor in reducing the stress associated with parenting (Suzuki, Holloway, Yamamoto, & Mindnich, 2009). Women such as Asako whose husbands were involved and cooperative had someone to talk with about their problems and someone to take part in disciplinary interactions with their children. Other women, including Chihiro and Junko, found it impossible to count on their husbands to be involved in the daily rearing of their children.

Asako had the additional benefit of living close to her mother, sister, and mother-in-law, all of whom figured in her socialization efforts. However, she had little positive to say about her in-laws, and expressed relief that she was no longer living in their home. Virtually all the women whose mothers-in-law were still alive characterized the relationship as difficult. They perceived their in-laws as nosy and critical rather than supportive. They did not feel that their in-laws appreciated or respected them, nor did they value their in-laws' perspectives on child rearing. Even Miyuki, who demonstrated enormous patience in accommodating her demanding husband, found herself boiling with rage when her mother-in-law challenged her technique of putting a diaper on her baby.

The role of friends was important for many women, but it was not as salient as that of the husband. Asako mentioned that she could trust only the members of her own religious group, and tended to hold herself somewhat apart from the other mothers she met through her children. Junko had a close friend from whom she derived a great deal of support, but this woman was not someone who interacted with her children or husband; indeed, her friend had never entered her apartment, in spite of living in the same apartment complex. Chihiro, too, had friends, but she resisted exposing her problems to them. These women seem to fall into a pattern described by Imamura (1987) as "professional friendships," which are formed for the purpose of obtaining information about child care and education – and as such are part of the network of a "professional" housewife – but are not intimate (p. 102).

Thus, the picture that emerges is one in which women have inherited high standards regarding their role in socializing their children, but often lack a strong network of supportive relations to help them accomplish these goals. Women in previous eras may have encountered strong criticism of their *shitsuke*, but at least they had the benefit of knowing that other adults were available to interact with their children. In contrast, the contemporary women in our study are still highly aware of the judgment of *seken*, those imaginary members of their community with the moral authority to evaluate and sanction their parenting actions (Sugimoto, 2003), but do not have the network that was available traditionally. Their husbands and mothers-in-law often convey their criticisms openly and strongly, yet there are fewer adults around to mitigate the mothers' sense of isolation or interact with their children. In the best-case scenario in our study, represented by Asako, she has the benefit of a supportive husband who is available in the evenings and on weekends. But for others whose husbands are physically or psychologically distant, their resulting emotional stress interferes with the goal of being a calm, cheerful, and wise mother.

8

Maternal Involvement in Children's Schooling

> I am not smart, so I can't teach my child like other mothers can.... I feel
> that I cannot do that. I feel that my child will have to do that by herself.
> (Kayoko, middle school educated, low self-efficacy mother of two)

> I read to him every night.... We go to the library every weekend and
> check out books.... I let him choose books himself. He chooses very
> quickly. It's really fun to do that. (Masayo, college educated, high self-
> efficacy mother of two)

> Having a brain is not necessary for girls, who will do housework and
> raise kids. I don't want girls to think about difficult things. I want my
> daughter to build up her body so that she can have many children. But I
> want to make my son study... For my daughter, education is the second
> priority. For my son, I value education. (Hiromi, high school graduate,
> high self-efficacy mother of two)

The excerpts quoted at the beginning of this chapter illustrate how parents' education background affects their ability to help with their children's
schooling. Kayoko, the least well-educated mother in our sample of 16, felt
severely hampered in her ability to help her daughters with their schoolwork
due to her own lack of schooling. Conversely, Masayo, a university graduate, not only felt confident helping with homework but also greatly enjoyed
reading with her sons. The constructs of gender and socioeconomic status –
and the interaction between the two – emerge as important themes in this
chapter, more so than in the previous ones.

I begin with a history of schooling in modern Japan, showing how it
began as a decentralized network of institutions that primarily served boys
from elite families. The current system was designed to serve girls as well
as boys from all socioeconomic levels, but gender differences in attainment remain and a social class gap is once again emerging in the types
of schooling available to different groups. I also show how, throughout

the latter half of the twentieth century and into the current decade, mothers have played a significant role in their children's academic achievement and I discuss how the structure of schooling has contributed to mothers' perceptions of their role in this regard.

To develop these themes, I turn to our survey data, which gave us a close look at the aspirations that women held for their children's education and the ways in which they chose to become involved in their schooling. Examination of the survey data reveals that the gender of the child and the mother's socioeconomic status played a strong role in the mothers' beliefs and actions related to their children's schooling. In the final section of the chapter I show how and why mothers with higher parenting self-efficacy became more involved in their children's schooling.

Schooling in Modern Japan[1]

Prior to the Meiji Restoration, educational opportunities in Japan were allocated along gender and social class lines. The country was divided into approximately 280 feudal domains, each of which provided schooling for the sons of the samurai class. The primary purpose of these schools was to produce individuals who were virtuous and effective administrators with a sense of loyalty to established authority. Confucian studies formed the centerpiece of education. According to Rohlen (1983), "The crucial emphasis was thus on moral education, with the classics as guides and daily conduct in the school as the mirror" (p. 49). Complementing the focus on Chinese scholarship was rigorous preparation in martial arts, which was seen to embody essential Japanese qualities of simplicity, affinity for nature, and directness of emotion. As mentioned in Chapter 7, an underlying Confucian assumption guiding socialization and education processes was the belief that human nature was inherently good and could be perfected through rigorous training and the experience of hardship.

During the feudal era, commoners sometimes attended temple schools, where they received informal instruction in basic literacy and mathematics as well as guidance concerning the development of virtues such as thrift, persistence, and meticulousness. Approximately one quarter of the students enrolled in temple schools were female. After age seven, students attended separate classes divided by gender. By the time of the Meiji Restoration,

[1] For a comprehensive history of Japanese education, please refer to the following sources, which were consulted for this discussion: Horio (1988); Okano and Tsuchiya (1999); Rohlen (1983).

roughly one-third of young people were receiving some type of primary education but less than 1 percent attended secondary school.

In contrast to the decentralized, informal, class-based education system of the feudal era, the Meiji government aspired to create a single system of elementary education that would help produce citizens who identified with the nation rather than just with local leaders. In 1872, the government put forward an education policy that was intended to give all children (but particularly boys) the opportunity to attend school regardless of class background. Policy makers drew upon Western models of pedagogy and emphasized instruction in Western science and technology.

The new policies proved to be controversial. For one thing, families were required to bear the cost of schooling, and this imposed a financial hardship on them, particularly since parents no longer had the benefit of their children's labor once they became students. Additionally, many parents reacted negatively to the imposition of foreign ideas, many of which were not well understood and hence poorly taught by Japanese teachers. Conservatives in particular wanted to preserve the more traditional moral focus of the feudal schools. In 1890, in an effort to resolve some of these tensions, the national government issued the Imperial Rescript of Education, asserting full control over educational objectives and methods. The rescript reinstated Confucian teachings while continuing to import curriculum and pedagogical techniques from the West.

Growing national prosperity enabled more and more children to attend school and allowed the government to offer free primary schooling. By 1905, enrollment rates in the elementary schools had reached 87 percent, up from 52 percent just ten years earlier. The field of education continued to experience numerous tensions and conflicts during the early twentieth century as the government persisted in its attempt to synthesize Confucian elements with Western pedagogical content.

At the end of the nineteenth century, the government created a system of middle schools, which were designed to prepare boys for entering elite universities. The boys who graduated from these schools were well positioned for subsequent employment, and the subset who entered the university were virtually guaranteed the highest positions available in business and government upon graduation. The government also launched a system of low-status "youth schools" largely designed for rural boys, who received some vocational and military training on a part-time basis.

The use of examinations to determine admission to these prestigious middle schools and universities was a key development in the modern education system. This device assured that the selection was merit-based and offset the personal connections and other advantages available to students from elite families. Girls in the Meiji era also experienced increased opportunities to attend primary school. Those who completed primary school could opt to attend a private or public girls' secondary school, but these schools offered fewer academic subjects than boys' schools did, and they were not intended to lead to university education. In order to become "good wives and wise mothers," girls were expected to study ethics, child care, home economics, and the like. At the turn of the century, only three colleges were open to girls.

During the 1930s, the increasingly nationalistic government revamped the curriculum to emphasize ethics and the history of Japan. During the early part of the decade, despite the military's encroachment into the curriculum, the basic educational system continued to expand and deepen in some ways. Increasingly, the government responded to Western practices and the demands of the growing urban middle class in Japan by accepting child-centered methods of pedagogy but regulating them to prevent deviation from a single national standard. But by the end of the 1930s, military goals were paramount and conventional schooling was all but suspended as student labor was utilized in service of the war effort.

Subsequent to the end of the war, guided by the U.S. occupation forces, the education system underwent another major reform. The American system of six years of elementary school, three of junior high, three of high school, and four of college was adopted, and attendance made mandatory for the first nine years. The government combined boys' and girls' secondary schools into a single institution and integrated the various tertiary institutions into a system of four-year universities and two-year junior colleges. For a brief period, local control was encouraged and progressive teaching methods were fostered, but then the pendulum swung back toward a centralized approach. Rather than designing comprehensive high schools to serve a geographic locale, following the U.S. system, the government opted to allow high schools to admit students on the basis of entrance examinations taken in middle school. These high schools provided higher-achieving students with a college preparatory experience, which culminated in another set of entrance examinations for university. A system of lower-status vocational schools was developed for students with less academic promise.

In subsequent decades, as enrollment increased and competition to attend higher education became more intense, the educational system became increasingly oriented toward formalized preparation for high school and university entrance examinations. In the 1960s, in response to industry and business pressures, the system was further reformed to ensure that the education process would better meet the need for a trained workforce.

The specific objectives were teaching the kind of knowledge that would be needed in the coming industrial age and working out a more efficient way to sort youth in the service of these needs. Meanwhile, the government's strong control of education was resisted by the teachers' union as well as by parents who wanted more opportunities for their children to pursue an academic rather than a vocational track. In spite of internal political turmoil, Japanese schools and students gained an international reputation for high achievement in the 1980s and 1990s.

As I have previously noted, the reputation of Japanese students has been somewhat tarnished in recent years. Their ranking in international examinations has dipped somewhat, and schools have experienced an increase in peer-related violence, disobedience toward teachers, and absenteeism. Furthermore, the achievement gap between more advantaged and less advantaged students has grown considerably, due to a number of factors including the increasingly important role of supplementary schooling (sometimes called cram schools) in preparing students for the high school and university entrance examinations.

Another cause of concern is the persistence of strong gender differences with respect to tertiary schooling. As we learned in Chapter 5, parents of girls are reluctant to bear the cost of a four-year university education, given the poor prospects for young women to find and keep a high-paying job after marrying and having children. The two-year junior college is thus the main track for women, whereas the university is the major track for men. One-third of Japanese women attended a four-year college after graduating from high school in 2004, as compared to half of men. Male and female students differ significantly in terms of the subjects that they study in college. Among those students attending a four-year university, one-third of young women major in literature and arts while less than 10 percent of young men do so. Only 5 percent of females (compared to one-third of males) study engineering (Ministry of Education, Culture, Sports, Science, and Technology, 2005).

The Role of Mothers in Supporting Their Children's Schooling

During the late Edo and early modern period, it was fathers rather than mothers who played the major role in children's education, particularly in elite families. Because mothers were perceived as relatively incapable of reasoning about moral issues, they were not seen as appropriate tutors for their children. Thus, fathers were charged with providing moral guidance to their sons and teaching them about the history and customs of the household. Girls were largely left out of this process, in part because they were expected to learn the habits and customs of the household that they married into, not the one in which they were born.[2]

In the Edo period, there were four official castes (gentry, peasantry, artisans, and merchants); this system in turn contained numerous subdivisions whose members were ranked and had little social mobility. Subsequent to the Meiji Restoration, this social status system broke down and was gradually replaced by a system of social class that depended on material wealth and educational attainment (Sand, 2003). During this time of social upheaval, a powerful ideology of self-advancement (*risshin shusse*) emerged. Parents' role in schooling became much more explicit and more important as their children's future quality of life became increasingly dependent on educational attainment. Women's educational opportunities expanded quickly in the early modern period. By the early 1900s many young women were able to attend school, where they learned modern techniques of household management and child rearing, and could access a growing number of books, newspapers, and magazines on these topics.

In the immediate postwar period, the role of the mother became even more pointedly associated with supporting children's achievement. With the rise of large corporations and their alliance with government officials determined to convert the rural Japanese populace into workers with the habits and skills to work in factories and offices, educational attainment took on even greater importance. This phenomenon culminated during the 1980s, when Western scholars and media depicted Japanese mothers as the powerhouse behind the extraordinary achievement of Japanese students. These "education-oriented mothers" (*kyōiku mama*) were depicted as rendering faithful service to their hardworking children, poised to provide a word of encouragement or to prepare a nutritious snack for the child studying late into the night. In subsequent years, the reputation of the *kyōiku mama* suffered; they have been blamed in the media for focusing on educational achievement to the neglect of social competence, for depriving their sons and daughters of a joyful childhood and stifling their creativity, and for creating a generation of stressed-out, socially immature young adults.

There are, nevertheless, numerous ways in which contemporary Japanese mothers are expected to support their children's academic achievement. Above all, mothers have been charged with creating a stable, calm atmosphere in the home. They receive explicit written instructions from the school on how to reinforce the school routine at home. The schools expect

---

[2]   I did find some memoirs by women whose fathers had taken a particular interest in their education, but this was clearly the exception to the rule (e.g., Sugimoto, 1927).

them to help their children maintain the same eating and sleeping schedule, whether they are on vacation or attending school. Allison (1991) has argued that schools are asking mothers to offset the alienating effects of an elementary system in which children are offered little individual attention and a middle school system characterized by increasingly intense preparation for the high school entrance examinations. Mothers who resist going along with this system are made to feel that they are doing a poor job of parenting and putting their children's future at risk.

Mothers also spend a significant amount of time preparing materials for the children's use or consumption at school. For instance, when their children are in preschool, mothers are expected to sew or at least put labels on a variety of items including hand towels, smocks, and cloth bags for storing possessions. Additionally, many preschools require the child to bring a box lunch (*obentō*) every day and expect the mother to provide a wide array of healthy foods prepared in a visually pleasing manner (e.g., cutting apple slices to resemble rabbits) (Allison, 1991). The unpaid labor of mothers thus constitutes an important underpinning of the smooth functioning of the classroom. And, women's contributions in this regard are visible to school personnel making mothers feel as if they are being evaluated and constituting a source of self-evaluation as well.

Japanese schools offer clear, uniform expectations concerning communication between teachers and parents. Parents are expected to visit the school during scheduled observation days, as well as attend the school's annual field day and other special performances. Parents of preschool and elementary students are expected to attend an annual parent-teacher conference, and they also receive specific reports on their own child through the use of a school notebook which the child takes from home to school every day. Mothers and teachers can make entries in the notebook about the child's activities, mood, health, and any other information likely to affect his or her performance in school. An implicit assumption underlying parents' involvement with the schools is that teachers are experts who impart information and advice to parents, who are viewed as novices with little to contribute to the exchange. Recently as parents have become more outspoken and demanding, education professionals have reacted with alarm rather than reconceptualizing the notion of parent education as a partnership among equals ("Japan's 'monster' parents take centre stage," 2008).

Still another important form of parental involvement takes place outside the purview of the regular school. Many parents enroll their children in supplementary lessons run by private companies or offered by individuals. Preschool children often take swimming, gymnastics, martial arts, and piano lessons. When children enter elementary school, they frequently attend supplementary classes (*juku*) in academic subjects, sports, or the arts after school and on the weekends. According to a recent national study of nearly 10,000 students, 37 percent of elementary students, 43 percent of junior high school students, and 25 percent of high school students participate in supplementary classes (Benesse Educational Research Institute, 2008a).

Parents enroll their children in supplementary classes for several reasons. Some may be seeking intellectual enrichment for their children. Others are trying to boost the achievement of those who are having trouble in the regular classroom. With class size averaging 28.6 students per class in primary education and 34.0 per class in lower secondary education – one of the highest levels for any OECD country – it can be difficult for children to get individual attention from their regular teacher (Ministry of Education, Culture, Sports, Science, and Technology, 2006). Still other parents are hoping that preparatory classes will help their children obtain a favorable score on the examinations that determine where they will be able to attend high school. Mothers are usually responsible for determining what forms of supplementary education are available, selecting options that are appropriate for the child's needs and within the household's budget, and monitoring the child's progress. According to Hirao (2007b), sending a child to supplementary school requires "tremendous input on the part of parents" (p. 178).

In sum, the school system depends heavily on the labor of mothers but approaches them as novice learners who need detailed, specific guidance to ensure that their contributions are adequate.[3] As I noted in Chapter 4, Merry White has argued that this "manual syndrome," with its blend of "performance perfectionism, a curriculum of conformity, and high demands," can undermine rather than build mothers' confidence (1995, p. 271). As we will see, some mothers feel comfortable engaging in the activities that the school demands of them, while for others it is one more aspect of parenting that makes them feel insecure and anxious.

Social Class and Parental Involvement in Schooling

As *juku* attendance becomes increasingly common, one major concern is that, unlike regular public school education, it is available only to parents who can afford it. A wide variety of educational services are available,

---

[3]   A form of ritual formalism also emerges in the way that schools treat students. Schools often provide students with manuals containing detailed behavioral guidelines for everything from packing their school bags to shampooing their hair on school field trips (Feiler, 1991; Holloway, 2000).

with concomitant variability in cost and quality. In 2006, the annual cost to families of enrolling their children in supplementary classes was estimated at 142,000 yen (approximately $1,235) for elementary school students, 246,000 yen ($2,139) for middle school students, and 224,000 yen ($1,948) for high school students (Ministry of Education, Culture, Sports, Science, and Technology, 2006). The high cost of supplementary classes is frequently cited as a factor parents consider when deciding whether to have additional children. On average, Japanese households spend 22 percent of their education expenses on supplementary classes (Hirao, 2007b). The cost of these lessons is a burden to many families, and there is increasing concern about the role of supplementary lessons in widening the achievement gap between children from wealthy and less wealthy families.

Indeed, research in the past decade has begun to reveal significant academic discrepancies associated with family socioeconomic status, in spite of the relatively egalitarian school system and the common perception of postwar Japan as being a "middle-class society" (Hashimoto, 1999; Kariya, Shimizu, Shimizu, & Morota, 2002). For example, powerful effects of family income on parent involvement in schooling were noted in the context of the Third International Mathematics and Science Study: "The most striking effects we noted through our observations were differences in opportunity for education associated with income and wealth. Economic background appeared to influence parental participation in school activities, the rate of students holding part-time jobs as well as parents' and students' academic aspirations" (LeTendre, 1998, p. 11).

The psychological mechanisms by which family background translates into educational opportunity in Japan are not yet well understood, but it appears that more highly educated parents assist their children by spending more time engaged in cognitively stimulating activities than less educated parents. Teachers tend to value the type of knowledge that children derive from these activities, and consider it in making judgments about a student's academic potential (Yamamoto & Brinton, 2010). In the remainder of this chapter, I further explore the ways that parental involvement in children's schooling is related to the family's social class background as well as the gender of the child.

Parental Aspirations for Children's Schooling:
Evidence from the Surveys

The construct of *parental aspirations* usually refers to the idealistic hopes or goals that parents may form regarding the future attainment of their children. Psychologists find that high aspirations appear to catalyze parental

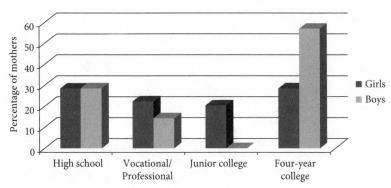

FIGURE 8.1. Mothers' Educational Aspirations for Their Childrens' Education by Gender of Child.

efforts to engage their children in home learning and lend support to the school. It is frequently assumed that in Japan, a so-called "education-credential society" (*gakureki shakai*), parents must hold high aspirations for their children's education. In fact, our survey data found that many mothers did *not* aspire for their children to attain a college education. Forty-seven percent stated that it would be acceptable to them if their child obtained a high school degree and did not attend college. The rest said they would not be satisfied unless their child attended either junior college or university. Maternal aspirations were significantly higher for boys than for girls, as indicated in Figure 8.1 (see also Holloway, Yamamoto, & Suzuki, 2005). More highly educated mothers were more likely to have high aspirations than were those with less education. Our findings echo those of a large study on parental views and practices which found that Japanese parents reported lower educational aspirations than parents in the United States, Thailand, Korea, France, and Sweden (International Comparative Research on "Home Education," 2005).

When we examined the types of intellectual activities that mothers made available to their children at home, socioeconomic status also came into play. Wealthier mothers signed their children up for more lessons during the preschool period than did lower-income families. Wealthier mothers also purchased more educational magazines and workbooks for their children, and took them on educational excursions to zoos and museums more often. When the children were in second grade, the wealthier mothers continued to sign their children up for more lessons and spent more money on these activities than did mothers in lower-income families.

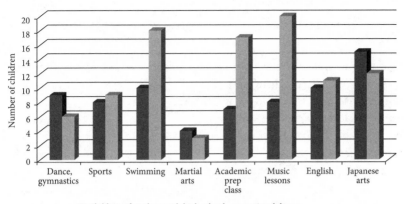

FIGURE 8.2. Extracurricular Activities in Second Grade by Educational Level of Mother.

Mothers' educational level was also related to several aspects of parental involvement in children's learning. We compared mothers with a high school education and those who had received a junior college or four-year college degree. Whereas 41 percent of the mothers with a high school diploma or vocational training reported *never* reading to their children, only 21 percent of the more educated mothers so indicated. Mothers who were more educated signed their children up for more supplementary activities during the second grade, as they had during the preschool period (see Figure 8.2). Here, too, the more highly educated mothers spent more money on lessons than did the less educated mothers. This effect of education held up even when we controlled for family income. So, while the more educated mothers did have more income at their disposal, our findings suggest that it was not money alone that drove them to sign their children up for more lessons and activities.

Contrary to our expectations, we found that the less educated mothers reported participating in more activities at their child's preschool than did the more highly educated mothers. This conflicts with studies in Western countries which find that more educated mothers feel more comfortable interacting with teachers, are more familiar with school life and routines, and hence are more likely to find ways of being present and involved at the school site (Lareau, 2003). Presently, when we look at the mothers' narratives, we will be able to get a clear sense of how it is that mothers' education affects their willingness and ability to engage in certain kinds of activities.

Is Parenting Confidence Related to Involvement in Children's Schooling?

Another question of deep interest pertains to the association between mothers' sense of parenting self-efficacy and their involvement in children's schooling. One could argue that mothers' ability to be effective in guiding children through the education system is based on their own experiences in school and from having the resources to enroll their children in supplemental schooling. But another argument focuses on the fact that those resources are deployed within the context of an ongoing personal relationship. If, as Allison argues (1991), children's emotional reserves are depleted by the Japanese school system, then mothers must be able to identify what their children are feeling and figure out how to help them feel confident and energized in their approach to school. This would suggest that effective parental involvement hinges on mothers' ability to form and sustain a close relationship with their children. Thus, in our research we wanted to examine whether or not the mothers' sense of their efficacy in parenting was associated with their engagement in their children's schooling.

We found strong evidence of this association in our survey data. At the preschool level, we found that mothers with higher parenting self-efficacy more often read to their child at home, and they engaged in a more thorough search for a good preschool before enrolling their child (Yamamoto, Holloway, & Suzuki, 2006). When the child was in second grade, we found that mothers who felt more efficacious as parents were more likely to engage in cognitively stimulating activities with their children. This relation held up even after we statistically controlled for mother's education, family income, and family size (Holloway, Yamamoto, Suzuki, & Mindnich, 2008).

In summary, the survey data suggests that some forms of parental involvement are more common among higher socioeconomic status families, and that maternal education level is a particularly robust predictor of parent involvement. We also suspect that mothers' aspirations for their children are contingent not only on mothers' education level but also on the child's gender, with mothers of girls holding significantly lower aspirations than mothers of boys. And finally, we found an intriguing association between mothers' sense of parenting self-efficacy and their engagement in activities to support their children's education. Let us now turn to the narratives to obtain a more detailed understanding of how and why mothers' actions are shaped by these structural and psychological forces.

Why Do Japanese Mothers Hold Low Aspirations for Their Children?

Mirroring the survey findings, the narrative data revealed that only four of the 16 mothers believed that attending college was crucial to their children's future success. Most mothers emphasized that they were more concerned that their children develop moral qualities than that they pursue certain academic or professional credentials. As Asako said about her son, "I do not care much about fame and status. I just want him to be respected and trusted by people. That is all I wish." Mari articulated a similar idea. Even though she was more strongly oriented toward her children's education than anyone else in the sample, she nevertheless thought that her ultimate goal was to help her children learn how to live in society:

Recently I was told that the knowledge about how to live, or just manners at home, are the most important things in a person's life, and I really think this is true ... Children who can study but do not have good manners are not really fully human. I think that people who can do things properly and not cause trouble for others have studied properly. That's something I really understand.

Most women wanted their children to find something they were strongly interested in and pursue it wholeheartedly. They said that their own preferences were less relevant than those of their children. Three of the women, including Asako, harbored hopes that their sons would become professional athletes, but only if the sons themselves wanted to pursue this dream as well. Junko strongly believed that her son should find a job that would be meaningful to him and did not want to pressure him to go into the family business:

It is OK with me [if he enters the family business] as long as he is convinced that the job is [right] for him. Otherwise he would fail to perform well at work. He would always think that, "I had actually really wanted to do that [other] job instead."

Parental aspirations concerning their children's education appear to have been affected by the financial downturn of the 1980s and 1990s. Noting that many companies were being restructured to cope with these economic challenges, these mothers believed that the days of lifelong employment with a single company were over. Some thought that individuals with a specific vocational skill would be better prepared for the future job market than those with a university degree. Naoko expressed her opinion that her son may not need to go to a four-year university, even though both she and her husband had done so:

It's been said that this is a society of education credentials (*gakureki shakai*). But even if you go to college and enter a good company, it doesn't mean you can necessarily establish good relations with colleagues, and recently, you know, there has been some personnel restructuring within companies. Stable enterprises go bankrupt. So it is better if you have practical knowledge, skills, and specific knowledge.

These women were aware of the risks that their children would be taking if they experimented with unconventional alternatives and experienced the consequences of their choices. Most mothers believed that boys were more able to endure the hardship and failure that such experimentation might involve. For example, Yasuko thought that it would be better for her son (but not her daughter) to take a difficult and unpredictable path than to live a "mediocre" life:

To some degree, it's good to get off the path sometimes. I don't expect him to stay on top of a rail and walk straight on … For girls, I don't want them to go through hardship. But for boys, I don't expect a boy to stay in the "socially expected path" all the time. He should rather live a checkered life than a mediocre life so that he would be a man rich in experience.

Careful analysis of these data by Yoko Yamamoto (2006) for her doctoral dissertation revealed some of the reasons why less educated mothers were more likely than more educated mothers to articulate low educational aspirations for their daughters. One argument for providing boys with a college education was based on the perceived utility of education for boys. Boys were expected to support themselves and their family when they became adults, whereas girls were expected to work for only a short time before having children. This view was expressed in clear terms by Hiromi, a high school graduate, in the quotation at the beginning of this chapter. Even when the more educated mothers planned to encourage their daughters to attend college, they did not necessarily think that this college experience would lead to professional opportunities. Rather, they saw college as a useful way to make friends and cultivate skills that would be useful for raising children.

Chihiro wanted her daughter to go to college, not so much for her professional and intellectual development but because attending college would give her daughter "opportunities to meet various types of people and to make lifelong friends." Chihiro was also planning to require that her daughter live at home while attending college. This was the same restriction that Chihiro's father had imposed, which had forced her to give up her goal of becoming an architect because no institutions in her immediate area offered a degree in that field. Chihiro did not think it was important for her son to live at home when he was in college; to the contrary, she wanted him to experience the difficulty of surviving on his own:

I don't want my daughter to live by herself because there are many schools around here. My son, well, boys need to move out. They need experiences. As a parent, it's scary, but ... even if they have to eat only miso and tofu, that's fine. Boys need that kind of hardship. But for girls, they don't have to go through that. They will probably have a family, and they can put all their effort into their husband and children.

In light of the frustration that Chihiro expressed about being a housewife, and her regret at having decided against applying to graduate school, it is quite striking that she nevertheless assumed that her daughter would follow the same path.

Chihiro and several other mothers indicated their awareness that gender norms were changing somewhat in Japan but nevertheless expressed different goals and standards for their sons than for their daughters. For example, here again are the comments of Yasuko:

Well, for girls, my expectation is not high. People say men and women are equal, but I think that there are different roles for men and women. I expect boys to see and think ahead. I couldn't say that I don't have that desire [for my son]. But as for girls ... if they like studying, parents can support them. But if they say they don't like studying anymore, then they can head in another direction, they can head toward another interest. After all, boys and girls are a little different. My opinion may sound strange to others. In a time of equality between men and women, my [ideas] are old-fashioned.

Only two of the 16 mothers – both relatively well-educated women who had daughters as well as sons – did not think that girls should be steered in the direction of homemaking. Both of them hoped their daughters would attend college and find a rewarding career. One of them, Reiko, was socializing her son to take responsibility for domestic chores so that he would be a supportive husband rather than someone who expected his wife to do all the housework (as did her husband). She strongly believed that her daughter should have the same career and lifestyle choices as her son:

I do not think that [my daughter's] educational background depends on her gender. I think it depends on the individual person. Because children do not know about the possible choices yet, I can, want, to show them that there are a lot of interesting choices.

The second mother, Beni, also articulated a clear vision for her daughter's educational and occupational future. Because Beni had a slight physical disability, her parents had not expected that she would marry or have children. They had encouraged her to pursue her education seriously and hoped that she would be able to find a job that would enable her to be economically self-sufficient as a single person. Her successful career ended up being cut short when, counter to her parents' expectations, she did marry and have children. Beni's own experiences appear to have shaped her views about the potential of her daughter. Beni was hoping that her daughter would have an opportunity to consider a wide variety of jobs, including those in the international arena: "It's up to my daughter, but I want her to know that there are so many jobs she can try.... If possible, she can have a job through which she can contribute to society."

In summary, the lasting impression that we gained from listening to these women is that most had modest aspirations for their children. Most of them did not want their children to be geniuses in school, or to be particularly high achieving in some future profession. They also expressed little interest in enhancing the occupational opportunities available to their daughters; with a few exceptions, they expected them to focus on household responsibilities and parenting rather than building a career. Yet, it was evident that most women thought it quite difficult to help their children attain even an average lifestyle. They thought it was hard to raise a child who was empathic, optimistic, and energetic, and they thought it would be hard to help their children discover the path to a happy and comfortable life. Thus, mothers often applied perfectionist standards to their *own behavior* in rearing their children, but they did not expect extraordinary achievement on the part of the children themselves.

In the next section of the chapter, my goal is to obtain a more detailed understanding of how mothers' own educational experiences and their sense of parenting self-efficacy shaped the type of involvement they had in their children's education. I approach this by contrasting the narrative of Junko, whose negative experiences in school significantly undermined her sense of efficacy in supporting her son in preschool and the primary grades, with that of Miyuki, who left school with a sense of positive accomplishment that set the scene for her energetic and persistent attempts to boost her son's achievement in the early grades.

Junko: Negative Academic Experiences and Low Parenting Self-Efficacy

Junko repeatedly described herself as a student who hated school even as early as the second grade: "I, myself, hated studying. I even hated looking at the textbooks.... I hated studying science when I was a second grader." The reason she hated school so early is that she often did not understand what was happening in class:

Even though I did the work, I didn't really understand the content. I really didn't understand the meaning in my head. My parents were oblivious to the fact that I didn't understand the concepts. They just thought that I should be able to do it.... I kept on telling them that I didn't understand, but my parents just thought that I didn't want to do it.

Junko's difficulties in school can be attributed at least partly to her social class background. Her parents were not well equipped to support her during her academic struggles, although they tried to do so. Her mother had only gone as far as junior high school. Her father had attended a vocational high school and had bitter memories of being ridiculed for not being completely literate. She reported that her parents constantly scolded her for not doing her homework, but appeared to have no way to help her understand the material. Her teachers did not provide much support other than to pressure her to stay in school:

I made my junior high school teacher worry because I didn't want to go to high school. I told my teacher I would rather become a dishwasher.... Even though I did not want to go [to high school], I was forced to go and since I was forced to go, I don't really have any fun memories [from high school].

Junko expressed doubt that her son would do well even before he started elementary school. During the first interview, when he was six years old, she described him as an amiable bumbler, saying, "He is kind of clumsy and sort of slow. I think he is just like his parents." Junko did not feel that intellectual development and academic attainment were particularly important goals for her son. Her objectives were for him to be healthy and to behave well. She believed that "studying was a secondary issue" and that "it didn't matter whether he was clever or not." She stated that she would be satisfied if her children learned basic academic skills and nothing more: "I hope my kids will learn the important things in order for them to survive, which I failed to learn."

Not surprisingly, given her own experiences and opinions about school, she had no particular desire for either her son or her daughter to attend college. She expressed a willingness to finance her son's education through high school if he were willing to put in the necessary effort to succeed. But she did not intend to "force" him to go even to high school if he didn't want to, believing that it would be a waste of the family's money to do so. She expressed some willingness to pay for college, again with the caveat that her assistance would be contingent on his level of effort.

Although her aspirations for him were not high, she assumed that supporting him in school was part of her role. She thought he would need her help even to attain an average level of performance. During his last year in preschool and first two years in the primary grades, she made sporadic efforts to involve him in educational activities at home, but rarely felt she was successful. Junko might have been more able to overcome her insecurities about her own intellect and ability to support her son if she had felt more emotionally connected to him. However, as we learned earlier, she also lacked confidence in her ability to communicate with him and to discipline him, and believed that he preferred the company of his friends to being with her. There seemed to be few activities that the two of them enjoyed doing together, and she lacked a basis for constructing a dialogue or interaction about schooling. Thus, her lack of agency with regard to parenting also contributed to the difficulty of supporting his work in school.

When he was in preschool, she bought a subscription to an educational magazine but told us that he didn't read it. Her attempts to teach him the basic Japanese syllabary were also deemed unsuccessful: "He didn't like [me teaching him] so I just dropped it. Then his friend's older sister taught him. I think it was easy for him to learn from that friend's sister." While she used to read a book to him every night, by the time he was in the last year of preschool she had tapered off, reading "twice a week at most." One of the more positive experiences she reported was enrolling him in an English class, which he seemed to enjoy. She also reported taking him to the library regularly to borrow comic books.

Junko had selected her child's preschool on the basis of its proximity to their apartment and because, looking at it as she passed by on the street, it seemed to have a relaxed atmosphere. Seeing the abundance of equipment in the playground, she and her son both decided that it looked like a fun school:

I thought it fit his personality, with a relaxed orientation. There are preschools where the children have to be orderly and where the mothers have to visit a lot or have to hand sew their children's bags [for storing personal possessions]. This preschool is not like that at all. It lets you take it easy.

She described herself as too busy to attend many of the school's activities for mothers. She preferred to communicate with her son's teachers through the daily notebook and was certain that the teacher was living up to her promise to "pay attention to my child and look after him." She avoided participating in the PTA, and noted that she was not the only one to do so: "Everyone wants to avoid being in the PTA and usually it's really hard to decide who will be in it. So we decide by playing 'rock, paper, scissors.'"

When we spoke with her just before her son started first grade, she appeared to be quite uncertain about her role and was avoiding certain types of engagement. She reported that she had been trying to talk about the new school with other mothers in her neighborhood, but didn't feel she had learned very much: "I don't quite understand the stuff they talk about. I don't understand the various details." In the month before school started, she put off the purchase of a school backpack, hoping that her mother-in-law would offer to buy it for him. And unlike every other mother we spoke with, she had decided not to buy a desk for him when he started elementary school "because he will not be studying that much in the beginning." Anticipating his enrollment in elementary school, she worried that he would find it difficult and stressful. She conveyed her reluctance to force him to study against his will: "I have no intention to be serious about at-home education, but I will at least help him understand the textbooks." Once he actually started school, she continued to worry about putting pressure on him, telling us that she'd decided not to say too much about studying for fear that he would start to hate it.

After her son began first grade, she told us that she had not sought out specific information about the school curriculum, activities, or policies. She tended to see the teachers as the experts, and felt comfortable with any decisions they made, including those pertaining to corporal punishment. She was impatient with parents who criticized teachers for using physical punishment, telling us, "If my kids really did something bad, then it is right for the teacher to hit them on the head."

In summary, there can be little doubt that Junko's own history of difficulty in school, combined with her feeling that she was not skillful in providing basic *shitsuke* to her son, undermined her ability to support his early forays into the school system. She was so worried about her son repeating her own pattern that she avoided some forms of engagement in his schooling. She made sporadic attempts to support him at home, but dropped them at the slightest sign that they were not working. In general, she had few resources for getting support or assistance with these parenting activities. As we saw previously, her husband was not involved in caring for the children. She did not seem to develop a close or trusting relationship with any of her children's teachers. Although she did have one friend whom she trusted and could confide in, in general she felt uncomfortable interacting with other mothers concerning academic issues. All these factors combined to impede her from feeling effective and capable in helping her child, and led her to develop a "hands-off" approach to his education.

Miyuki: Positive Educational Experiences and High Parenting Self-Efficacy

Miyuki's social class origins were similar to those of Junko, but whereas Junko was not able to move much beyond her parents' class position, Miyuki was upwardly mobile. Furthermore, she had obtained a degree in the area of early childhood education. It seems that her advanced degree in this field assisted her in feeling generally efficacious as a parent and also specifically contributed to her ability to support her children's education.

Miyuki's parents both grew up in large families and were unable to continue their own education past junior high school. Her mother was employed when Miyuki and her sister were young, but managed to balance her job responsibilities with being strongly present in the home. Miyuki described herself as "an average girl with no special ability," but when she was in junior high school she decided to become a teacher. She bought a book explaining how to enter a teacher preparation program, studied hard, and passed the entrance examination for an appropriate high school. Impressed by her hard work and determination, her parents agreed to take out a loan to pay for a piano so that she could take lessons, a requirement for preschool teachers in Japan. She did well enough on the college entrance examinations to receive an offer of admission from a junior college, from which she ultimately obtained a degree in early education. She enjoyed college and was delighted to take a job as a child-care provider, the profession that had been her dream for so many years.

Miyuki was much more confident in her ability to communicate with her children than was Junko. The cornerstone of her confidence lay in her conviction that there are "various kinds of mothers" and many different ways to succeed as a parent. As we learned in the previous chapter, although her son was quiet and did not reveal his emotions readily, Miyuki felt that she could usually understand him using her intuition.

She perceived her son as a somewhat easygoing child who did not worry too much about doing well in school. She noted that he "somehow learns, although he does not seem very motivated [to do it by himself]." She expected that he would probably be "average" in school. His moderate, relaxed approach was acceptable to her because she "had learned that kids are all different and that one has to value the differences. Because of my teaching experience, I learned not to compare my three kids and force them to do something beyond their ability." He learned to read by playing with alphabet (*hiragana*) blocks, watching educational videos, and playing card games with his sisters. She avoided taking a didactic approach to his early learning, confident that he would learn to read and write correctly when he started first grade.

Miyuki's approach to supplementary lessons was more aggressive than Junko's. As she had done for his older sisters, she signed her son up for supplementary lessons in math and reading during his last year of preschool. Miyuki believed that available family resources should go into supporting his success in school, saying: "We want to spend our money on our children's education rather than spending it on ourselves." After her son entered the first grade, she continued sending him to supplementary lessons.

In general, Miyuki's attitude toward school was more positive than Junko's. When her son was about to enter first grade, she made sure to communicate the idea of school being a fun place: "I told him that school was a place to make friends ... and that it wouldn't be so hard in the beginning. I said that even if you have to study, it is more like playing, so you should just enjoy it."

There were many indirect ways in which Miyuki supported her son as he began the transition to elementary school. The connection between parenting self-efficacy and support for schooling was evident in an anecdote that Miyuki related about her son's first week in school. She said that after the first day she asked him how school had been, and he said that he didn't know. She then asked him many detailed questions about his day and was surprised when he became angry with her. Upon reflection, she realized that "he became angry because he didn't know how to explain his experience, and after being nervous all day at school, he was thinking that he was just really relieved to come home, so why was he being asked all these questions? So I thought to myself that I shouldn't ask him any more!" After a short time, he felt comfortable enough to volunteer information about what was happening at school. Miyuki's thoughtful reflection and sensitivity to her child's feelings helped her to formulate a more supportive way to find out about his daily activities.

Miyuki kept track of what each of her children was learning in each subject at school and in their supplementary lessons. She expected her children's teachers to keep her informed about their progress. Unlike Junko, she was sharply evaluative of teachers who did not appear to be attending carefully to her son. When her son's preschool teacher did not offer any specifics about his progress in his first year at the school, she felt frustrated and began to mistrust the teacher. When she then learned the teacher had not noticed that her son was writing with his left hand rather than his right, as is preferred in Japanese schools, she fully realized that "it is parents' responsibility to raise their kids. It is of no use to ask his teachers to take over this role." She reported advising other mothers to be assertive in support of their children, even if it might result in "being marked as a nagging mother" by school staff. She took on a leadership position in her son's preschool in order to stay abreast of what was going on there. She was in charge of collecting and depositing parents' tuition checks, a highly challenging task due to the number of parents who were not always able to pay in a timely manner. She was later pressured into accepting a role in the PTA when her son was in second grade, even though she was busy with three children and a part-time job.

In summary, it is evident that Junko and Miyuki had very different experiences in school that affected how they approached their own children's schooling. Miyuki had much more confidence about her ability to engage her son in educational activities, and so she tended to stick with her chosen approach to helping him rather than shifting erratically if she ran into a temporary roadblock. Her attitude toward school was positive and optimistic, and she was determined to communicate that perception to her son. And she felt comfortable interacting with his teachers and the mothers of his classmates. In addition to all these specific factors that contributed to her ability to support her son, she also had a general sense of parenting efficacy that guided her in the many small decisions and adjustments she had to make to help him negotiate the demands of schooling.

Exceptions to the Pattern: Asako and Chihiro

Mothers like Miyuki, whose own experience in school had been positive and who also felt confident in their general child-rearing abilities, were likely to take on a wide variety of parent involvement activities. Those like Junko, who had not been successful in school and doubted their child-rearing capabilities, had trouble knowing how to support their children in the academic domain. The question is whether a mother who had confidence in her parenting could overcome her own lack of educational background to become fully involved in her children's academic life. Indeed, there were several women who did manage to find a way to overcome any disadvantage they may have experienced as a result of their less extensive educational background.

Asako provides one clear example of this pattern of resilience. Like Junko, Asako had disliked school and terminated her formal education after receiving a high school diploma. Unlike Junko, however, she felt a strong emotional connection to her son. She emphasized that, for her, the primary goal of parenting was being able to understand what her child was feeling by "seeing into his heart and soul (*kokoro*)." Her empathy toward her son led her to support his early learning in ways that built on his capabilities and interests. She seemed to enjoy finding creative and fun ways to engage in stimulating and educational experiences. For example, noting his obsession with trains as a toddler, she read him children's books about trains as well as magazines for adult model train enthusiasts. She and her husband indulged his desire to go on long train and subway rides, and built on his curiosity about train travel, even teaching him to read the names of the stations.

Asako's responsiveness to her son's interests and feelings also led her to advocate for him at school in ways that were different from those of other women with less schooling. Her son's second grade teacher was known to be a harsh disciplinarian and impatient with students who were slow at grasping the lessons. Asako viewed him as a dangerous and ineffective teacher, and worked hard to find ways of supporting her son without directly challenging the teacher's authority. She became a more active volunteer in the classroom so that she could monitor the situation, and both she and her husband tried to develop a good relationship with the teacher in the hope that he would in turn look favorably upon their son.

We also wondered if there might be any mothers who, despite lacking a sense of parenting self-efficacy, managed to be highly involved in their children's education. Chihiro fits this pattern. As we have already learned, she did well in college, received a bachelor's degree, and was very confident in her role as an employee. Throughout our conversations, she emphasized her feeling of inadequacy as a mother. She particularly focused on her inability to connect with her daughter, remarking that she often had trouble understanding what her daughter was thinking or feeling. However, the feeling that she could not connect with her daughter did not inhibit her from engaging in many forms of parent involvement. Not surprisingly, the aspects of parent involvement that she felt most drawn to were those that occurred in the context of the school. She volunteered to be in the PTA at her daughter's preschool. Unlike most mothers, who saw the job as intimidating or tedious and time consuming, she thought PTA activities were fun and rewarding: "I like events like festivals. It's a feeling of exuberance and release.... Ever since I was a student I've always enjoyed getting together with everyone at events like cultural festivals and having a great time." She was prepared to volunteer again when her daughter started first grade. She enjoyed getting to know the teachers and had learned to like public speaking, because "talking in front of everyone becomes one more kind of pleasure after a while."

Chihiro's participation in these events helped her become knowledgeable about what was happening at the school. She drew on that knowledge to engage in an informal monitoring of her own children's classes. Having heard at one point that bullying had become a problem in her son's class, she took every opportunity to observe how the teacher was handling the situation:

I would go to the school many times at that time. I used to go to see the class and ask the teacher how he was doing or something like that.... Even when there was no particular reason or thing for me to go for, I would peek in as if I had just dropped by. And I would ask the teacher, "What are you teaching now?" ... I also secretly looked into the class at other times, too.

Chihiro found it possible to engage in many forms of parental involvement, particularly those that focused on the school institution. She also had the financial resources to encourage her children's participation in various types of supplementary activities. She was therefore able to partially overcome the serious problem that she faced as a result of feeling emotionally disconnected from her daughter. Her case illustrates that, while a mother's own education background and sense of efficacy in child rearing are important contributors to the way she supports her children's education, it is nevertheless possible for those who lack these advantages to find ways to make a positive contribution to their children's development.

Conclusions

A primary goal of this chapter was to examine mothers' aspirations for their children. The most striking finding there was that many parents – particularly those of girls – did not strongly aspire for their children to attend college. Our findings are supported by other research. In the large survey of parents in Japan, the United States, Thailand, Korea, France, and Sweden mentioned earlier, Japanese parents expressed the lowest educational aspirations of any nation in the survey, with 45 percent wanting their children to attend university and just 2 percent wanting them to attend graduate school (International Comparative Research on "Home Education," 2005). Additionally, Japan was the only country in which parents expressed lower aspirations for girls than for boys, with 66 percent of parents with sons aspiring for them to attend university versus 37 percent of those with daughters. By comparison, regardless of children's gender, more than 80 percent of Korean parents said they wanted their children to go to university or graduate school. And finally, Japan was also the only country to report an average *decrease* in parental aspirations over the ten-year period between two administrations of the survey.

Undoubtedly the reverberations of corporate restructuring and Japan's ongoing economic challenges played a significant role in this national pattern. The mothers in our survey also drew our attention to other types of goals, including a desire that their children become humble, kind, and ordinary adults. Additionally, they made it clear that they were trying to be realistic. In talking about their children's future, some stated how fearful they were that their children might end up with serious emotional problems or with their name splashed across the television screen for committing a crime. To these mothers, raising a child to become productive and ordinary did not necessarily seem simple or easy to do, and they sometimes went to extraordinary lengths to ensure that they would excel within the relatively constrained parameters of their role. Muriel Jolivet (1997) has also noted that Japanese women's aspirations for their children are modest, saying that they "yearn to have children who are neither better nor worse than the others." She points out that their demanding vision of what it takes to turn out an "ordinary" child requires mothers to give up their dreams of doing anything other than raising children and she calls their dream of raising a child who is stable and productive "the expression of the purest wisdom since it is modest, realistic and therefore human" (p. 187).

When we delved into the actions that mothers took to realize these modest aspirations for their children, we saw the importance of their early experiences in school in shaping their own attitudes about school and their evaluation of their ability to support their children academically. The less educated mothers sometimes emerged from their own school careers with a feeling of intellectual inferiority that undermined their sense of competence in supporting their children's school achievement (Yamamoto, 2006). Our findings illustrate the associations between class membership and forms of cultural capital – dispositions, values, taste, and attitudes – that can affect parental involvement in the educational system (Bourdieu & Passeron, 1977). Forms of capital that have legitimacy within the school system are less often found in lower class homes, and the less educated mothers we interviewed expressed less confidence about interacting with school staff, whom they perceived as intimidating and difficult to challenge or even understand.[4]

While our findings about the connection between mothers' educational background and their support of children's schooling generally mirrored the results from studies in Western countries, there was one exception, which pertained to involvement in activities at school. The survey analyses revealed that mothers who were *more* highly educated were *less* likely to participate in activities at the school. In the interviews, several mothers mentioned that participation in PTA activities was highly demanding, reduced the resources available for their own children at home and prevented them from undertaking activities more directly beneficial to their children's schooling. We suspect that the less educated mothers may have found it more difficult than their more highly educated counterparts to resist pressure from preschool staff to participate in the PTA. More highly educated mothers appeared to feel less intimidated by the teachers and were more successful in refusing to take on time-consuming activities. Additionally, the more highly educated mothers appeared to be more consumed with the individual "cultivation" of their own child's skills and less oriented toward the general welfare of the school and all of the students. These findings are consistent with research in Japan suggesting that more highly educated parents are in general more involved in their children's education *in the home setting* than are their less educated counterparts (Iwamoto, 2000).

Our interview data indicated that parenting self-efficacy played a significant role in shaping mothers' involvement in their children's schooling. The survey findings suggested that parenting self-efficacy was strongly associated with frequency of mothers reading to their children and exerted its influence independent of mothers' educational level (Yamamoto, Holloway, & Suzuki, 2006). In the United States, research suggests that mothers with low parenting self-efficacy find it difficult to create the emotional connection needed to make reading a mutually enjoyable experience (Bus & van IJzendoorn, 1988). Thus, mothers who feel a strong emotional connection to

---

[4] Research in the United States has frequently shown that less educated mothers question their right or ability to register complaints with the school or to advocate for their child (Lareau, 2000; Okagaki & French, 1998; Stevenson & Baker, 1987) and often feel less confident in their ability to engage in activities at home that will support their children's school achievement (Cutrona & Troutman, 1986; Froman & Owen, 1989; Jackson, 2000; Machida, Taylor, & Kim, 2002).

their children, are able to communicate with them, and have developed an effective system of guiding their behavior are clearly at an advantage when they attempt to engage them in the process of schooling.

The most involved and supportive mothers in our study were those like Miyuki who reported feeling successful in their own educational careers and who experienced a sense of general parenting self-efficacy. But having both forms of self-efficacy did not appear to be essential. Mothers like Asako also appeared to be able to function quite effectively at this stage in their children's schooling even though they had not themselves done well in school. And highly educated women like Chihiro who felt confident in the school setting were effective in supporting their children's academic achievement even though they lacked a feeling of confidence regarding the affective aspects of parenting.

In summary, we found that mothers expressed modest educational aspirations for children, particularly girls, but a heightened sense of the difficulty of helping their children do well in school. Consistent with a cultural predilection for role perfectionism, mothers saw themselves as having an important role to play but were often unsure how to go about it. The tendency of some mothers to flail about in attempting to find constructive ways of supporting their children seemed partly to result from the nature of parent-teacher relations in Japan. Mothers were expected to play a large role in their children's schooling and were given explicit instructions in how to do so. As I discussed in Chapter 3, the tendency to focus on doing things "one best way" may sometimes have the opposite of its intended effect: the learner feels unable to conform to the blueprint but not empowered to figure out an alternative route.

In fact, there are signs that the expert-novice dichotomy may be breaking down in Japan as more and more women attain an education level equivalent to that of the teacher. Some of the more highly educated, confident parents have begun to challenge teachers and subvert the assumption that the teacher is always right – even when they know that they may be branded as troublemakers, and even when they fear possible negative repercussions on their own children. It will be interesting to see whether Japanese educators can successfully develop a more egalitarian and supportive partnership with parents.

We also saw gender dynamics operating in deep and pervasive ways, extending beyond the education system to other social institutions. In particular, the ongoing Japanese view of men as breadwinners and mothers as homemakers continues to shape contemporary mothers' aspirations for their sons and daughters. The women we spoke with did not express discomfort with their role in reproducing gender-related inequities in schooling, even when they themselves had been forced to relinquish their own educational goals, as in the case of Chihiro. They viewed themselves as bowing to the reality of the Japanese workplace, which makes it difficult to balance work and family life. In the next chapter, I delve more deeply into the topic of women's labor force participation, in order to get a better understanding of how Japanese women are currently conceptualizing the possibility of balancing family life and employment, both now and in the future when their own sons and daughters will face these challenges.

9

Balancing Work and Family Life

> After five years, I was one of the most experienced employees at my
> workplace.... I didn't want to quit my job when I got married ... My
> boss was a career-oriented single woman. She worked so hard. For her,
> the job was the first priority. She told me that I should be ready to do
> overtime even after getting married ... Six months after I got married I
> was asked to be part of a new project team. I was given one condition for
> joining. I was not supposed to become pregnant for two years ... When
> I was told that I could not get pregnant for two years, I had to reconsider
> the offer ... In the end, I declined the offer. And I ended up quitting the
> job because I was not feeling comfortable working there. (Beni, college
> educated, low self-efficacy mother of three)

Beni, quoted above, is typical of many Japanese women, in that she held
a full-time job for several years after finishing school and then left the
workplace upon getting married. In fact, Japan is one of the few countries
where a graph of women's employment trajectory over their lifetime still
forms an "M" shape, with high rates of employment prior to child rearing, a deep dip during the childbearing years, and a rise when the children
begin school (Brinton, 2001; Choe, Bumpass, & Tsuya, 2004; Macnaughtan,
2006). In Japan, only 22 percent of women with preschool-aged children are
employed, compared to 60 percent in the United States, 56 percent in the
United Kingdom, and 42 percent in Taiwan. Japanese mothers of adolescents are more likely to be employed (52 percent) than those with young
children, a figure similar to that of the United States (59 percent) and the
United Kingdom (70 percent) (Shirahase, 2007). However, it is important
to note that in Japan the second "hump" of the M-shaped curve is "not only
lower, but also qualitatively inferior to the first," because many women re-
entering the job market take part-time work with lower wages and benefits
than they had in their prior full-time job (Rosenbluth, 2007, p. 13).

Whereas women in most countries are achieving increasingly better conditions in the labor force, Japanese women's status is declining with respect to key benchmarks. For example, in 1965, fewer than 10 percent of women were nonregular (i.e., part time and not permanent), but by 2001, this share had increased to over 45 percent (Macnaughtan, 2006). Part-time workers in Japan tend to work long hours – six per day on average – but are paid less per hour and receive smaller annual bonuses than full-time employees do. In 2000, female part-time workers received only 67 percent of the wages of female regular workers and 44 percent of the wages of male regular workers. The economic picture is not particularly good for full-time female workers, either. In 2007, the average wage of Japanese women workers was about two-thirds that of men's, as compared to 81 percent in the United States and 83 percent in Britain (Tipton, 2008). In addition, only 10 percent of Japanese women attain managerial positions, compared to 30 percent in Western countries (Tipton, 2008).

To understand the issues that face Japanese women as they attempt to balance work and family responsibilities, I first examine historical trends in women's employment. A quick overview makes it clear that at the same time that societal expectations for women have expanded regarding the role of mother, they have contracted with respect to the role of worker. In contemporary Japan, the needs of business and industry largely determine the structure of the workplace, and this factor has resulted in a number of policies that ensure a large pool of part-time female employees, who can be hired and laid off as required by companies. Other structural factors reinforce this low rate of participation in the workforce, including the demand for women's participation in supporting their children's schooling and a shortage of child-care and elder-care services.

After examining these historical trends regarding women's work, I explore the employment trajectory of the mothers we interviewed. I focus on the life histories of Miyuki and Chihiro, whose narratives illustrate the barriers that Japanese mothers face when it comes to sustaining meaningful employment. Their cases show how being employed can boost the life satisfaction of women and their perception of themselves as good parents.

Women's Work in Prewar Japan: A Focus on Productivity over Domesticity

Prior to the twentieth century, Japanese women worked alongside men in a variety of occupations – farming the land, diving for shellfish, and even working in coal mines (Mathias, 1993). As Japan began to modernize in the late 1800s, many families migrated to the cities, and the nature of women's labor-force participation started to change. Japanese women often took jobs in textile factories, where the workforce was 60 to 90 percent women (Nolte & Hastings, 1991, p. 153). Others were engaged in piecework at home (Hunter, 1993; Uno, 1991, 1993). Paid very little, they had to work 12-hour days merely to contribute 10 to 25 percent of the household's income (Uno, 1993).

With the formulation of the Meiji Constitution in 1889, the state began to articulate the family's role in contributing to the nation. As government officials moved to capitalize on the economic potential inherent in the traditional family structure, two competing visions emerged concerning the role of women. As discussed in Chapter 3, in the Ministry of Education, officials emphasized domesticity and actively supported the notion that education should help girls learn skills related to housekeeping and parenting. Alternatively, in the Interior Ministry, officials articulated a vision of women's contribution that focused on productivity rather than domesticity. In particular, Interior Ministry officials sought to increase women's ability to manage the home efficiently and participate in civic activities: "[T]he ideal woman was one who attended girls' higher school, spent an appropriate amount of time on organized philanthropic and patriotic activities, and used the postal savings system" (Nolte & Hastings, 1991, p. 171). At this early stage, the Interior Ministry did not try to discourage women from taking jobs in order to contribute to the family's economic stability.

These competing visions – a focus on productivity versus a focus on domesticity – continued to affect state actions toward women into the mid-1920s. Employment opportunities were expanding during that era, permitting women to participate in areas that had not been previously available to them. Teaching positions for women opened up in the early decades of the twentieth century, as the number of girls attending schools grew and as many men left teaching to take jobs in the expanding private sector (Nagy, 1991). Women were also drawn to the occupation of nursing – which expanded four-fold between 1911 and 1926 – as well as to white-collar office work. Many women continued to work in textile factories, where conditions had improved since the early days of the Meiji era (Molony, 1991). Increasingly, women viewed employment as essential to attaining and maintaining the middle-class status that many had achieved in the boom years during the First World War. Employers found it cost-effective to hire women, given that the cost of female labor was approximately one-third the cost of male labor.

[handwritten margin note: more jobs for women]

Even as women's labor-force participation was expanding, social analysts began to express ambivalence about the movement of middle-class women into the workplace. Some voiced concern about threats to women's physical and moral welfare as they moved about the public sphere. Others, influenced by the Western focus on the mother as primary caregiver for children, worried about the welfare of children whose mothers were employed (Uno, 1993, 1999). In the 1910s, a few prominent Japanese education experts who had been exposed to German ideas about child development began to emphasize the harm to infants caused by daily separation from their working mothers. Initially, these views were not well received by the broader education community, who were still promoting the importance of child-care centers in enabling impoverished women to contribute to the household income. However, by the 1920s, several prominent Japanese Christian women who had founded or directed the earliest preschools had accepted the position that mothers should have primary responsibility for rearing children.

[margin note: job vs. caring for children]

Yuki Tokunaga was one such pioneer in the early childhood movement in Japan. She directed one of the first preschools in Tokyo from 1910 until 1973. Western religious beliefs as well as Western feminist thinkers such as Ellen Key influenced her ideas. Following Key's line of thinking, Tokunaga emphasized women's contribution to society as mothers and focused on improving working conditions within the home. This particular strand of Western feminism – which accepted women's domestic destiny while also seeking to expand the range of socially permissible activities for women – continues to be relatively influential in contemporary Japan (Mackie, 2003).

[margin note: compromise to be able to do both]

As men's unemployment rose toward the end of the 1920s, the economic incentives for businesses to reduce women's role in the workplace began to outweigh the savings created by their low wages. Accordingly, the government moved to create jobs for men, on the one hand, and redoubled its efforts to train housewives to run their households with modern methods that would eliminate unnecessary expenses, on the other (Nagy, 1991). In the 1930s, the government began to draft men to serve in the invasion of Manchuria. The Ministry of Education – ever insistent on the domestic aspect of women's contributions – responded to men's absence from family life by crafting policies that shifted the role of child rearing from fathers to mothers. This move represented the final phase in a long series of government efforts to promote women as caregivers. The role of the family had thus been transformed from the locus of moral socialization (formerly the province of men) to the seat of warm emotion, a function that only women were seen as capable of fulfilling (Miyake, 1991).

[margin note: weren't mothers primarily caring for their children anyways?]

As Japan's government stepped up its military initiatives during the early 1940s, officials became particularly eager to foster growth in the birth rate. A mandate issued by the Ministry of Welfare recommended a number of policies to strengthen families and encourage childbearing: provide matchmaking services in municipal agencies, reduce marriage expenses, provide information about child rearing and hygiene to girls in school, prohibit employment to women over the age of 20, introduce tax incentives and family allowances to reward large families, and prohibit birth control (Miyake, 1991). Miyake claims that, "the state's intervention into women's reproductive roles by pronatalist policies, in conjunction with other repressive state policies, restructured the family system so that it could function as an arm of the state" (p. 281).

At the same time as they were being encouraged to step more fully into the role of family leader, Japanese women were also being called on to take over jobs vacated by men who were serving in the military. During this period of increasing economic hardship, some women welcomed the income, but they were frequently underpaid, treated poorly, and subjected to harsh and often dangerous conditions (Miyake, 1991). Partner's compelling biography of a rural woman in the Tōhoku region of northern Japan describes how, in 1943, she was hired to unload coal from ships, alongside American and Chinese prisoners of war and Korean forced laborers. While the physical demands of the job almost ruined her health, she earned five yen per day – "an almost unheard-of sum for casual labor" (Partner, 2004, p. 98). At the close of the war, the government fired about 3 million women to accommodate men returning from battle (Miyake, 1991).

When American occupation forces drafted a new Japanese constitution after the war, they included a clause – Article 24 – establishing the equality of men and women: "With regard to choice of spouse, property rights, inheritance, choice of domicile, divorce and other matters pertaining to marriage and the family, laws shall be enacted from the standpoint of individual dignity and the essential equality of the sexes." The equal-rights clause was drafted by Beate Sirota Gordon, a young American woman who had grown up in Japan, spoke fluent Japanese, and was one of the few members of the drafting committee to have any actual knowledge of Japanese society and the plight of women at the time (Gordon, 1997). This clause has frequently been blamed by contemporary conservative politicians for causing many of the problems faced by Japanese families (Brooke, 2005). In spite of this constitutional assurance of equal rights for men and women, women have not achieved full parity with men in the subsequent decades, particularly with repect to the workplace.

Women and Work in the Postwar Era: Shift toward Domesticity

In the years following the war, women continued to be employed as teachers and nurses in the many industrial settings and businesses that were springing up in metropolitan areas. However, by this time, the "wise mother" aspect was becoming the dominant element of the "good wife, wise mother" edict. As we saw in Chapter 3, the notion of a hardworking mother who watched her children from afar was being replaced by an ideal in which the mother was deeply and exclusively involved in every aspect of her children's care. The increasingly demanding standards for being a mother in Japan made it correspondingly difficult for women to combine parenting with employment (Hirao, 2001; Yu, 2001).

Cultural attitudes about motherhood are only part of the reason that Japanese women are more likely than women in other countries to leave the workforce when they have children. In some other Asian countries, men and women hold similar attitudes to the Japanese about gender roles, but women nonetheless participate in the labor force during their childbearing years. Yu (2001) argues that certain structural features of the Japanese labor market diminish women's participation. For example, in Japan the business world is dominated by large corporations with inflexible hiring and promotion practices; by contrast in Taiwan there is a mix of large firms and small, family-run businesses whose less formal practices accommodate women's needs to balance employment and child care. Another factor that contributes to higher participation by young Taiwanese mothers in the workplace is that in Taiwan, men's salaries are often not sufficient to maintain a middle-class lifestyle, as they are in Japan. A third factor is that Japanese corporations need skilled rather than nonskilled workers, whereas in Taiwan, many businesses use less skilled workers and continue to employ home-based pieceworkers, who are typically women.

In the postwar years, the Japanese government has largely upheld corporate policies, even when the resulting practices have severely disadvantaged women in terms of salaries, work conditions, and opportunities for engaging in meaningful work. Most analysts agree that it was *international* perceptions of widespread discrimination against Japanese women in the workplace that led to the passage of Japan's Equal Employment Opportunity Law (EEOL) in 1985 (Brinton, 1993). This legislation encouraged firms to treat women equally and to avoid discrimination but stipulated no penalty for failure to comply. In 1999, the EEOL was strengthened, but it still has not been sufficiently enforced to have an impact on women's opportunity for equal pay or advancement (Rebick, 2006; Schoppa, 2006).

While the traditional practice of hiring women only for low-level clerical work has been supplanted by a supposedly gender-neutral tracking system, in practice, most women are still funneled into the administrative track, which features routinized work and little opportunity for promotion. Men, meanwhile, are directed to the professional track, which requires overtime and possible transfer but leads to managerial positions and higher salaries. Another area in which change has been more superficial than real is the continuing practice of hiring young women and then pressuring them to quit after less than ten years (usually upon marriage), rather than allowing them to remain on the job and thus benefit from accrued seniority. Companies may not formally advocate the practice, but corporate cultural norms continue to push women out of the workplace when they get married or become pregnant.

[handwritten margin note: why do they do this?]

Another aspect of the Japanese labor market that is disadvantageous to many women with children is the widespread practice of age discrimination. A government poll released in 2001 found that more than 90 percent of firms had an age limit, and that the average cut-off age for hiring new employees was 41 (Sakuraba, 2009). Historically, firms preferred to hire young college graduates, socialize them into workplace norms, and teach them occupational skills through on-the-job training. Educational institutions also show a preference for hiring only young employees; in an earlier study of Japanese preschools, I noted that directors of private schools preferred to hire recent graduates rather than those who already had teaching experience. The directors believed that it would be easier to train inexperienced teachers because they would have no particular beliefs or teaching techniques that might be at odds with the norms of the new workplace (Holloway, 2000). As we will see later in this chapter, Miyuki ran into an age barrier when she sought to return to a position as a child-care teacher after her third child entered elementary school.

Technically, there are laws on the books that prohibit age discrimination. The Employment Measure Act (EMA), enacted in 1966 and amended in 2001, required that firms "endeavor" to avoid age discrimination (Hamaguchi, 2007; Sakuraba, 2009). In light of the ongoing employment crisis that left many middle-aged workers unemployed and unable to find work due to age limits, the government decided the law needed more teeth. The EMA was revised again in 2007 in a way that reduced the number of exemptions to the basic principle of age-based hiring, and that allowed individuals to sue for age discrimination. However, some legal analysts still find that the law contains too many exemptions to provide adequate protection for older workers (Sakuraba, 2009).

The basic conditions of employment in Japanese corporations are not particularly attractive to many women: long hours, mandatory socialization, stressful conditions, and frequent relocations (Iwao, 1993). During the 1980s and early 1990s, Japanese women became even less eager to participate in full-time salaried work than they had been in earlier decades as they came to realize that workplace norms continued to make it difficult to work and have children without extreme personal sacrifice (Rosenberger, 2001). Another problem is that women are still expected to care for their elderly parents, and thus many women anticipate having to leave the job market when their parents or in-laws require their assistance (Brinton, 1993).

Yet another factor contributing to women's difficulties in remaining employed after they marry and have children is a shortage of center-based child care. Existing centers do not offer enough hours of care to serve full-time employees. Informal care by nannies or babysitters is not customary in Japan, nor is there a pool of immigrant female labor to fill those positions, as there is in many other countries. Even if more child care were made available, it is not clear that this would resolve the problem, because, as we saw in the preceding two chapters, Japanese mothers have extremely high standards regarding child rearing. This makes it difficult for many of them to imagine that child-care professionals could really be an adequate substitute for maternal care (see also Yu, 2001).

Women's Perspectives on the Benefits of Work

In our surveys and interviews, we wanted to understand the unfolding of women's work and family lives from a longitudinal standpoint, exploring their early thoughts and ambitions about work, their involvement in the labor force prior to marriage, and their approach to work activities subsequent to having children. We were interested in learning what lay behind their motivation to work at various points in their lives and in examining the dynamic interaction between their own desires and those of others – particularly their parents and husbands. With respect to their current situation, we hoped to gain a clear idea of how working affected their sense of themselves as women, wives, and mothers. We were particularly interested to learn how the experience of working was related to their sense of parenting self-efficacy.

On our second survey, administered when the focal children were in the first grade, a total of 43 percent of the women indicated that they were employed in some capacity. Twenty-one percent of the women in the sample had part-time jobs, 14 percent were engaged in piecework at home, and 8 percent were working full time. By the next year, the number of employed women had increased to 55 percent, most of them working part time. The employed women reported working an average of 17.96 hours. These figures are comparable with national statistics; data from 1995 showed that 55 to 60 percent of Japanese women in their thirties were participating in the paid labor force (Brinton, 2001).

To learn more about the importance that these mothers attached to work, we asked them to indicate what activities they were currently involved in and to rate the personal importance of each activity on a five-point scale. Notably, they awarded the highest rating of importance to working (3.61), followed by attending a class (3.29), participating in sports (3.21) or the PTA (3.21), and participating in children's community activities (2.91).

To gain further insight into the psychological effects of working, we examined the association of work status to women's parenting self-efficacy and life satisfaction. We found that employed women expressed greater satisfaction with their lives than did those women who were full-time homemakers. In fact, work status was a significant predictor of life satisfaction even after controlling for mother's education, family income, financial strain, number of children, and beliefs about whether women should work outside the home and commitment to the role of mother (Holloway, Suzuki, Yamamoto, & Mindnich, 2006). This was a powerful finding, particularly given the fact that most of these women were engaged in routine jobs that would appear to afford relatively little opportunity for self-expression or personal autonomy.

such simple jobs, yet happier

Life on the M-Shaped Trajectory

We looked to the interviews to better understand what it was about working that fostered such a deep and pervasive sense of satisfaction in so many women. Among the 16 mothers we interviewed, only Masayo held a full-time job at the start of the study. Six of them worked part time while the target child was in preschool. By the third interview, when the children had started elementary school, three additional mothers started part-time jobs, and one changed from part-time to full-time work. Five women did not take any jobs over the course of the study; two of these (Asako and Miho) were caring for an infant during this period. With the exception of one participant who was a teacher, the women were engaged in a variety of less skilled jobs, including assembly work at home or in a factory, home-based or door-to-door sales, and office work. For some of them, as we will see in the cases of Miyuki and Chihiro, their re-entry jobs were significantly less challenging and well paid than the jobs they had held prior to getting married.

When these women were young girls, their aspirations had been quite variable. However, these aspirations bore little relation to the employment they held as adults, due to the particular conditions underpinning women's labor-force participation in Japan. Thus, as I have just noted, there was relatively little variability in what they ultimately ended up doing when they re-entered the job market. We begin with the case of Miyuki, mother of three, who worked briefly in a child-care center before getting married.

Giving Up a Dream: Miyuki's Education and Employment Story

We learned some of the basic facts about Miyuki's childhood in Chapter 5. Her parents were generally supportive of her desire to go to college. Each of her parents had grown up in a family of 11 children, and neither had had the opportunity to get much more than a middle school education. Their lack of education made it very hard for them to find employment when they first moved to the Osaka area as a young married couple. The memory of this difficult experience prompted them to encourage their daughters to obtain at least a two-year college degree in order to be assured of finding a good job.

As Miyuki moved through school, her parents were closely involved in her career plans. They provided her with the necessary tuition to attend a junior college, where she received certification to teach in child-care centers (*hoikuen*). Their economic support gave them power over her academic choices. She became interested in becoming a special education teacher, but they opposed the plan, arguing that working with disabled children would be too physically taxing for her. She acceded reluctantly to their wishes, recognizing that she was completely dependent on them to fund her education, and remained in the field of regular rather than special education.

When Miyuki graduated, she took a job at a child-care center not far from her home. She found the job to be exhilarating and challenging. When there was a special event at the center, she was sometimes so busy that she got only two hours of sleep at night. Miyuki loved working with children, and she got along well with her co-workers. But after only two years on the job she became engaged to be married and was immediately faced with a decision about whether or not to quit. Her husband did not want her to keep working, nor did her parents. She reported that her parents told her, "You are clumsy. We do not think you can handle both housework and your job." Her husband agreed with this characterization, telling her: "New computers can do so many things simultaneously, right? But old ones can handle only one thing at a time. You are an old computer." Her co-workers at the child-care center also discouraged her from staying on the job, including one woman who had suffered a miscarriage, which she attributed to working, and had never been able to become pregnant again. Faced with all of this pressure and advice, Miyuki made the tough decision to quit what she characterized as her "dream job."

Miyuki had hoped to return to the classroom when her children started school. But after her three children were born, there was never a time she felt that she could manage both her home responsibilities and a teaching job. In addition to learning how much work was involved in caring for three children, she had also come to believe that "the husband comes first in my family." The task of caring for him was particularly challenging, given his lack of knowledge concerning the details of daily home life, as she noted: "After all, he can't cook or do laundry. He doesn't understand how to operate the washing machine. He cannot figure out which button to press to get it started."

has to take care of both 3 children + husband

During the third interview, when her youngest child was in first grade, she acknowledged longing to return to teaching or some other type of work, admitting that "staying home and dealing with my kids all day long bores me." While she rarely experienced stress when she worked as a teacher, she realized that she did become stressed at home: "I get very stressed out, and wonder why I am not as tough as before, or as patient as before." She was also eager to be able to contribute to her family's economic resources, because she worried that her husband's health might give out, leaving the family without a source of income. In spite of her desire to work, she also knew that whatever job she took was likely to be temporary, since she would be expected to care for her husband's mother eventually: "Since my husband is the only one among his siblings who is married, I probably will be the one that has to look after his mother. That's why I think that in the future I will be more busy taking care of old folks than being a mother or a wife."

surprising that home life is more stressful than work was.

Initially she attempted to find a job as a child-care provider. But by then she was nearly 35, and she was told that the child-care centers in her community did not hire teachers over the age of 33. To her dismay, she seemed to run into age limits in nearly every job she applied for. Apparently, even the position of part-time receptionist at a dentist's office was limited to applicants under the age of 30. Eventually, she was able to obtain a part-time job in a convenience store, working the early morning shift – 6:30 to 9 a.m. – three or four days a week. She reported waking up at 4 o'clock in the morning in order to prepare her husband's lunch, walk the dog, and get ready for work. She relied on her older daughter to wake up the rest of the household, and they fixed themselves a minimal breakfast of bread, butter, and jam. She expressed appreciation – and some amazement – that her family had adapted so well to their new morning routine. She was particularly surprised that her husband was willing to carry his dishes from the table to the sink, telling him it was a "great development." She was amazed that he didn't realize he had never helped before: "He asked me if he hadn't done anything before, and I said, 'No, you didn't! Weren't you aware of that?'"

According to Miyuki, she and her family experienced a number of benefits from her taking a job. First of all, she believed that working helped her become a better mother. She had an opportunity to observe families who came into the store, and she learned how different parents handled their children. She also began to appreciate more deeply her husband's contribution to the family. She came to realize how hard he had worked for the previous 24 years, and how difficult it was to earn enough to support their family. She expressed considerable regret for not managing his hard-earned money more prudently in the past. Among other things, she vowed to start darning her children's socks rather than throwing them out at the first sign of wear, declaring to us, "Darning is great!"

Miyuki was also proud of learning how to use the computerized cash register. Her husband, she reported, had said that she "had improved amazingly" in her ability to listen to verbal instruction, take accurate notes when something was being explained to her, and keep her notes and other materials in order. Summing up her views about the job, she remarked, "Although it's tough, it gives me a sense of spirit, instead of staying home all day long. Getting some excitement makes the fun times incredibly fun, but when I am tired, I feel incredibly tired. It's strange, but I enjoy it even when I am exhausted."

Miyuki's buoyant spirit enabled her to make the best of almost any situation, but it will be easy for most readers to identify the things that are wrong with this picture of a highly trained, dedicated teacher being forced at age 34 to take a job in a convenience store. In her story we can identify the key elements that combine to create the powerful force field that repels so many Japanese women from professional employment after they are married. A similar constellation of cultural attitudes and workplace conditions came into play in the case of Chihiro, which we turn to next.

Longing for Engagement and Stimulation: Chihiro's Story

As we learned in Chapter 5, Chihiro had wanted to become an architect when she was a high school student. When it came time to select a college, her father insisted that she restrict her search to colleges within commuting distance of their home. He thought that she would be lonely if she lived away from home, and he also worried that there would be no one to take care of her if she became ill. Although she had been looking forward to meeting new people living away from home, she ended up giving in to her parents. As was also true of Miyuki, Chihiro depended on her family to pay for college tuition, so she had no choice but to accede to their wishes.

Since no college in the area offered a degree in architecture, she decided to apply to a school of industrial design. She was eventually admitted to a college that was a two-hour commute from home each way. She studied hard and graduated with honors in four years. Her academic advisor encouraged her to pursue a graduate degree, and in retrospect she wished that she had taken his advice: "If I had kept studying, I could have become an assistant professor or something. So I wonder whether I would be leading another life if I had done that. It might be more fun, you know ... I think I made a mistake." She believed that her parents would have supported her if she had chosen to go to graduate school, saying, "They would let me be myself as long as I wasn't doing things against the norm." But her friends wanted her to join them in the job market and told her that they could not remain friends if she started "hanging out with a professor." She ultimately decided to take a job in product design. Although she found it stressful due to the pressure of developing new products and the long hours, she loved her work, and particularly enjoyed interacting with her colleagues and customers.

Soon after she began working, she met her husband on the job. After a three-year courtship they decided to marry. Her father was concerned about her health and encouraged her to quit work before she became seriously ill. So, at age 25, she left her job and got married. Like Miyuki, Chihiro was very frustrated with the life of a stay-at-home mother: "Well, I think that I'm longing for a stimulation that I'm not getting from life now. I want to see the outside world. I feel that there are so many things I can learn, like going to school, studying, getting a job."

When her younger child was in first grade, Chihiro began to think about looking for work. She briefly considered running for local office, which would have made good use of her energy, outgoing personality, and leadership skills. However, she doubted that she would get support from her family for such a plan, saying, "I think my husband would be against it. My children would oppose it, too. They would be totally against it.... It would destroy our family life, right?" She contemplated a wide variety of jobs, and even considered working as a dishwasher or selling box lunches at the train station. Like Miyuki, she also had to consider the possibility that she would be called upon to care for her parents should they become ill.[1]

---

[1] Traditionally, the job of caring for elderly parents has fallen to the wife of the oldest son, but Chihiro, as an only child, is responsible for her parents' care. Also, several women in our study noted that their elderly parents preferred to be cared for by their own daughter rather than by the wife of a son.

Ultimately, a part-time job fell into Chihiro's path. A friend of hers was working at a copy shop, and when an opening came up she asked Chihiro if she would be interested in taking the position. Chihiro agreed to take it even though the work neither drew upon her expertise or intellect nor called for the type of leadership skills she had demonstrated in her volunteer work in the schools. Unlike Miyuki, she didn't find the job particularly rewarding. She worked six days a week, anywhere from two to five hours a day. Because her schedule was never fixed in advance, it was difficult for her to plan her time. She felt lucky that because they lived with her parents she never had to worry about the children coming home to an empty house. She thought that her children might derive some benefit from her working because they were forced to be a bit more mature if she wasn't always at home.

In the future, Chihiro planned to continue her part-time job and eventually hoped to take another leadership role in the PTA. At one point she mentioned hearing somewhere that husbands were not getting overtime pay anymore and were starting to come home earlier than their wives who worked long hours at "part-time" jobs. She had heard that some of these men were taking on dinner preparation, doing the laundry, and preparing a bath for their wife. Chihiro said, with a laugh: "I don't think that happens, you know. It's like a dream, it is like a dream."

Youthful Dreams and Variable Support from Parents

Miyuki and Chihiro are two examples of women who developed specific career aspirations by the time they were in high school. However, both had to modify their goals to accord with their parents' views about the type of schooling and the type of career that would be appropriate for a young woman. In Japan, students' parents usually have to pay most or all of their college expenses. Few fellowships or scholarships are available to offset tuition costs. The prospect of incurring these expenses motivates parents to reflect carefully on the likely return on their investment. In our sample, parents also restricted their daughters' career options to jobs that matched their views about what females were capable of physically as well as psychologically.

A few of the women in our study were able to overcome these social norms through sheer force of will. For example, Masayo, who was a teacher, had received no encouragement from her parents to pursue an education beyond high school. She described her father as a "traditional man" who "said that women need no education." Her mother, although somewhat more supportive of Masayo's schooling, expected her to "be feminine, help with the housework, and find a husband." Masayo's parents discouraged her from studying hard in high school; in the evenings, they would literally turn off the lights when she was trying to do her homework. However, Masayo was ambitious and determined to pursue her education: "I was a rebel. I had a strong will to go to the university. I was in a stage of resistance.... I felt like, why do I have to lose to men [in terms of achievement]?" An unexpected twist of fate – the death of her father when she was in high school – made her eligible for tuition assistance from the government to the college of her choice. Her mother, in the meantime, had become more supportive of Masayo's educational ambitions and did not oppose her plan to attend college.

Unlike Miyuki, Chihiro, and Masayo, several ambitious dreamers were not able to realize their career goals due to unstoppable opposition from their parents. Junko, as we have seen, hated school and had little confidence in her intellectual abilities. In junior high school, she was attracted to a career in the fashion industry and wanted to attend a high school with a program in fashion design. Her parents did not feel they could afford the tuition and sent her instead to a vocational high school focusing on business skills. Upon graduating, she told the job placement staff that she particularly did not want to be placed in a job that involved accounting:

I was asked if I liked working with the abacus or not. I told them: "I don't like to at all. Not only that, I don't like the computer or bookkeeping, either. I don't understand them." But I ended up receiving a notification that I would work in the accounting section. It was the worst feeling.

Not surprisingly, she disliked her job. With almost no opportunity to select a line of work that matched her own interests, Junko was not sad about becoming a full-time mother, but by the time her younger child was in preschool, she was already feeling bored and beginning to think about finding work.

The Difficulty of Maintaining Good Human Relations on the Job

A second theme that emerged in many of the narratives concerns the difficulty of managing social relationships in the workplace. In Japan, social relations at a place of employment are strongly structured in terms of the individual's tenure at that site. An employee always has to deal with three types of co-workers: those who joined the firm at the same time as the employee (*dōki*), senior colleagues who joined prior to the employee (*senpai*), and the junior colleagues who joined subsequently to the employee (*kōhai*). These structural relations govern many facets of behavior, including whom one socializes with and the language used in speaking with each other. Two other structural criteria that affect social relationships at the workplace are education level and age. When these various criteria are at odds with each other, interpersonal tensions are exacerbated, leading to confusion about the pecking order within a group of individuals who are all doing the same job. Based on her extensive fieldwork in a Japanese office, Ogasawara (1998) argues that female workers frequently fail to support each other on the job, not because of their "inherent female nature," as many of the women themselves believed, but because of "company policies that created complex lines of division among the women" (p. 68).

Junko, for example, reported having this type of difficulty when she was a full-time employee prior to getting married. She had been bothered by the tendency of certain junior colleagues (*kōhai*) to try to dominate members of her cohort. For example, when a junior co-worker found fault with her for bringing food to the office, Junko was annoyed because this person had joined the company a year later than she had, and hence had no right to criticize her. Junko also had problems with male colleagues who did not understand the "system" that the female workers had developed among themselves for getting work done: "We female workers had our own codes for working together ... When a male worker who didn't understand what we were going through messed up our system, I really hated it. It could destroy our relationships, you know."

Asako also alluded to the sensitive matter of getting along with co-workers but said that she did not have a problem in this regard. After graduating from high school, she selected a job based on two criteria: an informal dress code and close proximity to her home. She found a job as an office assistant in a small company that suited her well and she experienced few adjustment problems:

I have been learning about the pecking order (*jyoge konkei*) since I was a child thanks to my soccer activities. I was raised to be respectful toward my elders. It made it easier for me to start working full time for the company. I could fit myself into the work environment without any trouble. I had no trouble with human relations. I did not go through any mental problems such as a sense of failure or "beginner's hypochondria," all of which contemporary young people tend to suffer from.

Some women in our sample reported feeling pressure to work long hours. Miyuki experienced this when she was working as a child-care provider, particularly when teachers were preparing an event for the parents. Although the phenomenon of putting in a lot of overtime is more often associated with full-time corporate jobs, it appears to characterize some lower-level jobs held by the women in our sample as well. However, it was sometimes difficult to tell whether women were working overtime because of actual job demands or to fulfill their own perfectionist standards. For example, prior to marrying, Miho worked as the manager of a clothing shop and was expected to put in many hours of overtime. She appeared to have taken on more responsibility than was strictly necessary:

When I was still working, I had to check the sales slips after the shop was closed. I sometimes had to bring work back home. My first priority was my job. My husband was of secondary importance. I even went to the shop on my day off to see if everything was going all right or not. I had to leave the shop before the manager showed up, because I was not supposed to be there. I knew my home would be of secondary importance if I kept working. I thought it was inappropriate ... Since the job was really hard, I was always ready to quit and get married. It was a hard job. I remember that I cried a lot. Looking back, it was not worth it. It was tears of bitter disappointment after trying really hard.

Even though Miho seemed to indicate that her own sense of responsibility was driving her to work so hard, most of the women in our study did not view their work conditions as self-imposed, and, therefore, they did not expect to be able to negotiate any changes at the workplace to make the job more compatible with having a family. As we will see in the next section, these perceptions, along with the women's familiarity with the demands that the workplace placed on their husbands, contributed to the view of most women that combining full-time work with parenting would be all but impossible.

Pressures from Family and Employers in "Deciding" When to Quit Work

Japan is one of the only modern capitalist societies in which women are actively pushed out of the workplace when they get married or become pregnant. While most Japanese companies no longer have an official policy of firing women for these reasons, many still encourage women to effect a "harmonious separation" (*enman taisha*) from the workplace when they become engaged. Most companies find it more economical to employ young women than to continue paying those who have accumulated seniority, and executives find it desirable to hire and lay off part-time workers as company needs warrant (Ogasawara, 1998). In some cases, employers are willing to keep a married woman or a woman with children as long as the employee can assure the employer that her performance will not be affected by her new status. For example, as noted in the excerpt at the beginning of this chapter, Beni had been employed for four years at a company at the time she got married. The company offered her a promotion at that time, but only on the condition that she didn't get pregnant for two years. When she realized that they expected her to "sacrifice the family, no matter what," she decided to quit rather than make this demanding commitment.

Only one woman in our sample, Masayo, kept working continuously after getting married and having children. As a teacher who had struggled hard to overcome her parents' objections to her obtaining a university degree, Masayo did not want to quit work when she got married, although her husband preferred that she do so. She resorted to the indirect strategy of postponing a clear decision about the matter:

I did not want to resign. Well, I did think about quitting, but I decided to wait to do so until after getting pregnant. Then, after we had a kid, I waited again until the end of my paid maternity leave. So in the end, I just kept on putting off quitting my job. [Laughs.] He [her husband] gave up on that for me.

As we learned in Chapter 6, Masayo was one of the few women whose husbands were willing to do housework. Her success in remaining on the job thus depended on their partnership as well as her own determination. Additionally, she had the advantage of working for the public schools, where employment policies and practices tend to be more progressive than in many private sector firms.

Most of the women we interviewed expressed a sense of ambivalence about continuing to work after getting married. They frequently characterized themselves as torn between their sense of responsibility toward their family duties and their desire to remain on the job. They typically described talking with family members around the time they became engaged or pregnant and receiving advice (or pressure) to quit. Most of the women believed that their primary responsibility was to care for their husbands and children. Several women mentioned that their husbands had memories of being alone in the afternoons while their mothers worked, and these men didn't want their own children to have the same experience. The majority of women characterized themselves as having made the decision themselves, rather than being forced to quit, but most expressed some sadness about leaving their work.

Some of those who left their jobs came to regret their decision, as we saw in the case of Chihiro. Another person who expressed regret was

Mari. A forceful and ambitious woman, who described herself as really good at "ordering people to do things," Mari had been promoted rapidly at a large company and by age 25 was already supervising ten employees. Nevertheless, she quit working when she became engaged, with the support of her fiancé and her parents. According to her, the decision was based on her belief that "my husband could demonstrate his ability 120 percent if I stayed home for him." Although he did become very successful at his job, she experienced great frustration with life as a housewife and sometimes found herself thinking that she should have been the one to stay in the business world instead of him. While committed for the present time to promoting her children's educational progress, she dreamed of some day opening her own store and eventually "having franchises all over Japan." Mari, like so many other mothers, seemed to respond to cultural expectations about women's role by "choosing" to stay at home, but then found herself frustrated with the role of wife and mother. Even though these women were motivated to undertake child rearing with a seriousness born of their perfectionist standards, they longed for more challenge and stimulation.

[handwritten margin note: choose to stay home, but then regret it almost]

[handwritten margin note: like a job would give them]

Returning to the Workplace

For the women we interviewed, the idea of going back to work became increasingly attractive as their children became older and more independent. The logistics of returning to work were complicated by the fact that most of their husbands opposed their wives working or accepted it only if they were able to carry out all of their household responsibilities in addition to taking on a job (see Chapter 6 for more on this issue). The issue of child care did not pose a severe problem for those women who wanted to work part time. Most preschools offered an extended care program, available on an "as-needed" basis for an additional charge. At the elementary school level, after-school programs were available in many cases. Sometimes women's work interfered with their ability to take their children to lessons, but they often found it possible to ask an older sibling to take on this responsibility or to schedule lessons in the late afternoon or on weekends.

[handwritten margin note: high expectations]

Many of the women wanted to return to work for the companionship and stimulation it afforded, as well as the extra money. Like Miyuki and Chihiro, they expressed a desire to supplement their husband's income in order to pay for their children's after-school activities and supplementary classes. Yuri, saddled with a bad marriage, was particularly eager to supplement her husband's income, because she disliked having to ask him for anything:

[handwritten margin note: help support family too]

[handwritten margin note: & own spending $$$]

My husband makes only a certain amount of money each month because he is a sarariiman. On top of that, our relationship is not so good. It is hard for me to ask him to buy me something. And I would be mad if he refused to do so.... Now, I can afford my own things.... As for my child, for example, since my husband's salary is set, if she said she wanted to take ballet lessons and I didn't work, then she wouldn't be able to take lessons.

As we saw in the cases of Miyuki and Chihiro, many of the women found staying at home all day boring and stressful, and were eager to take a job no matter how menial. This was also true for Junko, whose interest in the fashion industry had been sidetracked into accounting in high school. When her younger child started attending preschool, she wanted to find a part-time job in a dress shop, but her husband told her not to "be silly," and insisted that she could make more money helping him handle the accounting in the family business. Once again, she felt compelled to set aside her own preferences and heed someone else's request: "Ever since then I have had no choice but to go there and help them."

Eager to earn more money and find work that did not involve her husband, she decided to take a home-based piecework job in addition to her accounting work. She told us that the job was "interesting" and that she found it "useful to get rid of stress," even though it was not particularly remunerative and the chemicals in the materials she worked with irritated her skin. She felt motivated by the fact that her paycheck directly reflected the amount of time she put into the job, and she was happy that she didn't need to get dressed up or deal with co-workers. She thought this job helped her children understand the value of money, because they could see what was involved in earning a paycheck. Taking this job – however humble it may have been – was one of the few instances when Junko had been able to make a plan and implement it without being criticized or derailed by someone who thought she should be doing something else. That fact alone must have contributed to her enjoyment of it.

Are Working Moms Better Moms?

As we have seen, prior to taking a job, some of the women worried that working would undercut their ability to care effectively for their husband and children. Few husbands other than Asako's and Masayo's were willing to do any housework or take on any serious child-rearing responsibility. How did these mothers manage it? What was the effect of working on their daily routines and, more important, on their sense of competence as a parent?

As we have seen, Miyuki and Junko both thought that working helped them to become better mothers by reducing their stress and helping them model the virtues of hard work and thrift. Reiko was even more emphatic in describing the positive effects of work on her ability to be a good mother. She had been very unhappy as a full-time housewife when her children were young: "I had shut myself in the house, so I was really irritated, and so I took out my stress on the kids, and the kids didn't listen to me. We had this vicious cycle going on." She described herself as almost having a "child-rearing neurosis." She ultimately decided that it was "not right to devote all of myself to children, while killing myself and what I wanted to do." Against the strong wishes of her husband and the advice of her mother, she started working in direct sales for a cosmetic company. Through this work she was able to meet women with children of all ages, and thus had "many opportunities to listen to their stories." She believed that these conversations helped her to reflect on and improve her *shitsuke*: "I used to scold my children in a half-hearted way. I was tentative, and my kids didn't really understand why I was upset. But now, I don't withdraw. I make sure and tell them what I need to say."

Reiko identified other benefits of her work as well. She enjoyed being able to pay for her children's supplementary classes and activities, and she also believed that the job benefited her children by allowing them to see their mother "working hard and having a dream," and getting rewarded for it.

A few of the mothers pointed out some of the drawbacks of being employed. For Hiromi, who moved from part- to full-time work when her younger child entered first grade, the motivation for working was financial. Her husband's salary could not cover the growing financial needs of their family, particularly their mortgage and the cost of their children's supplementary classes and sports activities. She chose an evening shift, in order to be home during the afternoon when her children came back from school. But this grueling schedule left her tired and emotionally unstable, and she regretted that her children could not have friends over if no one was available to supervise them. Although her husband was emotionally supportive, she found it difficult to live up to her own high standards for being a good mother.

Conclusions

Mary Brinton (1993) has written that the role of Japanese women in the workplace is constrained in two fundamental ways: first, by early socialization experiences in the family that discourage women from pursuing serious professional work, and second, by workplace policies that route them into

· discouraged
· gov't (?) policies

low-paying, part-time work. Our findings support this conclusion and add new dimensions.

To begin with, women are disadvantaged by the way that higher education is funded in Japan. The government contributes relatively little to education compared to other similar countries. In 2004, overall government expenditure on education represented 4.8 percent of the GDP, as compared to 7.4 percent in the United States and 7.2 percent in Korea (OECD Factbook, 2008). In Japan, the majority of students attend private universities, but the vast majority of the government's contribution to higher education goes to the national universities. Figures from 2000 show Japanese students covering 40 percent of the total cost of higher education, whereas in the United States, students covered just 26 percent of the cost (Asonuma, 2002). Given the heavy cost burden, Japanese families weigh the benefits of a college education carefully. This has meant that for females, families frequently make the decision to fund two rather than four years of college, thereby curtailing their access to most professions, which require a four-year degree.

A second type of disadvantage for women is related to role perfectionism, both at work and with regard to child rearing. Because of stringent workplace demands and high standards for *shitsuke* and supporting children's schooling, most women believe they cannot balance full-time employment and child rearing when their children are young (Yu, 2001). Their plight is further complicated by the fact that few can count on receiving any assistance from their husbands. Indeed, according to a recent government report, Japanese men in double-income families contributed only 12.6 percent of the housework and child-rearing hours, compared to figures of 37 to 40 percent in the United States, Australia, Sweden, and Norway (Japanese Cabinet Office, 2007).

We found that when the women in our study sought to return to work after their children entered school, some of them encountered company policies that discriminated against older applicants. The discriminatory practices that Miyuki reported encountering are now officially prohibited under the most recent version of the Employment Measure Act. However, the law has not succeeded in eliminating the widespread practice of favoring young applicants (Hamaguchi, 200; Sakuraba, 2009). One reason for its ineffectiveness is that the law contains many exemptions, allowing employers to hire young workers for a wide variety of reasons. For instance, the law permits employers to "recruit only new graduates who are youth, or below certain ages, in order to give them the opportunity to develop and improve their occupational abilities over a long period of service" (Sakuraba, 2009, p. 62).

This type of exemption could be used by a preschool director to justify a disinclination to hire older, more experienced teachers such as Miyuki.

If they did manage to find a job, our participants faced the difficult obstacle of figuring out how to manage their household responsibilities (usually single-handedly) while also holding down a job. They came face to face with the extraordinary demands placed on employees in a country where even part-time jobs require an average of 30 hours a week (Jolivet, 1997). And they also faced the possibility that in the future they might need to quit if their parents or in-laws needed their care; without long-term prospects, it was more difficult to commit wholeheartedly to a demanding job.

As Miyuki's story makes clear, however, the women themselves saw a number of benefits to working before they got married and when their children were no longer babies. Having a job affected not only their general sense of well-being but also their parenting self-efficacy. They could contribute financially to enable their children to take lessons and participate in sports. They felt calmer and less stressed in their interactions with their children. They had opportunities to connect with other women and obtain information about children as well as to receive emotional support. These findings are further supported by the results of a longitudinal study finding that maternal employment before children were three years old was not associated with Japanese children's externalizing problems (e.g., disobedience, social aggression) or depression at age ten (Sugawara, 2005).

And the women in our study do not seem to be exceptional in their desire to work even if conditions make it difficult to do so. A survey of 872 Japanese women, reported by Choe, Bumpass, and Tsuya (2004), found that 83 percent of full-time housewives said they wanted to find work. A report published by the Japanese government in 2004 concluded that when the percentage of unemployed women with young children who wanted to work was added to the percentage of women who were actually working, the characteristic "dip" in the employment M-curve disappeared, making Japan look similar to other countries of comparable wealth and education levels (Japan Cabinet Office, 2004).

In spite of their interest in working, the women in our study expressed an understanding of the hardships associated with full-time employment. Their own early work experiences had left them with the clear impression that in Japan the job comes first, and they were not willing to make this type of sacrifice. We did not get the sense that most women longed to work under the same conditions endured by their husbands, even if it were possible. Our findings thus suggest that policies designed to expand women's participation in the workplace need to include basic changes that make work more compatible with family life, for men as well as women.

Our data augment the analysis of Rosenbluth (2007), who found a strong statistical association across many developed countries between a *higher* national birth rate and a *greater* female participation in the workplace. She argues that most women prefer to work as well as raise a family, but that if they have to choose between the two, they will suppress their wish for more children in order to participate in the workplace, and thereby gain "household bargaining leverage and exit options that come with an outside source of income" (p. 5). According to her analysis, women faced with very challenging employment conditions will not stay home and have babies, but rather will spend more effort "to get in the door, climb the promotion ladders, and struggle against glass ceilings" (p. 4).

While we agree that Japanese women are highly motivated to work, our data suggest that they are not particularly worried about having "exit options" from their marriages. Only one woman in our sample – Yuri – hinted at having considered divorce, and she seemed to have rejected the idea, at least for the present. But she did seem motivated by the notion of "household bargaining leverage" in the sense that she preferred to pay for household incidentals and her daughter's lessons herself rather than having to ask her husband for the money. A couple of women, including Miyuki, mentioned that they wanted to have some kind of job skills in case their husband died or lost his job. And as the story of Miyuki and Chihiro suggests, Japanese women do not seem to be struggling against glass ceilings, so much as struggling to get in at the ground level. But their determination to pursue a life that includes more than staying at home with children is clearly signaled by their general disinclination to jump early and often into the business of making babies.

What are the future prospects for women in the Japanese workplace? With the proportion of workers continuing to shrink relative to the retiree population, there is a growing need for women to participate in the labor market. Whether or not they can enter and remain in that market depends on whether the government can improve the child-care system, develop and enforce policies that make the workplace more amenable to employees who are also active parents, and devise an elder-care system that does not hinge on the unpaid labor of middle-aged female relatives. Some opportunities may also accrue to women from the current dismantling of Japan's lifetime employment system, which has tended to disadvantage those leaving and then re-entering the workplace.

Rosenbluth (2007) has summed up the future for women and employment with a somewhat grisly yet ultimately optimistic metaphor: "We can expect the eventual demise of lifetime employment contracts for core male employees and, as a result, easier access for women into the labor market. Japanese fertility rates may be in for some recovery, but we have to wait first for the old institutions to gasp their last breath. They are still gasping" (p. 16). As we have seen in this chapter, many Japanese women will indeed be happy when these "patients" take their last breath.

[handwritten note:] must wait for older, traditional values/opinions to "die out" before things can improve.

10

Women and Family Life: Ideology, Experience, and Agency

As the preservers of home life, our women are still held subject to the old family traditions, while modern capitalism, on its invasion into our country, has ruthlessly taken advantage of their cheap labor and patient and inexhaustible industry. (Mishima, 1941, p. 232)

In her memoir, writer Sumie Seo Mishima calls attention to changes in women's lives during the first three decades of the twentieth century, when the new economic and political forces of the modernizing society were transforming traditional family structures and cultural patterns. Remarkably, Mishima's observations also ring true in today's Japan: women continue to fulfill a cultural mandate to take on nearly all the domestic responsibilities for their families and corporate interests continue to expect women to fill in as cheap part-time workers at their beck and call. And yet, we can also detect significant changes in women's lives, beginning with a simple demographic fact: women are increasingly postponing marriage and parenthood, and limiting their family to one or two children. Many dream, too, about having professional careers, although their plans are frequently derailed by a combination of domestic pressures and workplace exigencies.

The story of Japan's rapid transformation from an isolated federation of fiefdoms to a modern industrialized democracy is nothing short of extraordinary. An essential aspect of this transformation was the government's manipulation of family structure and family practices to create an allegiance to the modern state and to harness the energy and competencies of women. The government continues to try to shape the contours of family life, with strategies ranging from sharp criticism of women for not bearing more children to the imposition of tax penalties on dual-career couples. Thus, it is tempting to agree with Bernstein's observation about Japanese government's manipulation of family life: "The issue of how women should behave and *always decided (for them)*

what they should do and should not do has rarely been left either to chance or to individual choice" (1991, p. 13).]

But, while government policies and business interests have clearly exerted a powerful influence on women's lives over these decades, Japanese women have themselves exerted personal agency to create their own choices and possibilities. My goal in this book is to investigate how individual "meaning making" and action are affected and enabled – not unilaterally determined – by the surrounding social structures and cultural models (see also Frank, 2006; Swidler, 2001). Accordingly, I have focused on how individual women interpret available cultural models of parenting within institutional constraints and opportunities. This analytic frame has given us a way to understand the reasons why many women in Japan appear to derive much anxiety and little satisfaction from the role of mother, and yet others find a way to become not necessarily the kind of mother idealized by government officials or by school administrators but rather – in the words of Miyuki – to be "my kind of mother."

Cultural Models of Parenting: Ambitious Standards for Mothers

I began this volume with an exploration of women's views about what it takes to be a good mother. The mothers in our sample were quick to identify their own child-rearing practices as a crucial ingredient determining the success of their children's development. Their vision of what it takes to be a good mother contained some traditional elements as well as others that appeared to be more attuned to contemporary norms. We saw the theme of emotional self-regulation emerge again and again in these narratives. These women believed that ideal mothers were busy, confident, and above all cheerful. They themselves sought to achieve a balance between the older custom of watching from afar (*mimamoru*) and having a more hands-on, interactive style. And, they hoped to develop a consistent and effective disciplinary style characterized by calm reasoning rather than emotional response or corporal punishment. Mothers' preoccupation with emotional self-regulation is a historical legacy of premodern Japan, when suppression of personal desires and emotions was expected of all women, but especially young mothers. Other attributes of the ideal mother – particularly the focus on fostering communication – seem to represent a more contemporary approach.

What type of child were these women hoping to raise? Overall, the impression that we gained from listening to them talk about their goals for their children is that they were hoping to rear a normal, average child, not an extraordinary one. The goal of most of them was to help their children develop the social competence needed to get along with others. They hoped to inculcate such attributes as empathy, compassion, and sensitivity to others. They were strongly motivated to impress upon their children the desire and the ability to avoid causing trouble to others. At the same time, they did not want their children to be passive and dull – rather, they valued children's energy and wanted them to be assertive and accepting of challenge, especially if they were boys. They did not value behavioral compliance if it was not accompanied by an understanding and acceptance of why a certain behavior was desirable. They considered academic competence desirable, but many parents did not strongly aspire for their children to pursue higher education. On the whole, these findings are quite consistent with earlier work, and they suggest that parents' ideas about what it means to be a "good child" have remained fairly stable over the past 50 years in spite of such social shifts as a decrease in family size and a stronger emphasis on individualistic achievement in school (Hendry, 1986; White & LeVine, 1986).

Some of the women found it difficult to put the old models of child rearing into play. It was hard for them to adhere to the traditional norms of endurance and self-repression, even if they thought that they should do so. Chihiro, for example, was doing her best to suppress her own desire to have a job that made use of her intellectual abilities and talent for leadership. Rather than crediting herself for the strong self-discipline this required, she criticized herself for failing to feel more warmly toward her daughter. Junko, too, was attempting to suppress her personal needs, and criticizing herself for lapses in her ability to do so. She was enduring a profoundly unsatisfying marriage to a man who made little attempt to communicate or interact with his family, yet she criticized herself for losing her temper with her children rather than acknowledging all that she was successfully doing to hold her family together.

In addition to these specific ideas and ideals pertaining to child rearing, the women in our study also drew upon more general cultural tools such as the tradition of self-reflection, or *hansei*. Traditionally, the practice of *hansei* involved comparison of oneself to an ideal model, with the goal of using the model as a guide to one's future actions. While every mother seemed to participate in the practice of *hansei*, we noted some crucial individual differences between mothers who were able to use self-evaluation in a constructive way and mothers who were unable to move beyond self-recrimination and ended up floundering as they searched for alternative solutions to the problems that were bothering them or their children.

The women who were perfectionists in their quest to be a good mother often had a hard time feeling efficacious as parents. Role perfectionism led some mothers to exhausting and extreme behavior, as exemplified by Yuri's frantic consultations about how to breastfeed her newborn daughter or Mari's dogged insistence that her son fill every spare moment with a supplementary course or lesson. When their unstinting efforts did not pay off as anticipated, these mothers were subject to emotional self-recrimination and often felt angry and disappointed with their children as well.

In contrast, other women seemed more accepting of their imperfections and mistakes. Miyuki provided an example of this latter pattern, acknowledging that she sometimes lost her temper with her children but excusing these outbursts as an inevitable consequence of interacting with three lively children 365 days a year. She assumed that her children were resilient and could withstand her temper tantrums and did not let feelings of guilt or anxiety stand in the way of pursuing her parenting goals.

Another trap for some mothers was buying in to the cultural norm of following a model or a blueprint for how to be a good parent. Some mothers experienced a sense of uneasiness and anxiety because they could never seem to find the "one right way" to accomplish a child-rearing objective. For example, Junko castigated herself for not knowing the right way to scold her children and compared her lack of skill to the more professional approach of preschool teachers. Chihiro repeatedly asserted that she felt sorry for her children because of her lack of parenting skills and observed that she lacked the "qualifications" to be a good parent.

In contrast, higher efficacy mothers preoccupied themselves less with comparing themselves to a universal standard and were more open to pursuing the pathway that seemed to work for themselves and their children. Miyuki and Asako, for example, focused on trying to understand their own particular children and figuring out how to tailor their parenting to meet their children's needs, and did not worry about how they were doing relative to other mothers. In short, women who believed that there are "many kinds of mother" were able to avoid the self-recrimination that accompanies the futile quest to copy a generic standard.

It may be tempting to assume that the more efficacious mothers, like Asako and Miyuki, were somehow more "individualistic" and therefore more "Westernized" whereas the less confident mothers who tried to stick to an established standard were more "traditional." In fact, the notion of ritual formalism allows for individual ingenuity on the part of the learner, who can develop an idiosyncratic approach to a task even while remaining within established parameters. Hori (1996) illustrates this notion with the example of a monk preparing vegetables for the evening meal; there is a clear standard for what the dish is supposed to look like and how it is supposed to taste, but the exact process by which the product is achieved is up to the creativity of the cook. By the same token, women like Asako and Miyuki who confidently sought their own way of rearing socially responsible, well-adjusted children were not necessarily less "traditional" than those who were desperately looking for a child-rearing "how-to" manual. Rather, they were able to utilize culturally constructed strategies – including self-reflection – to come up with their own approach to rearing their children.

What I am arguing here is that Japanese mothers hold high standards of parenting that lead them to perceive it as grueling and difficult to manage successfully (see also Hirao, 2007a). Additionally, the clashes and inconsistencies between older and newer cultural models of parenting can themselves create stress and anxiety as women seek to reflect on their actions and evaluate themselves according to self-generated standards. And finally, the general tendency to engage in intense and frequent self-evaluation *vis-à-vis* an ideal model puts women in danger of succumbing to self-recrimination and subsequent floundering unless they have some ability to forgive their imperfections and make room for an idiosyncratic approach to child rearing. In sum, these culturally based norms constitute one important set of factors that contribute to contemporary women's ambivalent feelings about parenting and family life.

The Role of Social Support and Criticism

A central goal of this book has been to examine the social context in which women take on the day-to-day activities of parenting. In Japan, as we have seen, many people accept the idea that negative evaluation by others can lead one to heightened effort and improved performance; this cultural model underlies the notion of "mutual polishing" in the Zen Buddhist tradition (Hori, 1996). In contrast, within Western psychological theory, the assumption is that other people's positive rather than negative judgments give rise to a positive self-evaluation, which in turn motivates an individual to persist and do well. Most notably, Albert Bandura has proposed that a key determinant of self-efficacy is the evaluation and support provided by others (Bandura, 1997).

While parents – and mothers in particular – receive a lot of criticism in many societies, Japanese women seem to be subjected to an extraordinary degree of excoriation. At the highest levels of government, politicians worry about the declining birth rate, which they routinely attribute to women's laziness or lack of patriotism. In one famous instance, former prime minister Yoshiro Mori asserted that women without children shouldn't be given government pensions when they become elderly, because "they haven't contributed anything to society"]("Severe Acute Ridiculousness Syndrome," 2003). As Jolivet (1997) documents in detail, physicians and educators have written countless books in which nearly every childhood ailment and problem is attributed to mothers' ignorance or laziness. Many preschool directors also tend to view mothers as young and clueless, or as narcissistic and irresponsible (Holloway, 2000). In very recent times, "monster parents," as they have been dubbed in the media, have come under attack for openly criticizing teachers whom they perceive as ineffective ("Japan's 'Monster' Parents Take Centre Stage," 2008).

Certainly, it is worth considering whether this critical treatment is one factor contributing to women's discouragement about family life and disinclination to engage in child rearing. In this book, I have examined the support and criticism that women have received from various quarters, beginning with their most intimate relations and moving to more distal institutions. Of key importance was the way that the women interpreted messages they received from others and the effect of these interpretations on their perceptions of parenting and family life.

I focused first on the degree of support and encouragement that women experienced as children and adolescents from their own parents. Most of the women felt loved and protected by their own mothers. They commonly viewed their mothers as doing the best they could under difficult circumstances created by such things as poverty or an unappreciative husband. In contrast, remarkably few of the women experienced a close relationship with their fathers. At best, they perceived their fathers as distant but well-intentioned men preoccupied with earning a living. Several reported receiving harsh treatment that bordered on abuse from their fathers, and the number of fathers who appeared to struggle with alcoholism was noteworthy. The ultimate effect of such difficult family circumstances appeared to depend on the women's ability to understand and come to terms with the way they were treated as children. Women who had come to realize the ways in which their parents' behavior had reflected affection and commitment to their children's welfare were better able to resolve their feelings of anger and approach parenting with a more confident attitude.

The educational and vocational opportunities that these women were given when they were growing up seemed to hinge on the gender-role stereotypes of their parents – particularly their fathers – in combination with the family's financial status. Some of the women were prevented from following a preferred career path because one or both parents deemed it unsuitable for a woman. Chihiro had to curtail her ambition to be an architect when her father insisted that she live at home during college so that she could be protected from loneliness and financial hardship, and later she quit her job partially in response to his concern that it would have a deleterious effect on her health if she tried to combine work and married life.

Other women did not experience any barriers in this regard or received support from their mothers even if not from their fathers. Asako's father did not believe that she should devote herself to soccer, but her mother ignored his misgivings and the criticism of others, and helped her to reach her goals. Masayo's father had refused to allow her to go to college, but when he died unexpectedly and government funds became available to cover the cost of tuition, her mother was willing to go along with her educational goals.

Some of the women told us that their parents tried to ensure that they would see a financial return on their investment in tuition for their children. Few of the parents expected their daughters to remain in the workplace after getting married, and most were aware that jobs for less educated women were more prevalent than jobs for those with advanced degrees. Pragmatic reasons such as these explained why Junko's parents were reluctant to spend money on a vocational program in fashion design and instead enrolled her against her own wishes in an accounting program. However, some parents wanted to be sure their daughters had the ability to be financially independent and were willing to take on debt in order to fund their higher education. Having experienced firsthand the difficulty of making ends meet without an advanced degree, Miyuki's parents took out a loan to purchase the piano she needed in order to pursue her dream of becoming a preschool teacher and then provided the financial resources to meet the tuition payments for her two-year college program.

The fate of these women in terms of their ability to pursue a chosen career thus seems to have depended on such factors as whether or not their father had strong ideas about appropriate jobs for a woman and whether or not their mother was willing to advocate on their behalf. Some were able to obtain a college degree and find a job doing what they enjoyed, at least for the brief time prior to getting married. Even for these relatively lucky individuals, the lifetime impact of this vocational training and experience was less profound due to the pressure to quit once they got married. It took extraordinary determination to continue along a path deemed unsuitable by family members and friends. As we saw, only Masayo – the teacher – succeeded in remaining in her chosen field after having children. The others saw little hope of reconciling the demands of career and family. Being faced with the stark choice between having a family and following a career path certainly contributed to their trepidation about marrying and having children.

Turning to the support and criticism that the women in our study were [least supportive] receiving in their current family context, we saw that <u>husbands turned out to be the most crucial actors</u>. This finding was surprising to us in light of many accounts downplaying the (salience) of marital relations in Japan. Contrary to the dominant stereotype, these women were preoccupied with their husbands and saw them as having a significant effect on their emotional well-being and sense of child-rearing efficacy. But unfortunately for many women, their husbands were frequently insufficiently attuned to their needs and often failed to provide the desired support.

Most of the women did not expect their husbands to participate extensively in housework, but they did want them to be actively involved with their children. The women also wanted their husbands to provide emotional support, mostly by listening carefully and sympathetically to their worries. [wanted husband to be able to give advice] The women hoped that by talking over matters with their husbands they would gain some perspective on their problems and develop confidence that they could come up with an adequate response. To a lesser extent, they expected to benefit from their husbands' specific suggestions and advice.

However, many of the women were disappointed with the quality and quantity of support provided by their husbands. Some described their husbands as immature and lazy. They characterized them as childlike and felt that wives were put in the position of nagging husbands to engage in basic [like ch. 6] daily life routines. Most of the women attributed these problems to their husband's own character rather than seeing their behavior as a function of structural conditions such as workplace demands. They also commonly reported that their husbands were emotionally and behaviorally disengaged, and they tended to respond to this treatment with sadness, loneliness, and even rage. In addition to feeling sorry that their own emotional needs were [No support from hubby → sad wife/mother → affects child(ren)] not being met, they worried that their children were being shortchanged as well. They also worried that their own precarious emotional state was undermining their ability to be cheerful and emotionally available to their children.

The unhappy wives were stymied about how to improve their situation. Those who did not find fulfillment in their marriage seemed to focus primarily on managing their own emotions. They did not report seeking help from professionals, and while they did not express much hope for change in the future, they did not express a serious intention of dissolving the marriage. This strong sense of dissatisfaction with their married life gives us another clue to Japanese women's increasing desire to postpone family life.

Our interview data revealed that <u>a few couples did actually function as a team</u>, frequently discussing their children and devising solutions for dealing with problems. This form of support from husbands seemed to enable these women to customize their child rearing, which helped them avoid the pitfalls inherent in taking a "standardized" approach to parenting. In general, these couples seem to be pushing toward some new ideas about marriage, moving away from an exclusive focus on economic stability and child rearing and moving toward a goal of emotional interdependence characterized by frequent and intimate communication.

The role of friends deserves a more complete investigation than we were able to manage in the current study. Remarkably little has been written about Japanese women's relations with their friends, either in contemporary times or in the past. On one hand, the literature suggests that Japanese women are now being encouraged to view friends as a source of support for parenting. Sasagawa (2006) has observed that, "Mothers are no longer expected to endure hardships in raising their children as they used to be, but are now encouraged to enjoy a 'happy' child-bound life by making friends and taking part in peer groups" (p. 143). On the other hand, the tensions that women experience with each other in the workplace are one clue that close relationships among women are not always supportive. Similarly, our data indicate that while some mothers derived comfort from talking with their peers about their family problems, others were wary of getting into a competitive relation with other mothers or falling into an intimacy that could then somehow be used against them (Yamamoto, Holloway, & Suzuki, 2009).

Institutional Factors Affecting Families: Demands from the Schools and the Workplace

Observers of Japanese society who note the relatively low status of Japanese women in terms of professional opportunity and political power (Hausmann, Tyson, & Zahidi, 2006) often predict that they will eventually "catch up" to women in Western countries, under the assumption of a standard, linear process of social evolution. Indeed, like their counterparts in Europe and the United States, Japanese women have generally gained greater access to education, have acquired control over their own fertility, and have expanded their legal rights. In spite of all these similarities, there are also some key factors that distinguish family life in Japan from that of Western capitalist democracies. One of the most important pertains to the strong alliance between government and corporate interests and its role in shaping the lives of men and women. Eager to move from the chaos of the 1940s to the wealth and stability of the 1970s, the Japanese government was willing to support corporate initiatives by structuring the tax code to ensure a pool of cheap part-time labor (chiefly women). Corporations attracted male employees with a guarantee of lifetime employment, and paid them enough to support a family on a single salary.

These structural features of the ("iron triangle") of corporations, government bureaucrats, and politicians have had a distinctive impact on family life. Certain characteristics of the corporations – including their demand for continuous service and exclusive allegiance from workers – have made it difficult for women to move in and out of full-time work. The failure of the government to pressure corporations into creating a more humane workplace with good conditions and reasonable hours has resulted in a decreasing rather than increasing interest in full-time employment on the part of women. In our data, we saw reluctance on the part of many women to take on full-time work when their children were still young. We also saw examples of women who wanted to remain in full-time jobs but had been pressured to leave them, as well as of women who wanted to re-enter the workforce after taking time off for child rearing but found that they were considered too old or otherwise unqualified for full-time work.

Most of the women in our sample wanted to work at least part-time in order to supplement the family income; in particular they saw their own employment as making it possible to enroll their children in supplementary classes and lessons. Some enjoyed the feeling of independence that came with earning a paycheck, particularly because they no longer had to ask their husbands about personal purchases for themselves or their children. Perhaps the most beneficial aspect of working, according to these women, was that it gave them the opportunity to interact with other people and see a bit of the outside world. We saw in the case of Miyuki that getting a job – albeit just as a clerk in a convenience store – boosted her confidence in her ability to learn new things. But it also contributed in a positive sense to her family life, as she felt more refreshed and energetic at home when she was not "cooped up" with the children all day every day.

School is another institution that deeply affected the lives of women in our study. Historically, to the extent that participation in the new corporate world required higher education credentials, Japanese mothers in the postwar years were increasingly asked to spend substantial time supporting their children through the education system. The schools continue to make detailed demands on mothers: to prepare materials for the children's use in the classroom, to regulate children's emotions and activities so that they can withstand the demanding school schedule, to monitor the children's homework, and to monitor (and fund) their participation in supplementary classes and lessons (Hirao, 2007b).

We saw that mothers' education level and family income influenced how they approached these educational activities. Highly educated women like Chihiro felt comfortable interacting with teachers and other school staff. She was a frequent visitor and active volunteer in her children's classrooms. Women who had not attended college, like Junko, were more likely to doubt their own understanding of educational matters and less likely to spend time at their children's school. Lower SES women more often faced financial pressures that prevented them from providing all the educational experiences and materials that they thought their children needed. Those like Hiromi who took on full-time work to meet these expenses then found they had less time to manage all the responsibilities engendered by this complex network of educational institutions.

The Japanese education system has frequently been praised and rightly commands the attention of education researchers throughout the world. However, when it comes to the role of parents, the system has some features that bear critical scrutiny. Our data point to two aspects that are problematic for some mothers. First, the precision and intensity of the requirements schools make of mothers are somewhat unusual, as is the recrimination that is directed at mothers who do not comply in a manner that schools deem satisfactory (Allison, 1991; Kazui, 1997). And second, the "top-down" nature of demands for school involvement – in which school officials position themselves as the experts and position mothers as novices – plays into the mothers' tendency to look to others for a guide or blueprint on how to interact with their children. Mothers who succumb to the "manual syndrome" in which they try to follow the manual rather than trust themselves to find the best way are more susceptible to anxiety and lack of efficacy in their parenting abilities.

Implications for Practitioners Seeking to Support Japanese Mothers

The insights gleaned from the thoughtful mothers in our study have a number of implications for practitioners in the fields of psychology, social welfare, and education. In recent years, municipal governments in Japan have initiated various types of programs to support mothers and help them address anxieties or "neuroses" about child rearing, but these playgroups and classes tend to promote the notion that child rearing should be "standardized and systematized" (Sasagawa, 2006, p. 142). Most activities are run by individuals with professional credentials, whose stance is to "teach mothers that they need to be instructed on how to behave as mothers" (p. 143). This fact-based, top-down approach to "the 'standard' way of raising children" may

create a temporary feeling of security among some mothers who "no longer need to worry about how big their children's preschool bag should be"
(p. 143). But, the cost of this expert-driven, standards-oriented approach may
be high. The findings from our research suggest that rather than giving them
a child-rearing *kata* for attaining this standard, it would be better to support
women's own efforts to articulate what it means to be "my kind of mother."
An approach that validates women's own knowledge of their children might
be used to break down the novice vs. professional dichotomy and serve to
bolster mothers' confidence rather than undermining it.

A second set of implications concerns the practice and promise of psychotherapy. One particularly interesting aspect of this research was the
paradoxical juxtaposition between mothers' bitterness regarding their
own thwarted childhood dreams and their acceptance of a restricted and
gender-stereotypical scenario for the future of their sons and daughters.
As mental health services become more commonly accepted in Japan,
women may have more opportunities for analysis of their own childhood
experiences, which may lead to a more clear and consistent integration of
their thoughts, experiences, values, and actions. We also noted the sense
of anger and loneliness expressed by many women in talking about (and
to) their husbands. While they reported that it was sometimes possible to
vent these frustrations in conversations with friends, they often added that
it was not always advisable to be candid with friends and that they sometimes experienced feelings of competition or inadequacy. The private and
structured opportunity for self-exploration in a therapeutic relationship
may offer possibilities for support and growth beyond what is afforded by
peer relationships.

Given the various institutionalized inequities in Japan that systematically
oppress women, the notion of offering them individual psychotherapy may
seem at best inadequate and at worst a way to drain the energy from wom-
en's discontent rather than mobilize it to work for social change. However,
Japanese women seem to be more attuned to an individualistic approach to
solving their problems, and less inclined to work toward broad social change
(Schoppa, 2006). Individual psychotherapy may help Japanese women find a
private solution to their problems and a way to satisfy their deep need to feel
cared for as well as to care for others (Borovoy, 2005). At the present time,
the feminist movement is not particularly powerful in Japan, nor are there
any other strong collective entities advocating for institutional change to
benefit women. Noting Japanese women's longing to escape the repressive
aspects of their lives at home by moving to the "West," Kelsky (2001) suggests that their actions imply an "intensive focus on the self and rejection of

communal identity, whether it is derived from national or feminist solidarity" (p. 221). As she eloquently concludes, "This revolution begins and ends in solitude, or at least not in the company of other Japanese" and can be seen as "'social movement' that denies sociality, a vision of emancipation that is relentlessly private" (p. 223).

The themes of alcoholism and domestic violence were more salient in these women's narratives than one might expect in a society that is often described as prioritizing interpersonal harmony. Indeed, [the strong societal pressure to conceal problems of this sort contributes to the difficulty of understanding and ameliorating them (Borovoy, 2005).]Often characterized as a private family matter, domestic violence has only recently been acknowledged as a public problem in Japan (Goodman, 2006; Nakamura, 2003; Shoji, 2005). In our study, the mothers who had grown up in troubled families worried that these patterns would be replicated in their interactions with their own children. Psychotherapy is, of course, a powerful way of addressing these issues. In addition, it seems that broader public health and perhaps legal initiatives should be considered to address the problems of alcoholism and domestic violence.

A third set of implications pertains to the ways labor policies can be altered to support rather than detract from family life. For women to be able to move in and out of the workforce, a number of serious changes have to be implemented in the Japanese workplace. First, as Rosenbluth (2007) has argued, corporate policy should stop making experience within a single firm the main criterion for advancement and remuneration, and it should start acknowledging experience garnered in other workplaces. Additionally, companies should reduce or eliminate such practices as mandatory overtime, after-hours socializing, frequent job transfers, and pressure not to take vacation days.

The government should step up its enforcement of the Employment Measure Act to discourage firms from discriminating against older workers (Hamaguchi, 2007; Sakuraba, 2007). The government should also continue taking action against companies that fail to offer equitable opportunities and remuneration to males and females. In 1997, progress was made in strengthening the Equal Employment Opportunity Law (EEOL) to enable parents to petition employers to exempt them from night shifts and to work shorter hours, and by encouraging employers to rehire workers who were attempting to return to work after taking a family-related leave. Further legislation approved in 2001 increased the penalties for companies that retaliate against parents who try to take child-care leave, and contained provisions addressed at fathers as well as mothers, such as a requirement that parents of young children can insist on limiting their overtime to 150 hours a year. However, employer discrimination continues to be directed toward women who get pregnant or take time off to care for their children and, as Schoppa (2007) writes, "the percentage of women in full-time, regular jobs staying in those jobs through marriage and child rearing is actually *lower* than it was in 1992!" (p. 178, emphasis in original).

Until jobs are structured in a way that makes them compatible with family life, it is not only unlikely that women will be able to participate in a meaningful way in the workplace but also unlikely that men will be able to participate in a meaningful way in the family. Even so, permitting men to be more available does not ensure that they will be more involved in family life. Several persistent stereotypes about males and females that we noted in this research need to be addressed: the idea that boys are somehow cuter than girls and more deserving of attention, the perception that young women are vulnerable while young men are tough enough to endure the challenges of living away from home, and the view that women are naturally more competent parents than men.

Theoretical Implications for Cultural Psychology

Our work revealed a number of cultural themes that guided the women in our study in their attempts to work out how to be good parents. They drew upon culturally constructed notions of what it means to be a good mother, a good child, and a good husband. Their approach also reflected culturally distinctive ideas about how to engage in self-reflection (*hansei*), when to stick to a routine (*kata*) and when to depart from it, and how high to set the bar for one's own performance in a role.

My study departs from some previous work on cultural models by highlighting how these models change over time, how they are interpreted and put into play by the individual, and how they are manipulated by powerful institutions. One fascinating example of historical change pertains to the evolving definition of marriage from a largely utilitarian partnership engineered by others to one characterized by romantic love. As I noted in Chapter 8, even the term for the love between husband and wife (*ai*) is a relatively recent addition to the lexicon, replacing an older term (*iro*) that referred primarily to physical attraction typically experienced outside the marital relationship. The ongoing tensions experienced by many of the women in our study suggest that the transformation is occurring along a different path – or at a different rate – for men and for women. This process of change illustrates clearly the basic point that a given cultural model is neither static nor monolithically endorsed by all members of a society at any particular point in time.

This study also illustrates the importance of investigating how individual agency operates within institutional constraints to adapt and alter available cultural models (Swidler, 2001). By acknowledging the degree to which these women were reflective and introspective, my research has focused on the ways in which the individual mother interprets the role expectations available to her. I have conceptualized and studied cultural models of parenting not as static determinants of behavior but rather as "themes of which people are generally cognizant but which can nonetheless be approached in multiple ways: embraced, negotiated, but also rejected" (Gjerde, 2004, p. 149).

The process of self-reflection has occupied a central position throughout this book, demonstrating the strong preoccupation of the women themselves with examining and evaluating their own parenting practices. In our investigation, the culturally salient practice of comparing one's own behavior to a culturally defined "ideal" turned out to be a complicated process that sometimes led to floundering and insecurity and sometimes energized women to engage in effective action. We saw many instances in which efficacious women were able to resist culturally based ideas about how a mother should act – as when Asako persisted in her desire to play soccer, when Masayo fought to become a teacher and would not be pressured into quitting when her son was born, and when Miyuki decided to take a job and let the members of her family cope with waking up and making their own breakfast. This focus on the power of the individual in selecting and appropriating cultural models of parenting – and the resulting variability from one mother to the next – extends the traditional cultural psychology approach in important ways.

Finally, this study speaks to the importance of investigating the way in which powerful social institutions are deeply implicated in developing the dominant discourses or models of what being a good parent means in a particular society. It is impossible to delve into the history of Japanese families without seeing how strongly the government has shaped people's views about the role of mother. The fact that Japanese people have themselves come to view socially constructed views about women and parenting as "natural" and "normal" should not mislead anyone into ignoring "the ways in which political forces frame developmental settings" (Gjerde, 2004, p. 139; also Rosenbluth, 2007).

The shifting interpretations of the phrase "good wife, wise mother" illustrate the broad outlines of government efforts in this regard. In the early days of the Meiji era, government officials emphasized women's competence in order to energize and organize their role as caregivers, financial managers, and members of the labor force. Proximal institutions conducive to those functions found government support – child-care centers were available, banking practices were set up to encourage household saving, and high school education was extended to girls in order to teach modern methods of child rearing and household management. As time passed, the government began to encourage women to focus exclusively on child rearing and home management and to abandon the idea of sustained full-time employment. Currently, tax policies, divorce law, workplace practices, and the nature of the education system make it extremely difficulty for women to break out of a more constricted definition of "good wife, wise mother."

[handwritten marginal note: Focus on home stuff instead of work]

Implications for Self-Efficacy Theory

Our work strongly supports the basic theoretical tenets put forth by Bandura in his voluminous work on self-efficacy (Bandura, 1997; Coleman & Karraker, 1997; Oettingen, 1995). We demonstrated significant variability in Japanese mothers' perceptions of their own parenting competence. We saw that this variable self-efficacy was partly a function of early experiences in their family of origin and partly due to the amount of support they were currently receiving from their husbands and other family members. And we saw that higher self-efficacy was associated with focused and sustained efforts to be a good parent. Thus, our findings show that individual parenting self-efficacy is a valid and important construct in the context of Japanese parenting.

Contrary to scholars who have argued that individual self-efficacy would have little psychological resonance in a "collectivistic" society such as Japan, we found that the mothers were quite aware of their own individual role in rearing their children. These mothers did not subscribe to the "it takes a village" notion of child rearing. They strongly believed that a personal failure to be a good parent would not only be judged harshly by those around them, but would also have a strong and potentially devastating impact on their child.

Although self-efficacy theory stood up well in this cultural context, our findings do depart from theoretical predictions with respect to the stability of parenting self-efficacy. In general, the theory proposes that individuals settle into typical cognitive patterns that lead to a relatively stable sense of efficacy with regard to a particular domain (Bandura, 1997). Each person develops an idiosyncratic interpretive lens that prompts attention to experiences that confirm the self-schema and diminish those that challenge it. Additionally, to the extent that people tend to remain in particular relationships over time, the perceptions and actions of those around them are also consistent and thus contribute to a stable perception of efficacy. When it comes to parenting self-efficacy in particular, a person's own early childhood experiences are assumed to be a major determinant of later parenting self-efficacy, again lending stability to later perceptions of the self.

Our findings suggest that mothers' sense of self-efficacy sometimes changes as their children make the transition from preschool to elementary school. When their children were in preschool, mothers typically focused on their social competence and experienced the greatest challenge in the area of disciplining their children. When their children moved into elementary school, the mothers' attention shifted to the child's academic progress. Women with less education or whose schooling had been compromised tended to worry that they would not be able to support their children's academic efforts fully. Junko, a clear example of this type of mother, worried whether she was intelligent enough to help her son and whether he was intelligent enough to succeed in school (after all, she reasoned, he probably inherited her lack of schooling ability). Her worries resulted in a somewhat erratic and half-hearted approach to parental involvement; overall, she preferred to leave the matter in the hands of his teachers.

Children's initial success or failure in school also provided mothers with new information that they used to evaluate their own performance in the role of educational consultant. We saw evidence of this phenomenon in the case of Mari, who stopped viewing herself as a competent mother when her bright preschooler hit a few bumps on the road to first grade. In general, our findings suggest that the stability of self-efficacy beliefs hinges on continuity in the individual's institutional context. When new institutions become salient in a person's life (or that of their child), new norms, and hence new sources of self-evaluation, are introduced and can result in a change in self-efficacy judgments.

Implications for Policies Related to Declining Fertility in Japan

I began this book with a discussion of the declining birth rate in Japan and emphasized the alarm that it has caused among citizens and government officials alike. Indeed, these major demographic shifts have serious consequences that need to be addressed. The government needs to ensure that there is an adequate number of workers to keep the economy going, it needs to balance the number of pension-drawing retirees with the number of people paying into the system, and it needs to find a way to care for its growing elderly population.

The women in our study help to shed light on the decision many Japanese women are making to postpone marriage and child rearing well into their thirties. To envision how conditions in contemporary Japanese society affect young women contemplating marriage and family life, picture a scenario in which an imaginary young college student named Aiko falls into casual conversation with Chihiro, the frustrated mother in our study. When Aiko mentions that she is studying consumer sciences at a nearby university, Chihiro begins to describe her former exciting career as a professional in the field of industrial design. She goes on to chronicle her subsequent departure from the workplace when it became apparent how difficult it would be to manage the job and perform all her household duties with little help from her husband. She describes her persistent sense of failure as a mother, her feeling of estrangement from her husband, and her boredom at her part-time job. By the end of the conversation, Aiko's mood is low. How will she ever reconcile her desire for a rewarding career with the desire to have a family? At least, she tells herself, she can postpone the inevitable choice by waiting as long as possible to give in to her boyfriend's desire to get married!

How realistic is this hypothetical scenario? I would argue that it provides a reasonable account of what is going through the minds of many young Japanese women as they approach the age when marriage and child rearing are on the horizon. My argument is based on three core assertions about the factors that affect Japanese women's decisions about fertility. Assertion one is that women's fertility decisions are based on structural features of the labor market and educational system. Current labor market conditions preclude women from taking on – and remaining in – psychologically and financially rewarding work. The education system creates a strong demand for mothers' voluntary labor in support of their children's schooling. This position is strongly supported by political economists like Rosenbluth, who argues that "fertility tends to be depressed where vested interests impede female access to the workforce, and higher where easy labor market accessibility and childcare support make it easier for women to balance family and career" (2007, p. 4). In Japan, corporate policies that offer men lifetime employment while relegating married women to the role of part-time employee require women who wish to remain employed throughout their adult lives in a well-paid, full-time position to opt out of family life.

The second assertion is that cultural discourses about parenting and work can exacerbate the negative effects of structural inequities on women's ability to balance work and family life. In the case of Japan, we have seen in our study how women's tendency to be self-reflective and perfectionist has resulted in their creating an extremely high standard for parenting. This makes it difficult for them to feel that anyone else could do the job well (i.e., a hired caregiver) and makes them more susceptible to the conservative ideology about the essential role of mothers in young children's development. The same capacity for self-criticism and perfectionism comes into play at the workplace, creating a sense that the demands of a job are so onerous that achieving success in the workplace is impossible if one cannot devote 150 percent of one's efforts to it. Miyuki, for example, remembered sleeping as few as two hours when her school was preparing for a big event. Chihiro nearly ruined her health during her years in the product design field and knew that she would not be able to maintain that level of commitment to work as a married woman. These cultural discourses serve to amplify the magnitude of the structural barriers to combining work and family.

The third assertion is that the declining birth rate also reflects a general disenchantment with married life. Japanese women seem to feel even more dissatisfied with their personal relationship to their husband than they do with the role of mother. In our survey, when we asked women to rate their satisfaction with marriage, it was the personal characteristics of their husbands that they found objectionable – more so than the couple's allocation of household and child-rearing responsibilities between husband and wife. We saw that the women in our study who were trapped in unsatisfactory marriages were extremely unhappy.

Thus, attempts to address the issue of the declining birth rate need to consider a complicated set of issues, some structural and some related to discourses about work and parenting. On the structural side, Rosenbluth (2007) argues that the biggest change will come when firms no longer offer a guarantee of lifelong employment, thereby creating a situation in which worker skills will be oriented toward a job sector rather than being tailored specifically to a particular firm. This change may remove some of the current disadvantage for women who drop in and out of the workplace. She also argues for "incentivizing" fathers to become more involved in child rearing by requiring firms to pay a "take-it-or-leave-it sum" for paternity leave (p. 211) and offers a plan for reducing the tax incentives to work very long hours.

On the cultural discourse side, it may be possible to work toward change by addressing some of these norms and ideologies in the ways I have already noted, including through new forms of parent education, through individual psychotherapy, and through grassroots community initiatives based on helping women find workable individual solutions to permit a balance of work and family.

Ultimately, my interest in the phenomenon of the declining birth rate is prompted less by concern for the Japanese economy than by an interest in what it says about the lives of contemporary Japanese women. The birth rate has become, effectively, a barometer of the social status of a society's female population. Throughout Europe and Asia, the more support there is for women's welfare, the higher the birth rate in that society (Rosenbluth, 2007). In Japan, women's growing access to educational opportunities has not been matched by their access to professional opportunities, nor have they escaped the old discourses about their natural and essential role as good wives and wise mothers.

The deep sadness of women like Junko, Chihiro, and the other anxious mothers in our study is palpable. How hard it must be to feel inept at being a mother – the one role that society willingly accords to women in Japan. And all the worse if it is a role that has been defined as "natural" and "normal" for their sex. How tragic to leave one's dream job forever, as Miyuki did after her husband compared her to an "old computer" that could not do more than one thing at a time. And yet Miyuki, Junko, Chihiro, and others acknowledged the paradox that only by working outside the home could they find enjoyment and satisfaction – and do their best – in the role of mother. The women in our study described a variety of experiences and differing levels of agency, but they did convey one thing quite clearly – namely, that it is imperative to heed their voices and respect their contribution to the ever-changing discourse about what it means to be a good wife and wise mother in Japan.

[handwritten margin note: feel like you're doing a "bad job" at the one thing you're meant to do.]

References

Allison, A. (1991). Japanese mothers and obentos: The lunch-box as ideological state apparatus. *Anthropological Quarterly, 64*, 195–208.

(1994). *Nightwork: Sexuality, pleasure, and corporate masculinity in a Tokyo hostess club.* Chicago, IL: University of Chicago Press.

(1996). Producing mothers. In A. E. Imamura (Ed.), *Re-imaging Japanese women* (pp. 135–155). Berkeley: University of California Press.

Ando, M., Asakura, T., & Simons-Morton, B. (2005). Psychosocial influences on physical, verbal, and indirect bullying among Japanese early adolescents. *Journal of Early Adolescence, 25*, 268–297.

Ardelt, M., & Eccles, J. S. (2001). Effects of mothers' parental efficacy beliefs and promotive parenting strategies on inner-city youth. *Journal of Family Issues, 22*, 944–972.

Asonuma, A. (2002). Finance reform in Japanese higher education. *Higher Education, 43*, 109–126.

Azuma, H. (1986). Why study child development in Japan? In H. Stevenson, H. Azuma, & K. Hakuta (Eds.), *Child development and education in Japan* (pp. 3–12). New York, NY: W. H. Freeman.

Bandura, A. (1982). Self-efficacy mechanism in human agency. *American Psychologist, 37*(2), 122–147.

(1997). *Self-efficacy: The exercise of control.* New York, NY: W. H. Freeman.

Bandura, A., Barbaranelli, C., Caprara, G. V., & Pastorelli, C. (1996). Multifaceted impact of self-efficacy beliefs on academic functioning. *Child Development, 67*, 1206–1222.

Bankart, C. P., & Bankart, B. (1985). Japanese children's perceptions of their parents. *Sex Roles, 13*, 679–690.

Bassani, D. D. (2007). The Japanese *tanshin funin*: A neglected family type. *Community, Work, and Family, 10*, 111–131.

Beech, H. (2005, August 22). The wasted asset. *Time Asia Magazine*. Retrieved from http://www.time.com/time/asia/covers/501050829/story.html

Behrens, K. Y. (2004). A multifaceted view of the concept of amae: Reconsidering the indigenous Japanese concept of relatedness. *Human Development, 47*, 1–27.

Behrens, K. Y., Hesse, E., & Main, M. (2007). Mothers' attachment status as determined by the Adult Attachment Interview predicts their 6-year-olds' reunion responses: A study conducted in Japan. *Developmental Psychology, 43*, 1553–1567.

Benesse Educational Research Institute. (2006a). Basic survey on young children's daily lives and parents' childrearing in five East Asian cities: Tokyo, Seoul, Beijing, Shanghai, and Tapei. Retrieved from www.childresearch.net/RESOURCE/RESEARCH/2006/ASIAN.HTM

——— (2006b). The first report on Japanese fathers' views on childrearing. Retrieved from www.childresearch.net/RESOURCE/DATA/SPECIAL/FATHER/index.html

——— (2008a). Trends in Japanese education – 2008. Retrieved from http://www.childresearch.net/RESOURCE/DATA/SPECIAL/TRENDS2008/index.html

——— (2008b). *First time parenting*. Research report retrieved from http://www.childresearch.net/RESOURCE/DATA/SPECIAL/PARENTING/PART1.html

——— (2008c). Dai 4 kai gakushū kihon chōsa [The fourth basic research on academic performance]. Retrieved from http://benesse.jp/berd/center/open/report/gakuki-hon4/hon/pdf/kou/data_03.pdf

Bernstein, G. L. (1983). *Haruko's world: A Japanese farm woman and her community*. Stanford, CA: Stanford University Press.

——— (1991). Introduction. In G. L. Bernstein (Ed.), *Recreating Japanese women, 1600–1945* (pp. 1–14). Berkeley: University of California Press.

Bornstein, M. H., Haynes, O. M., Azuma, H., Galperin, C., Maital, S., Ogino, M., et al. (1998). A cross-national study of self-evaluations and attributions in parenting: Argentina, Belgium, France, Israel, Italy, Japan, and the United States. *Developmental Psychology, 34*, 662–676.

Borovoy, A. (2005). *The too-good wife: Alcohol, codependency, and the politics of nurturance in postwar Japan*. Berkeley: University of California Press.

Bourdieu, P., & Passeron, J. (1977). *Reproduction in education, society, and culture*. Beverly Hills, CA: Sage Publications.

Bowlby, J. (1973). *Attachment and loss: Separation (Vol. 2)*. New York, NY: Basic Books.

Brinton, M. C. (1993). *Women and the economic miracle: Gender and work in postwar Japan*. Berkeley: University of California Press.

Brinton, M. C. (Ed.). (2001). *Women's working lives in East Asia*. Stanford, CA: Stanford University Press.

Brooke, J. (2005, May 28). Fighting to protect her gift to Japanese women. *The New York Times*. Retrieved from http://www.nytimes.com/2005/05/28/international/asia/28japan.html?pagewanted=print

Brownstein, M. C. (1980). Jogaku Zasshi and the founding of bungakukai. *Monumenta Nipponica, 35*, 319–336.

Bugental, D. B., & Shennum, W. A. (1984). "Difficult" children as elicitors and targets of adult communication patterns: An attributional-behavioral transactional analysis. *Monographs of the Society for Research in Child Development, 49*(1), serial no. 205.

Bumpass, L. L., & Choe, M. K. (2004). Attitudes relating to marriage and family life. In N. O. Tsuya & L. L. Bumpass (Eds.), *Marriage, work, and family life in comparative perspective: Japan, South Korea, and the United States* (pp. 19–38). Honolulu: University of Hawaii Press.

Bus, A. G., & van IJzendoorn, M. H. (1988). Mother-child interactions, attachment, and emergent literacy: A cross-sectional study. *Child Development, 59*, 1262–1272.

Chen, S. (1996). Are Japanese young children among the gods? In D. W. Shwalb & B. J. Shwalb (Eds.), *Japanese childrearing: Two generations of scholarship* (pp. 31–43). New York, NY: Guilford Press.

Choe, M. K., Bumpass, L. L., & Tsuya, N. O. (2004). Employment. In N. O. Tsuya & L. L. Bumpass (Eds.), *Marriage, work, and family life in comparative perspective: Japan, South Korea, and the United States* (pp. 95–113). Honolulu: University of Hawaii Press.

Cohn, D. A., Cowan, P. A., Cowan, C. P., & Pearson, J. (1992). Mothers' and fathers' working models of childhood attachment relationships, parenting styles, and child behavior. *Development and Psychopathology, 4,* 417–431.

Coleman, P., & Karraker, K. H. (1997). Self-efficacy and parenting quality: Findings and future applications. *Developmental Review, 18,* 47–85.

(2000). Parenting self-efficacy among mothers of school-age children: Conceptualization, measurement, and correlates. *Family Relations, 49,* 13–24.

Condon, J. (1985). *A half step behind: Japanese women today.* Rutland, VT: Charles E. Tuttle

Conroy, M., Hess, R., Azuma, H., & Kashiwagi, K. (1980). Maternal strategies for regulating children's behavior: Japanese and American families. *Journal of Cross-Cultural Studies, 11,* 153–172.

Crystal, D. S., Chen, C., Fuligni, A. J., Stevenson, H. W., Hsu, C., Ko, H., et al. (1994). Psychological maladjustment and academic achievement: A cross-cultural study of Japanese, Chinese, and American high school students. *Child Development, 65,* 738–753.

Cutrona, C. E., & Troutman, B. R. (1986). Social support, infant temperament, and parenting self-efficacy: A mediational model of postpartum depression. *Child Development, 57,* 1507–1518.

Deutsch, F. M., Ruble, D. N., Fleming, A., Brooks-Gunn, J., & Stangor, G. S. (1988). Information seeking and maternal self-definition during the transition to motherhood. *Journal of Personality and Social Psychology, 55,* 420–431.

Doi, T. (1986). *The anatomy of self: The individual versus society.* Tokyo, Japan: Kodansha International.

(2002). *The anatomy of dependence.* Tokyo, Japan: Kodansha International. (Originally published in English in 1973)

Dore, R. P. (1958). *City life in Japan: A study of a Tokyo ward.* Berkeley: University of California Press.

Education rebuilding council submits second report. (2007, June). Foreign Press Center of Japan. Retrieved from http://www.fpcj.jp/old/e/mres/japanbrief/jb_744.html

Everingham, C. (1994). *Motherhood and modernity: An investigation into the rational dimension of mothering.* Buckingham, England: Open University Press.

Feiler, B. S. (1991). *Learning to bow: Inside the heart of Japan.* New York, NY: Ticknor & Fields.

Field, N. (1993). *In the realm of a dying emperor: Japan at century's end.* New York, NY: Vintage Books.

Fernald, A., & Morikawa, H. (1993). Common themes and cultural variations in Japanese and American mothers' speech to infants. *Child Development, 64,* 637–656.

Frank, K. (2006). Agency. *Anthropological Theory, 6*(3), 281–302.

Frederick, J. (2003, July 21). Severe acute ridiculousness syndrome. *Time Magazine.* Retrieved from http://www.time.com/time/magazine/article/0,9171,465836,00.html

French, H. W. (2002, September 23). Educators try to tame Japan's blackboard jungles. *The New York Times.* Retrieved from http://query.nytimes.com/gst/fullpage.html?res=9E0DE3DA1739F930A1575AC0A9649C8B63

(2003, July 25). Japan's neglected resource: Female workers. *The New York Times.* Retrieved from http://query.nytimes.com/gst/fullpage.html?res=9506E7D8123FF 936A15754C0A9659C8B63#

Froman, R. D., & Owen, S. V. (1989). Infant care self-efficacy. *Scholarly Inquiry for Nursing Practice: An International Journal, 3,* 199–211.

Fuess, H. (2004). *Divorce in Japan: Family, gender, and the state 1600–2000.* Stanford, CA: Stanford University Press.

Fujita, M. (1989). "It's all mother's fault": Childcare and the socialization of working mothers in Japan. *Journal of Japanese Studies, 15,* 67–91.

George, C., & Solomon, J. (1999). Attachment and caregiving: The caregiving behavioral system. In J. Cassidy & P. R. Shaver (Eds.), *Handbook of attachment: Theory, research, and clinical applications* (pp. 649–670). New York, NY: Guilford Press.

Gjerde, P. (2004). Culture, power, and experience: Toward a person-centered cultural psychology. *Human Development, 47*(3), 138–157.

Gonzales, P., Guzman, J. C., Partelow, L., Pahlke, E., Jocelyn, L., Kastberg, D., et al. (2004). *Highlights from the Trends in International Mathematics and Science Study (TIMSS) 2003.* Washington, DC: Institute of Education Sciences, U.S. Department of Education.

Goodman, R. (2006). Policing the Japanese family: Child abuse, domestic violence and the changing role of the state. In M. Rebick & A. Takenaka (Eds.), *The changing Japanese family* (pp. 147–160). Oxon, England: Routledge.

Gordon, B. S. (1997). *The only woman in the room: A memoir.* Tokyo, Japan: Kodansha International.

Grusec, J. E., Hastings, P., & Mammone, N. (1994). Parenting cognitions and relationship schemas. In J. G. Smetana (Ed.), *Beliefs about parenting: Origins and developmental implications* (pp. 73–86). San Francisco, CA: Jossey-Bass.

Hamada, T. (1997). Absent fathers, feminized sons, selfish mothers and disobedient daughters: Revisiting the Japanese *ie* household. *Japan Policy Research Institute Working Paper No. 33,* Retrieved from http://www.jpri.org/publications/ workingpapers/wp33.html

Hamaguchi, K. (2007). Nenrei sabetsu [Age discrimination]. *Hōritsu Jihō, 79*(3).

Hara, H., & Minagawa, M. (1996). From productive dependents to precious guests: Historical changes in Japanese children. In D. W. Shwalb & B. J. Shwalb (Eds.), *Japanese childrearing: Two generations of scholarship* (pp. 9–30). New York, NY: Guilford Press.

Harkness, S., & Super, C. M. (1992). Parental ethnotheories in action. In I. Sigel, A. V. McGillicuddy-DeLisi, & J. Goodnow (Eds.), *Parental belief systems: The psychological consequences for children* (2nd ed., pp. 373–392). Hillsdale, NJ: Erlbaum.

(2002). Culture and parenting. In M. H. Bornstein (Ed.), *Handbook of parenting: Biology and ecology of parenting* (2nd ed., Vol. 2, pp. 253–280). Mahwah, NJ: Erlbaum.

Harvey, P. A. S. (1995). Interpreting *Oshin* – war, history and women in modern Japan. In L. Skov & B. Moeran (Eds.), *Women, media and consumption in Japan* (pp. 75–110). Honolulu: University of Hawaii Press.

Hashimoto, K. (1999). *Gendai nihon no kaikyū kōzō: riron, hōhō, keiryō bunseki.* [Class structure in modern Japan: Theory, method and quantitative analysis]. Tokyo, Japan: Toshindo.

Hausmann, R., Tyson, L. D., & Zahidi, S. (2006). *The global gender gap report 2006.* Retrieved from World Economic Forum Website: www.weforum.org

Heine, S., Lehman, D., Markus, R., & Kitayama, S. (1999). Is there a universal need for positive self-regard? *Psychological Review, 106,* 766–794.

Hendry, J. (1981). *Marriage in changing Japan: Community and society.* Rutland, VT: Charles E. Tuttle.

(1986). *Becoming Japanese: The world of the pre-school child.* Honolulu: University of Hawaii Press.

Henman, P. (2006). Updated costs of raising children – June quarter 2006. Retrieved from http://www.uq.edu.au/swahs/costsofkids/CostsofRaisingChildrenJuneQuarter06.pdf

Hess, R. D., Azuma, H., Kashiwagi, K., Dickson, W. P., Nagano, S., Holloway, S. D., et al. (1986). Family influence on school readiness and achievement in Japan and the United States: An overview of a longitudinal study. In H. Stevenson, H. Azuma, & K. Hakuta (Eds.), *Child development and education in Japan* (pp. 147–156). New York, NY: W. H. Freeman.

Hess, R. D., Kashiwagi, K., Azuma, H., Price, G. G., & Dickson, W. P. (1980). Maternal expectations for mastery of developmental tasks in Japan and the United States. *International Journal of Psychology, 15,* 259–271.

Hirao, K. (2001). Mothers as the best teachers: Japanese motherhood and early childhood education. In M. C. Brinton (Ed.), *Women's lives in East Asia* (pp. 180–203). Stanford, CA: Stanford University Press.

(2007a). Contradictions in maternal roles in contemporary Japan. In T. W. Devasahayam & B. S. A. Yoh (Eds.), *Working and mothering in Asia: Images, ideologies and identities* (pp. 51–83). Singapore: NUS Press.

(2007b). The privatized education market and maternal employment in Japan. In F. R. Rosenbluth (Ed.), *The political economy of Japan's low fertility* (pp. 170–197). Stanford, CA: Stanford University Press.

Hitlin, S., & Long, C. (2009). Agency as a sociological variable: A preliminary model of individuals, situations, and the life course. *Sociology Compass, 3*(1), 137–160.

Holloway, S. D. (1988). Concepts of ability and effort in Japan and the United States. *Review of Educational Research, 58,* 327–345.

(2000). *Contested childhood: Diversity and change in Japanese preschools.* New York, NY: Routledge.

Holloway, S. D., & Behrens, K. Y. (2002). Parenting self-efficacy among Japanese mothers: Qualitative and quantitative perspectives on its association with childhood memories of family relations. In J. Bempechat & J. G. Elliot (Eds.), *Learning in culture and context: Approaching the complexities of achievement motivation in student learning* (pp. 27–43). San Francisco, CA: Jossey-Bass.

Holloway, S. D., Fuller, B., Rambaud, M. F., & Eggers-Piérola, C. (1997). *Through my own eyes: Single mothers and the cultures of poverty.* Cambridge, MA: Harvard University Press.

Holloway, S. D., Suzuki, S., Yamamoto, Y., & Behrens, K. (2005). Parenting self-efficacy among Japanese mothers. *Journal of Comparative Family Studies, 36,* 61–76.

Holloway, S. D., Suzuki, S., Yamamoto, Y., & Mindnich, J. (2006). Relation of maternal role concepts to parenting, employment choices, and life satisfaction among Japanese women. *Sex Roles, 54*(3/4), 235–249.

Holloway, S. D., & Yamamoto, Y. (2003). Sensei: Early childhood education teachers in Japan. In O. Saracho & B. Spodek (Eds.), *Studying teachers in early childhood education settings* [A volume in the *Contemporary perspectives in early childhood education* series] (pp. 181–207). Greenwich, CT: Information Age Publishing.

Holloway, S. D., Yamamoto, Y., & Suzuki, S. (2005). Exploring the gender gap: Working women speak out about working and raising children in contemporary Japan. Child Research Net Website: http://www.childresearch.net/RESOURCE/RESEARCH/2005/SUSAN.HTM

Holloway, S. D., Yamamoto, Y., Suzuki, S., & Mindnich, J. (2008). Determinants of parental involvement in early schooling: Evidence from Japan. *Early Childhood Research and Practice, 10*(1). Online journal: http://ecrp.uiuc.edu/v10n1/holloway.html

Hoover-Dempsey, K. V., & Sandler, H. M. (1997). Why do parents become involved in their children's education? *Review of Educational Research, 67*(1), 3–42.

Hori, G. V. S. (1996). Teaching and learning in the Rinzai Zen monastery. In T. P. Rohlen & G. K. LeTendre (Eds.), *Teaching and learning in Japan* (pp. 20–49). New York, NY: Cambridge University Press.

Horio, T. (1998). *Educational thought and ideology in modern Japan: State authority and intellectual freedom.* Tokyo, Japan: University of Tokyo Press.

Hunter, J. (Ed.). (1993). *Japanese women working.* New York, NY: Routledge.

Imamura, A. E. (1987). *Urban Japanese housewives: At home and in the community.* Honolulu: University of Hawaii Press.

Inoue, T., & Ehara, Y. (1999). *Jyosei no deeta bukku dai 3 ban.* [Women's data book] (3rd ed.). Tokyo, Japan: Yuhikaku.

International Comparative Research on "Home Education": Survey on Children and Family Life. (2005). Report by National Women's Education Center, Japan. Retrieved from http://www.nwec.jp/en/publish/page02.html

Ishigaki, A. T. (2004). *Restless wave: My life in two worlds, a memoir.* New York, NY: The Feminist Press. (Original work published in 1940)

Ishii-Kuntz, M. (1994). Paternal involvement and perception toward fathers' roles: A comparison between Japan and the United States. *Journal of Family Issues, 15,* 30–48.

(2003). Balancing fatherhood and work: Emergence of diverse masculinities in contemporary Japan. In J. E. Roberson & N. Suzuki (Eds.), *Men and masculinities in contemporary Japan: Dislocating the salaryman doxa* (pp. 198–216). New York, NY: Routledge.

(2008). *Sharing of housework and childcare in contemporary Japan.* Paper delivered at the Expert Group Meeting on "equal sharing of responsibilities between women and men, including care-giving in the context of HIV/AIDS" at the United Nations, Division for the Advancement of Women, Geneva Switzerland.

Ishii-Kuntz, M., Makino, K., Kato, K., & Tsuchiya, M. (2004). Japanese fathers of preschoolers and their involvement in child care. *Journal of Marriage and the Family, 66,* 779–791.

Ishimoto, S. (1984). *Facing two ways: The story of my life.* Stanford, CA: Stanford University Press. (Original work published 1935)

Ito, K. K. (2008). *An age of melodrama: Family, gender, and social hierarchy in the turn-of-the-century Japanese novel.* Stanford, CA: Stanford University Press.

Iwamoto, T. (2000). Katei kankyō to shingaku.[Home environment and college atten-dance]. In E. Kataoka (Ed.), *Kaisō bunka to raifu sutairu no shakaigakuteki kenkyū. Raifu sutairu to bunka kenkyūkai.* Osaka, Japan: Osaka University Department of Human Science.

Iwao, S. (1993). *The Japanese woman: Traditional image and changing reality.* Cambridge, MA: Harvard University Press.

Jackson, A. P. (2000). Maternal self-efficacy and children's influences on stress and par-enting among single black mothers in poverty. *Journal of Family Issues, 21*(1), 3–16.

Japan Center for Economic Research. (2007). *Long-term forecast of global economy and population 2006–2050: Demographic change and the Asian economy.* Retrieved from http://www.jcer.or.jp/eng/pdf/2006long_contents.pdf

Japan Institute of Labor. (2003). *Research report on the child-care leave system: Findings of a "Study of Women's Work and Family Life."* Retrieved from http://www.jil.go.jp/english/documents/JILNo157.pdf

Japanese Prime Minister's Office. (2000). The present status of gender equality and measures: Second report on the plan for gender equality 2000. Retrieved from http://www.un.org/womenwatch/confer/beijing/national/japan98.htm

Japan's " monster " parents take centre stage. (2008, June 7). Times Online. Retrieved from http://www.timesonline.co.uk/tol/news/world/asia/article4083278.ece

Jolivet, M. (1997). *Japan: The childless society?* (A. Glasheen, Trans.) New York, NY: Routledge.

Kaneko, R., Ishikawa, A., Ishii, F., Sasai, T., Iwasawa, M., Mita, F., et al. (2008a). Population projections for Japan 2006–2055: Outline of results, methods, and assumptions. *The Japanese Journal of Population, 6,* 76–114.

Kaneko, R., Sasai, T., Kamano, S., Iwasawa, M., Mita, F., & Rie, M. (2008b). Marriage process and fertility of Japanese married couples: Overview of the results of the thirteenth Japanese national fertility survey, married couples. *The Japanese Journal of Population, 6,* 24–49.

Kariya, T., Shimizu, K., Shimizu, M., & Morota, Y. (2002). Chōsa hōkoku: Gakuryoku teika no jittai [A report of declining academic performance]. *Iwanami Booklet* (Serial No. 578).

Kashiwagi, K. (1998). Life-span developmental and socio-cultural approach toward Japanese women/mothers: Conceptions and realities of Japanese women/moth-ers. *The Annual Report of Educational Psychology in Japan, 37,* 191–200.

Kazui, M. (1997). The influence of cultural expectations on mother-child relationships in Japan. *Journal of Applied Developmental Psychology, 18,* 485–496.

Kelsky, K. (2001). *Women on the verge: Japanese women, Western dreams.* Durham, NC: Duke University Press.

King, F. (1984). *Lafcadio Hearn: Writings from Japan.* London, England: Penguin Books.

Kojima, H. (1986). Child rearing concepts as a belief-value system of the society and the individual. In H. Stevenson, H. Azuma, & K. Hakuta (Eds.), *Child develop-ment and education in Japan* (pp. 39–54). New York, NY: W. H. Freeman.

(1996). Japanese concepts of child development from the mid-17th to mid-19th cen-tury. *International Journal of Behavioral Development, 9,* 315–329.

Kondo, D. K. (1990). *Crafting selves: Power, gender, and discourses of identity in a Japanese workplace.* Chicago, IL: University of Chicago Press.

Kosugi, R. (2006). Youth employment in Japan's economic recovery: "Freeters" and "NEETs." *Japan Focus, Article 572.* Retrieved from http://www.japanfocus.org/-Kosugi-Reiko/2022

Lanham, B. B., & Garrick, R. J. (1996). Adult to child in Japan: Interaction and relations. In B. Shwalb & D. Shwalb (Eds.), *Japanese childrearing: Two generations of scholarship* (pp. 97–124). New York, NY: Guilford Press.

Lareau, A. (2000). *Home advantage: Social class and parental intervention in elementary education.* Lanham, MD: Rowman & Littlefield

(2003). *Unequal childhoods: Class, race, and family life.* Berkeley: University of California Press.

Lebra, T. S. (1984). *Japanese women: Constraint and fulfillment.* Honolulu: University of Hawaii Press.

(1986). Self-reconstruction in Japanese religious psychotherapy. In T. S. Lebra & W. P. Lebra (Eds.), *Japanese culture and behavior: Selected readings* (Revised edition, pp. 354–368). Honolulu: University of Hawaii.

Lebra, T. S., & Lebra, W. P. (1986). Editorial note to part four. In T. S. Lebra & W. P. Lebra (Eds.), *Japanese culture and behavior: Selected readings* (Revised edition, pp. 339–343). Honolulu: University of Hawaii Press.

Lester, B. (2003). Adolescent suicide from an international perspective. *American Behavioral Scientist, 46,* 1157–1170.

LeTendre, G. (1998). *The educational system in Japan: Case study findings.* Washington, DC: National Institute on Student Achievement, Curriculum, and Assessment, Office of Educational Research and Improvement, U.S. Department of Education.

LeVine, R. A., Dixon, S., LeVine, S., Richman, A., Leiderman, P. H., Keefer, C. H., et al. (1994). *Child care and culture: Lessons from Africa.* Cambridge, England: Cambridge University Press.

Lewis, C. C. (1995). *Educating hearts and minds: Reflections on Japanese preschool and elementary education.* Cambridge, England: Cambridge University Press.

Machida, S., Taylor, A. R., & Kim, J. (2002). The role of maternal beliefs in predicting home learning activities in Head Start families. *Family Relations, 51,* 176–184.

Mackie, V. (2003). *Feminism in modern Japan.* Cambridge, England: Cambridge University Press.

Macnaughtan, H. (2006). From "post-war" to "post-bubble": Contemporary Issues for Japanese working women. In P. Matanle & W. Lunsing (Eds.), *Perspectives on work, employment and society in Japan* (pp. 31–57). Hampshire, England: Palgrave Macmillan.

Main, M., Kaplan, N., & Cassidy, J. (1985). Security in infancy, childhood, and adulthood: A move to the level of representation. In I. Bretherton & E. Waters (Eds.), *Growing points of attachment: Theory and research. Monographs of the Society for Research in Child Development, 50*(1–2), 1985, pp. 66–104.

Manzo, K. K. (2008). Trends in Japan: Japan continues search for academic triumph. *Education Week.* Retrieved from http://www.edweek.org/ew/articles/2008/04/23/34japan_Ep.h27.html

Mathias, R. (1993). Female labor in the Japanese coal-mining industry. In J. Hunter (Ed.), *Japanese women working* (pp. 98–121). New York, NY: Routledge.

McBride, B. A., Brown, G. L., Bost, K. K., Shin, N., Vaughn, B., & Korth, B. (2005). Paternal identity, maternal gatekeeping, and father involvement. _Family Relations, 54_, 360–372.

Miller, R. L. (2003). The quiet revolution: Japanese women working around the law. _Harvard Women's Law Journal, 26_, 163–215.

Minami, M., & McCabe, A. (1995). Rice balls and bear hunts: Japanese and North American family narrative patterns. _Journal of Child Language, 22_, 423–445.

Ministry of Education, Culture, Sports, Science, and Technology. (2005). School Basic Survey. Retrieved from http://www.mext.go.jp/english/statist/05101901/008.pdf

Ministry of Education, Culture, Sports, Science, and Technology. (2006a). Heisei 18 nendo kodomo no gakushuhi chosha [The report on Japanese children's academic expenses in 2006]. Retrieved from http://www.mext.go.jp/b_menu/toukei/001/006/07120312/001.htm

(2006b). Japan's Education at a Glance. Retrieved from http://www.mext.go.jp/english/statist/07070310/005.pdf

Ministry of Health, Labor, and Welfare. (2008). Effective April 1 2007 scope of coverage for the child allowance system will expand. Retrieved from http://www.mhlw.go.jp/english/topics/child-support/index.html

Mishima, S. S. (1941). _My narrow isle: The story of a modern woman in Japan._ Westport, CT: Hyperion.

Miyake, Y. (1991). Doubling expectations: Motherhood and women's factory work under state management in Japan in the 1930s and 1940s. In G. L. Bernstein (Ed.), _Recreating Japanese women, 1600–1945_ (pp. 267–295). Berkeley: University of California Press.

Mizuuchi, T., Kato, M., & Oshiro, N. (2008). Modantoshi no keifu – Chizu kara yomitoku shakai to kūkan [The lineage of modern cities – The society and space from maps]. Kyoto, Japan: Nakanishiya Shuppan.

Molony, B. (1991). Activism among women in the Taisho cotton textile industry. In G. L. Bernstein (Ed.), _Recreating Japanese women, 1600–1945_ (pp. 217–238). Berkeley: University of California Press.

Mori, K. (1993). _Shizuko's daughter._ New York, NY: Fawcett Juniper.

(1995). _The dream of water: A memoir._ New York, NY: One World/Fawcett Columbine.

(1997). _Polite lies._ New York, NY: Fawcett Books.

Morioka, K. (1986). Privitization of family life in Japan. In H. Stevenson, H. Azuma, & K. Hakuta (Eds.), _Child development and education in Japan_ (pp. 63–74). New York, NY: W. H. Freeman.

Morley, P. (1999). _The mountain is moving: Japanese women's lives._ New York: New York University Press.

Mouer, R., & Sugimoto, Y. (1986). _Images of Japanese society: A study in the social construction of reality._ London, England: Kegan Paul International.

Murase, T. (1986). Naikan therapy. In T. S. Lebra & W. P. Lebra (Eds.), _Japanese culture and behavior: Selected readings_ (Revised edition, pp. 388–397). Honolulu: University of Hawaii Press.

Murase, T., Dale, P. S., Ogura, T., Yamashita, Y., & Mahieu, A. (2005). Mother-child conversation during joint picture book reading in Japan and the USA. _First Language, 25_, 197–218.

Nagy, M. (1991). Middle-class working women during the interwar years. In G. L. Bernstein (Ed.), *Recreating Japanese women, 1600–1945* (pp. 199–216). Berkeley: University of California Press.

Nakamura, T. (2003). Regendering batterers: Domestic violence and men's movements. In J. E. Roberson & N. Suzuki (Eds.), *Men and masculinities in contemporary Japan: Dislocating the salaryman doxa* (pp. 162–179). New York, NY: Routledge.

Nakano, M. (1995). *Makiko's diary.* Stanford, CA: Stanford University Press.

National Institute of Population and Social Security Research. (2000). *The 2nd survey of Japanese family households report.* Retrieved from http://www.ipss.go.jp/index-e.html

(2003). *Child related policies in Japan.* Retrieved from www.ipss.go.jp/s-info/e/childPJ2003/childPJ2003.htm

(2006). Daisankai zenkoku kateidōkō chōsakekka gaiyō [A summary report of the 3rd survey of national households]. Retrieved from http://www.ipss.go.jp/ps-katei/j/NSFJ3/NSFJ2003.pdf

National Women's Education Center, Japan. (2005). *International Comparative Research on "Home Education" 2005 – Survey on Children and Family Life.* Retrieved from http://www.nwec.jp/en/publish/page02.html

Nolte, S. H., & Hastings, S. A. (1991). The Meiji state's policy toward women, 1890–1910. In G. L. Bernstein (Ed.), *Recreating Japanese women, 1600–1945* (pp. 151–174). Berkeley: University of California Press.

Oettingen, G. (1995). Cross-cultural perspectives on self-efficacy. In A. Bandura (Ed.), *Self-efficacy in changing societies* (pp. 149–176). New York, NY: Cambridge University Press.

Ogasawara, Y. (1998). *Office ladies and salaried men: Power, gender, and work in Japanese companies.* Berkeley: University of California Press.

Ogawa, N., Retherford, R. D., & Matsukura, R. (2009). Japan's declining fertility and policy responses. In P. Straughan, G. Jones, and A. Chan (Eds.), *Ultra-low fertility in Pacific Asia: Trends, causes and policy dilemmas* (pp. 40–72). New York, NY: Routledge.

Ohinata, M. (2001). Support for isolated mothers. *Child Research Net: Resources.* Retrieved from http://www.childresearch.net/RESOURCE/RESEARCH/2001/OHINATA.HTM

Okagaki, L., & French, P. A. (1998). Parenting and children's school achievement: A multi-ethnic perspective. *American Educational Research Journal, 35*(1), 123–144.

Organization for Economic Co-operation and Development (OECD) Factbook. (2008). Expenditure on education. Retrieved from http://dx.doi.org/10.1787/270504555680

Olioff, M., & Aboud, F. E. (1991). Predicting postpartum dysphoria in primiparous mothers: Roles of perceived parenting self-efficacy and self-esteem. *Journal of Cognitive Psychotheraphy, 5,* 3–14.

Organization for Economic Co-Operation and Development. (2003). Social expenditure – Aggregated data. Retrieved from http://stats.oecd.org/mei

Okano, K., & Tsuchiya, M. (1999). *Education in contemporary Japan: Inequality and diversity.* Cambridge, England: Cambridge University Press.

Organization for Economic Co-operation and Development Website. (2008). PISA 2006 results. Retrieved from http://www.oecd.org/document/2/0,3343,en_32252 351_32236191_39718850_1_1_1_1,00.html#ES

Official Website of Osaka City. (2008). Heisei 20 nendo gakkō kyōiku shishin [The official public education policy in 2008]. Retrieved October 11, 2008 from http://www.ocec.jp/shidoubu/index.cfm/1,0,34,html

Osaka prefecture results on national achievement test. (2008). Retrieved from http://www.nier.go.jp/08chousakekka/08todofuken_data/27_osaka/01_shou_27osaka.pdf

Otake, T. (2002, March 28). "Classroom collapse" gripping schools nation-wide: Teachers, parents, society all come under fire as experts remain unable to pinpoint cause. *The Japan Times*. Retrieved from http://search.japantimes.co.jp/cgi-bin/nn20020328b9.html

Ozeki, R. L. (1998). *My year of meats*. New York, NY: Viking.

Partner, S. (2004). *Toshie: A story of village life in twentieth-century Japan*. Berkeley: University of California Press.

Patessio, M. (2006). The creation of public spaces by women in the early Meiji period and the Tokyo Fujin Kyōfūkai. *International Journal of Asian Studies, 3*, 155–182.

Peak, L. (1991). *Learning to go to school in Japan: The transition from home to preschool life*. Berkeley: University of California Press.

Rebick, M. (2006). Changes in the workplace and their impact on the family. In M. Rebick & A. Takenaka (Eds.), *The changing Japanese family* (pp. 75–93). Oxon, England: Routledge.

Rice, Y. N. (2001). The maternal role in Japan: Cultural values and socioeconomic con-ditions. In H. Shimizu & R. A. LeVine (Eds.), *Japanese frames of mind: Cultural perspectives on human development* (pp. 85–110). Cambridge, England: Cambridge University Press.

Rohlen, T. P. (1983). *Japan's high schools*. Berkeley: University of California Press.

(1996). Building character. In T. P. Rohlen and G. K. LeTendre (Eds.), *Teaching and learning in Japan* (pp. 50–74). Cambridge, England: Cambridge University Press.

Rohlen, T. P., & LeTendre, G. K. (1996). Introduction: Japanese theories of learning. In T. P. Rohlen & G. K. LeTendre (Eds.), *Teaching and learning in Japan* (pp. 1–15). Cambridge, England: Cambridge University Press.

Rosenberger, N. (2001). *Gambling with virtue: Japanese women and the search for self in a changing nation*. Honolulu: University of Hawaii Press.

Rosenbluth, F. M. (2007). The political economy of low fertility. In F. M. Rosenbluth (Ed.), *The political economy of Japan's low fertility* (pp. 3–36). Stanford, CA: Stanford University Press.

Rothbaum, F., Pott, M., Azuma, H., Miyake, K., & Weisz, J. (2000). The development of close relationships in Japan and the United States: Paths of symbiotic harmony and generative tension. *Child Development, 71*(5), 1121–1142.

Sakuraba, R. (2009). The amendment of the Employment Measure Act: Japanese anti-age discrimination law. *Japan Labor Review, 6*, 56–75.

Sand, J. (2003). *House and home in modern Japan: Architecture, domestic space, and bourgeois culture, 1880–1930*. Cambridge, MA: Harvard University Asia Center.

Sasagawa, A. (2006). Mother-rearing: The social world of mothers in a Japanese sub-
    urb. In M. Rebick & A. Takenaka (Eds.), *The changing Japanese family* (pp. 129–
    146). Oxon, England: Routledge.
Scarborough, H. S., & Dobrich, W. (1994). On the efficacy of reading to preschoolers.
    Developmental Review, 14, 245–302.
Schooler, C., & Smith, K. C. (1978). "...and a Japanese wife": Social structural anteced-
    ents of women's role values in Japan. *Sex Roles, 4*, 23–41.
Schoppa, L. J. (2006). *Race for the exits: The unraveling of Japan's system of social pro-
    tection.* Ithaca, NY: Cornell University Press.
Shirahase, S. (2007). Women's economic status and fertility: Japan in cross-national
    perspective. In F. M. Rosenbluth (Ed.), *The political economy of Japan's low fertil-
    ity* (pp. 3759). Stanford, CA: Stanford University Press.
Shoji, J. (2005). Child abuse in Japan: Developmental, cultural, and clinical perspec-
    tives. In D. W. Shwalb, J. Nakazawa, & B. J. Shwalb (Eds.), *Applied developmental
    psychology: Theory, practice, and research from Japan* (pp. 261–279). Greenwich,
    CT: Information Age Publishing.
Shwalb, D. W., Imaizumi, N., & Nakazawa, J. (1987). The modern Japanese father: Roles
    and problems in a changing society. In M. E. Lamb (Ed.), *The father's role: Cross-
    cultural comparisons* (pp. 247–269). Hillsdale, NJ: Erlbaum.
Shwalb, D. W., Kawai, H., Shoji, J., & Tsunetsugu, K. (1995). The place of advice: Japanese
    parents' sources of information about childrearing and child health. *Journal of
    Applied Developmental Psychology, 16*, 629–644.
    (1997). The middle class Japanese father: A survey of parents of preschoolers. *Journal
    of Applied Developmental Psychology, 6*, 497–511.
Shwalb, D. W., Nakawaza, J., Yamamoto, T., & Hyun, J. (2004). Fathering in Japanese,
    Chinese, and Korean cultures: A review of the research literature. In M. E. Lamb
    (Ed.), *The role of the father in child development* (4th ed., pp. 146–181). New York,
    NY: Wiley.
Sievers, S. L. (1981). Feminist criticism in Japanese politics in the 1880s: The experience
    of Kishida Toshiko. *Signs, 6*, 602–616.
Silver, E. J., Bauman, L. J., & Ireys, H. T. (1995). Relationships of self-esteem and effi-
    cacy to psychological distress in mothers of children with chronic physical ill-
    ness. *Health Psychology, 14*, 333–340.
Smith, D., & Sueda, K. (2008). The killing of children by children as a symptom of
    national crisis: Reactions in Britain and Japan. *Criminology and Criminal Justice,
    8*(1), 5–25.
"Stabbing suspect aimed to harass relatives." (2001, June 14). *The Japan Times*. Retrieved
    from http://search.japantimes.co.jp/cgi-bin/nn20010614a6.html
Stevenson, D. L., & Baker, D. P. (1987). The family-school relation and the child's school
    performance. *Child Development, 58*, 1348–1357.
Stevenson, H., & Stigler, J. (1992). *The learning gap: Why our schools are failing and
    what we can learn from Japanese and Chinese education.* New York, NY: Summit
    Books.
Stroeber, M. H., & Chan, A. M. K. (2001). *The road winds uphill all the way: Gen-
    der, work, and family in the United States and Japan.* Cambridge, MA: MIT
    Press.
Sugawara, M. (2005). Maternal employment and child development in Japan: A twelve-
    year longitudinal study. In D. W. Shwalb, J. Nakazawa, & B. J. Shwalb (Eds.),

Applied developmental psychology: Theory, practice, and research from Japan (pp. 225–240). Greenwich, CT: Information Age Publishing.

Sugimoto, E. I. (1927). *A daughter of the samurai*. New York, NY: Doubleday, Page.

Sugimoto, Y. (2003). *An introduction to Japanese society* (2nd ed.). Cambridge, England: Cambridge University Press.

Suzuki, S. (in press). The effects of marital support, social network support, and parenting stress on parenting self-efficacy among mothers of young children in Japan. *Journal of Early Childhood Research.*

Suzuki, S., Holloway, S.D., Yamamoto, Y., & Mindnich, J. D. (2009). Parenting self-efficacy and social support in Japan and the United States. *Journal of Family Issues, 30,* 1505–1526.

Swidler, A. (2001). *Talk of love: How culture matters.* Chicago, IL: University of Chicago Press.

Tamanoi, M. A. (1990). Women's voices: Their critique of the anthropology of Japan. *Annual Review of Anthropology, 19,* 17–37.

Tanaka, Y. & Nakazawa, J. (2005). Job-related temporary father absence (*Tanshinfunin*) and child development. In D. W. Shwalb, J. Nakazawa, & B. J. Shwalb (Eds.), *Applied developmental psychology: Theory, practice, and research from Japan* (pp. 241–260). Greenwich, CT: Information Age Publishing.

Teti, D. M., & Gelfand, D. M. (1991). Behavioral competence among mothers of infants in the first year: The mediational role of maternal self-efficacy. *Child Development, 62,* 918–929.

Tipton, E. K. (2008). *Modern Japan: A social and political history* (2nd ed.). London, England: Routledge.

Tobin, J. J., Wu, Y. H., & Davidson, D. H. (1989). *Preschool in three cultures: Japan, China, and the United States.* New Haven, CT: Yale University Press.

Tobin, J. J., Yeh, H., & Karasawa, M. (2009). *Preschool in three cultures revisited.* Chicago, IL: University of Chicago Press.

Tsuneyoshi, R. (2004). The new Japanese educational reforms and the achievement "crisis" debate. *Educational Policy, 18,* 364–394.

Tsuya, N. O., & Bumpass, L. L. (2004). Gender and housework. In N. O. Tsuya & L. L. Bumpass (Eds.), *Marriage, work, and family life in comparative perspective: Japan, South Korea, and the United States* (pp. 114–133). Honolulu: University of Hawaii Press.

Tsuya, N. O., & Bumpass, L. L. (Eds.). (2004). *Marriage, work, and family life in comparative perspective: Japan, South Korea, and the United States.* Honolulu: University of Hawaii Press.

Tsuya, N. O., Mason, K. O., & Bumpass, L. L. (2004). Views of marriage among never-married adults. In N. O. Tsuya & L. L. Bumpass (Eds.), *Marriage, work, and family life in comparative perspective: Japan, South Korea, and the United States* (pp. 39–53). Honolulu: Universiy of Hawaii Press.

Ujiie, T. (1997). How do Japanese women treat children's negativism? *Journal of Applied Developmental Psychology, 18,* 467–483.

Uno, K. S. (1991). Women and changes in the household division of labor. In G. L. Bernstein (Ed.), *Recreating Japanese women, 1600–1945* (pp. 17–41). Berkeley: University of California Press.

(1993). One day at a time: Work and domestic activities of urban lower-class women in early twentieth-century Japan. In J. Hunter (Ed.), *Japanese women working* (pp. 37–68). London, England: Routledge.

(1999). *Passages to modernity: Motherhood, childhood, and social reform in early twentieth century Japan*. Honolulu: University of Hawaii Press.

U.S. Department of Agriculture, Center for Nutrition Policy and Promotion. (2005). Expenditure by Families on Children: 2005. Miscellaneous publication number 1528-2005. Retrieved from http://www.cnpp.usda.gov/Publications/CRC/crc2005.pdf.

Vogel, S. H. (1996). Urban middle-class Japanese family life, 1958–1996: A personal and evolving perspective. In B. J. Shwalb & D. W. Shwalb (Eds.), *Japanese childrearing: Two generations of scholarship* (pp. 177–200). New York, NY: Guilford Press.

Wagatsuma, H. (1978). Some aspects of the contemporary Japanese family: Once Confucian, now fatherless? In A. S. Rossi, J. Kagan, & T. K. Hareven (Eds.), *The Family* (pp. 181–210). New York, NY: W. W. Norton, Inc.

Weisner, T. S. (2002). Ecocultural understanding of children's developmental pathways. *Human Development, 174*, 275–281.

White, M. I. (1995). The marketing of adolescence in Japan: Buying and dreaming. In. L. Skov & B. Moeran (Eds.), *Women, media, and consumption in Japan* (pp. 255–273). Honolulu: University of Hawaii Press.

White, M. I. (2001). Children and families: Reflections on the "crisis" in Japanese childrearing today. In H. Shimizu & R. A. LeVine (Eds.), *Japanese frames of mind: Cultural perspectives on human development* (pp. 257–266). Cambridge, England: Cambridge University Press.

(2002). *Perfectly Japanese: Making families in an era of upheaval*. Berkeley: University of California Press.

(2005). The marketing of adolescence in Japan: Buying and dreaming. In L. Skov & B. Moeran (Eds.), *Women, media and consumption in Japan* (pp. 255–27). Honolulu: University of Hawaii Press.

White, M. I., & LeVine, R. (1986). What is an "ii ko" (good child)? In H. Stevenson, H. Azuma, & K. Hakuta (Eds.), *Child development and education in Japan* (pp. 55–62). New York, NY: W. H. Freeman.

Whiting, B. B., & Edwards, C. P. (1988). *Children of different worlds: The formation of social behavior*. Cambridge, MA: Harvard University Press.

Whiting, B. B., & Whiting, J. W. M. (1975). *Children of six cultures: A psycho-cultural analysis*. Cambridge, MA: Harvard University Press.

Williams, T. M., Joy, L. A., Travis, L., Gotowier, A., Blum-Steele, M., Aiken, L. S., et al. (1987). Transition to motherhood: A longitudinal study. *Infant Mental Health Journal, 8*, 251–265.

World Salaries Group. (2007). Total personal average income – international comparison. Retrieved from http://www.worldsalaries.org/total-personal-income.shtml

Yamamoto, Y. (2001). The duality of socialization and education: The impact of formal schooling on childrearing in Japan. *Harvard Asia Quarterly, 5*, 24–31.

(2006). Unequal beginnings: Socioeconomic differences in Japanese mothers' support of their children's early schooling. (Unpublished doctoral dissertation) University of California, Berkeley.

Yamamoto, Y., & Brinton, M., (2009). Cultural capital in East Asian educational systems: The case of Japan. *Sociology of Education, 83*(1), 67–83.

Yamamoto, Y., Holloway, S. D., & Suzuki, S. (2006). Maternal involvement in preschool children's education in Japan: Relation to parenting beliefs and socioeconomic status. *Early Childhood Research Quarterly, 21,* 332–346.

(2009). The dilemma of support: Parenting and mother-networks in Japan. Article posted online. http://www.childresearch.net/RESOURCE/RESEARCH/2009/ YAMAMOTO_HOLLOWAY_SUZUKI.HTM

Yamamura, Y. (1986). The child in Japanese society. In H. Stevenson, H. Azuma, & K. Hakuta (Eds.), *Child development and education in Japan* (pp. 28–38). New York, NY: W. H. Freeman.

Yoder, R. S. (2004). *Youth deviance in Japan: Class reproduction of non-conformity.* Melbourne, Australia: Trans Pacific Press.

Yoneyama, S. (2000). Student discourse on tokokyohi (school phobia/refusal) in Japan: Burnout or empowerment? *British Journal of Sociology of Education, 21,* 77–94.

Yoshizumi, K. (1995). Marriage and family: Past and present. In K. Fujimura-Fanselow & A. Kameda (Eds.), *Japanese women: New feminist perspectives on the past, present, and future* (pp. 183–197). New York, NY: Feminist Press of the City University of New York.

Yu, W. (2001). Family demands, gender attitudes, and married women's labor force participation: Comparing Japan and Taiwan. In M. C. Brinton (Ed.), *Women's working lives in East Asia* (pp. 70–95). Stanford, CA: Stanford University Press.

Appendix A

Berkeley Parenting Self-Efficacy Scale
(Preschool Version)

Maternal Strategy Subscale

❖ *How confident do you feel that you can use the following strategies with your child?*

	a little					very confident
Listen to my child	1	2	3	4	5	6
Understand my child's feelings	1	2	3	4	5	6
Control my emotions in front of my child	1	2	3	4	5	6
Avoid over-reacting when my child misbehaves	1	2	3	4	5	6
Create a peaceful, happy home	1	2	3	4	5	6
Set a good example by being polite and respectful to others	1	2	3	4	5	6
Explain things so that my child will understand	1	2	3	4	5	6
Praise my child when he/she does well	1	2	3	4	5	6
Discipline my child firmly when he/she misbehaves	1	2	3	4	5	6
Let my child know I love him/her	1	2	3	4	5	6

Child Outcome Subscale

❖ *How confident do you feel that you can teach your child the following things?*

	a little					very confident
To respect adults	1	2	3	4	5	6
To express thoughts clearly	1	2	3	4	5	6
To continue trying even when something is difficult	1	2	3	4	5	6
To figure out what behavior is called for in different settings (e.g., at the park vs. in the library)	1	2	3	4	5	6
To be polite (e.g., say "please" and "thank you")	1	2	3	4	5	6
To tell time	1	2	3	4	5	6
To avoid bothering others	1	2	3	4	5	6
To do things independently	1	2	3	4	5	6
To learn the alphabet	1	2	3	4	5	6
To get along with other children	1	2	3	4	5	6
To get enough exercise	1	2	3	4	5	6
To stay neat and clean	1	2	3	4	5	6
To eat a variety of nutritious foods	1	2	3	4	5	6
To avoid swearing and other rude language	1	2	3	4	5	6
To be interested in learning new things	1	2	3	4	5	6

Appendix B

Research Methods

We began this research in June of 2000 by interviewing 116 women – half from the large city of Osaka on the central island of Honshu, and half from Sapporo, the provincial capital of Hokkaido, a large island to the north of Honshu. All but one of the women were married. The women varied widely in their socioeconomic status. Their educational attainment, and that of their husband, can be found in Figure B.1. The modal household income was in the range of 5 to 7 million yen (approximately $47,170 to $66,038 in U.S. dollars at the 2000 exchange rate of 106 yen per dollar). The mothers' average age when we began the study was 35.6 years. Each had at least one child in preschool when the study began, and the average family size was 2.16 children. In the focal group of children, there were 59 girls and 57 boys, and their average age was 67.9 months.

We recruited families by asking nine preschool directors to invite mothers with a child in the final year of preschool to participate. We worked with several preschools serving working-class families and several located in middle-class neighborhoods. Virtually all the women who were invited to participate agreed to do so.[1]

Our initial goal was to elicit each woman's perspective on what she saw as the role of mother, what her challenges were in raising her child, and what her goals were for the child and for herself. At the time of first contact, we asked all 116 women to complete a one-hour structured interview as well as a survey focusing on these topics. When the target child was in first and second grade, we obtained two additional surveys from this group of women. In the later surveys, we asked about the mothers' early childhood years, including what sort of relationship they had with their parents and siblings. We also focused on their expectations about the role of husband

---

[1] The sample size for the second survey was also 116; sample size for the third survey was 98.

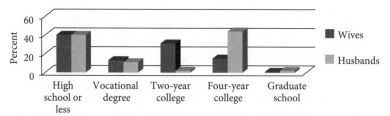

FIGURE (APPENDIX) B.1. Education Level of Survey Participants and their Husbands
Note: Sample size is 116.

and father. As it became clear that most of the women were extremely eager to share with us their perceptions – and frequently their disappointments – concerning married life, this aspect of the study was increasingly elaborated. Additionally, we queried the women at length about the forms of support they received from other actors, including friends, teachers, and extended family members. When the focal children entered first grade, we questioned the mothers extensively about their involvement in their children's schooling, and we also talked at length with those who had by that time entered the job market about work.

In order to obtain a deeper understanding of women's perceptions and experiences, we selected 16 mothers from the larger group to interview on three additional occasions over the course of the study. To ensure that we would hear diverse perspectives, we selected eight women with two- or four-year college degrees and eight who had stopped their education at high school or before. Because we were particularly interested in exploring the women's sense of parenting confidence, we selected eight mothers who scored above average on the parenting self-efficacy scale administered when the children were in preschool and eight who ranked below average in parenting self-efficacy (each group divided equally by education level).[2] Two of the 16 women (Masayo and Sakura) dropped out of the study after the second interview, but the rest participated in all four interviews.

The interviews were conducted by Yoko Yamamoto and Sawako Suzuki, native Japanese-speaking doctoral students attending UC Berkeley. I also participated in at least one interview with each mother. The interviews were wide-ranging conversations structured around central topics selected by the

---

[2]   The *child outcome* subscale assessed the mothers' confidence in helping their child master 15 different skills appropriate for a child that age, such as "do things independently." The *maternal strategy* subscale assessed mothers' confidence in enacting ten parenting behaviors, such as being able to "understand your child's feelings." The scale items may be viewed in Appendix A.

research team. Conducted in the privacy of the mothers' homes, the interviews typically lasted for about two hours each. We audiotaped the conversations, transcribed them and translated them into English. For an account of our analytic approach, see Yamamoto (2006).

The mixed-method approach proved to be an effective way of achieving a deep understanding of the themes of interest. The survey findings helped to place the interview responses into a larger perspective. We could, for example, read one mother's transcript to learn how she evaluated her own parenting skills and then examine her score on the parenting self-efficacy scale to see where she stood relative to others. Conversely, the interview data proved invaluable in interpreting the survey findings. When we found, for example, a surprising tendency for lower socioeconomic status (SES) mothers to be more involved in activities at their child's preschool than higher SES mothers were, we were able to read the interview transcripts for clues. Among other things, we noted that the less educated mothers reported having a hard time resisting pressure from the preschool staff to volunteer in the classroom. We have published the survey findings in a number of journal articles that are referenced in the book. Readers interested in getting a detailed account of the quantitative analyses may want to consult these sources.

Another valuable function of the interviews was to enable us to explore the cases of exceptional women whose beliefs or experiences did not match the general pattern. For example, the survey findings revealed that while generally mothers who had supportive husbands were more confident about their own parenting, there were also some confident mothers who did not have supportive husbands. We were able to go to the interview transcripts and explore the perspectives of "outliers" like Reiko, who expressed parenting confidence but had an unsupportive husband. We learned that Reiko depended on her friends at work to support her decision to take a job and give her child-rearing advice.

Index

achievement, academic
  Japanese, compared to international, 23
  in Osaka City, compared to
    Takatsuki City, 24
afterschool activities. *See* supplementary
  schooling
alcoholism, 78, 81–82, 88, 91, 201, 208
Allied occupation
  and democratization. *See* Constitution
    of Japan (1947), Article 24 of
  and education reform, 146
  and women's rights, 4, 10, 175
Allison, A., 79, 149, 154
amae (dependence and reception of
    indulgence), 36–37, 122, 126–130, 140.
    See also child rearing
  and autonomy, 126–130
attachment, parent-child
  Western theories concerning, 76, 89
autonomy, 122, 126–130, 179
Azuma, H., 79

Bandura, A., 6, 51, 200. *See also* self-efficacy
Behrens, K., 75, 89
Berkeley Parenting Self-Efficacy Scale,
  233–234
Bernstein, G., 196–197
birth order, 46–47
birth rate, 175, 212–215
  decline in, 3–5, 213–215
  and labor force participation, 194, 213–214
  and Ministry of Welfare, 175
  strategies to increase, 174, 212–213
Borovoy, A., 36

Brinton, M., 191–192
Buddhism, 54, 69, 108, 200
Bumpass, L., 193

child care. *See also* preschool
  cost of, 145
  government financial support of, 33
  insufficiency of, 4, 172, 178, 189
  quality of, 4
  working women and, 33, 49,
    96–99, 102
child rearing. *See also amae*; children;
    marriage; *shitsuke*
  and career. *See* employment
  and communication with children,
    41–43, 60–62, 131–134
  corporal punishment in, 22, 44, 62, 64,
    89, 119, 122, 130, 132, 161, 197
  cultural models of, 7–10, 29, 48–49,
    197–200
  ecocultural approach to study of, 8–9
  emotional rewards of, 6
  and emotional self-control, 44–45, 62,
    133–134, 140–141, 197
  and fathers. *See* fathers
  government allowance to offset
    costs of, 5
  maternal influence in, 45–48
  mimamoru (watching over), 39–42, 76,
    89, 197
  and mothers-in-law. *See* mothers-in-law
  "neurosis" *(ikuji fuan),* 7, 52
  perceived burden of, 96
  self-efficacy regarding. *See* self-efficacy